cut

Cathy Glass

Cut

The true story of an abandoned, abused little girl
who was desperate to be part of a family

HARPER
element

This book is a work of non-fiction based on the recollections of Cathy Glass. The names of people, places, dates and the detail of events have been changed to protect the privacy of others. The author has warranted to the publishers that, except in such minor respects not affecting the substantial accuracy of the work, the contents of this book are true.

HarperElement
An Imprint of HarperCollins*Publishers*
77–85 Fulham Palace Road,
Hammersmith, London W6 8JB

www.harpercollins.co.uk

and *HarperElement* are trademarks of
HarperCollins*Publishers* Ltd

First published by HarperCollins*Publishers* 2008

2

A catalogue record for this book
is available from the British Library

HB ISBN-13 978-00-728097-1
HB ISBN-10 0-00-728097-1
PB ISBN-13 978-00-728098-8
PB ISBN-10 0-00-728098-X

Printed and bound in Great Britain by
Clays Ltd, St Ives plc

To my family – with love

Acknowledgements

My continuing thanks to Carole Tonkinson and all the team at HarperCollins; my agent Andrew Lownie; and Anne Askwith for editing.

Prologue

When interviewed, I am often asked when and why I began fostering, all those years ago. This is the story of when and why; it is also the true story of Dawn. Dawn was the second child I fostered and nearly became the last. It is set at a time before the Children's Acts, when there was no training for foster carers, no record keeping, no meetings, no background information on the child, little accountability and no support. 'Dump 'em and run' seemed to be the philosophy of the social services at the time, and the more disturbed the child was, the faster and quicker the social services ran. Because of all the changes in fostering and social work practice, this story shouldn't happen now, although I fear there is a foster carer somewhere who can prove differently.

Certain details, including names, places and dates have been changed to protect the child.

Chapter One

In the Beginning

John, my husband, and I were trying to start a family, but it was proving difficult. We were doing all the right things (and often) but the longed-for baby hadn't arrived. One Saturday evening I was flicking through the local newspaper and saw an advertisement: *Could you offer a child a home? Mary desperately needs one.* There was an accompanying black-and-white photograph of a darling little girl, aged six months, reaching out with her arms and eyes to anyone who would look, together with the telephone number of the duty social worker.

I glanced up at John, who was sitting on the lounge floor trying to repair his electric drill. Lots of little metal bits were strewn across a sheet of old newspaper. Our first home together had been a DIY project, although now that we had been living in it since our marriage, two years previously, the worst was over. Most of the rooms were not only habitable but decorated, and although sparsely furnished, comfortable. I looked again at the social services advertisement, and to the small print under the main heading: *Little Mary requires a foster home while her mother recovers in hospital.*

'John?' I said tentatively.

'Mmm?' He glanced up, with the metal casing of the drill in one hand and a screwdriver in the other.

'What do you think about this?' I left the sofa and, careful not to tread on the assortment of drill parts, showed him the open page.

He read the advertisement and looked at me seriously. 'You'd never be able to give her back, would you?'

I paused for a moment, deep in thought. 'I guess you have to go into fostering aware that you are going to give the child back to the mother. What do you think? Is it worth a phone call to find out more?'

'What about your job?' he asked.

'I suppose I'd have to hand in my notice. I was going to give up work anyway when we had a baby.'

'It's not the same as having our own family, is it?' He was still looking at me, concerned. John could always be relied upon to view a situation objectively, seeing the pitfalls and problems when I had possibly rushed in.

'No, it would be as well as having our own family,' I said.

He looked down at the drill. 'I'm not sure about fostering. Let me think about it.' And if I was honest I wasn't sure either.

Could I look after a child that wasn't my own? Feed and change her, bond with her, knowing that at some point she would be returning to her mother? It was a huge emotional undertaking and a life-changing commitment, added to which, we needed the money from my job. Every penny counted, not only because of the cost of the house, but also as a nest egg for the day we did have a baby and I had to give up work. I closed the newspaper and dropped it into the magazine rack. 'Coffee?' I asked John.

'Yes please. And a doughnut if there's one left.'

It was John who raised the subject of fostering again, later that night as we climbed into bed, having obviously given the matter more thought. 'You know, I had an aunt who fostered,' he said. 'She looked after two boys. I don't know all the details. She lived in Scotland and we didn't really see that much of them, but they seemed happy enough.'

'Really?' I asked, intrigued, resting my head on the pillow.

'I suppose you could just phone, and find out more,' he said. 'They must have lots of enquiries that are never followed up.'

'If I have a chance I'll phone on Monday during my lunch hour,' I said. I worked for the civil service and the office manager didn't mind the staff making the occasional phone call as long as it wasn't overseas.

'And in the meantime, how about we have another attempt at starting our family,' John said with a smile. 'You know what they say – practice makes perfect.'

I laughed, and snuggling down into the bed felt John's strong warm arms encircle me and his lips lightly on mine.

I phoned the social services on Monday; it was an answer machine. I left my name and home telephone number, and said that I had seen their advertisement about fostering Mary and would like some more information. There was no dedicated line to the Children and Families team at that time. Now, if you phone to enquire about fostering, a social worker from the Children and Families team, with experience of 'looked after children', as they're called, will speak to you and tell you what you want to know. Well, that's the theory at least, although even now some councils are more efficient than others at recruiting foster carers. My message then would be picked up by the duty social worker with no knowledge of fostering who dealt with all messages coming into the social services offices, on all subjects.

My call wasn't returned for a month, by which time I had forgotten about fostering, or almost. A social worker phoned at 5.30 p.m. when I had just returned home from work. There was no apology for the delay in getting back to me. After she had given me her name she asked if we had ever fostered before, and I guessed my 'no' was the wrong answer. 'Oh,' she said clearly uncertain what to do next. All my questions were met with 'I'm sorry, I really don't know.' So when we said goodbye, five minutes later, I was none the wiser about fostering. However, she did say she thought there might be a leaflet somewhere, and that she would try to find it and send it to me, for which purpose I gave her our address.

Another week passed before the leaflet arrived – a single photocopied A4 sheet, showing pictures of smiling children with some general remarks that foster homes were needed for children who couldn't be looked after by their natural parents, but with no details about what was actually involved. On the reverse of the leaflet was a date (in ten days' time), together with a venue where an 'introductory evening' was to be held. I assumed this was an introduction to fostering, although it could have been about pig farming for all the information there was. I'd asked the social worker a number of specific questions, and the leaflet said nothing other than there were children of all ages who needed foster homes.

I left the leaflet with the other non-urgent mail on the shelf in the kitchen and thought no more about it. John and I were both busy with work and finishing the house. It wasn't until the day before the introductory meeting was scheduled that John raised the subject over dinner.

'Are you going to that meeting?' he asked as we ate. 'About fostering,' he added as I looked at him, non-plussed. 'It's tomorrow.'

'I hadn't planned to. We were going to finish the tiling in the bathroom tomorrow evening.'

'I can do the tiling, if you want to go,' John said. 'Or we could go together, and do the tiling on Saturday. I'm not playing golf.'

My enthusiasm for fostering had lapsed with the passing of time and the less than dynamic attitude of the social worker. 'Do you want to go?' I asked.

He nodded. 'May as well. Hear what they have to say. Otherwise we'll always wonder what we were missing.'

'OK,' I said. 'Fine.'

There were eleven of us in a church hall – five couples and a widow. The meeting was led by two social workers who spent half an hour explaining to us the reasons children came into care; the current policy that believed such children were better looked after in foster families than children's homes; and that all foster carers had to be interviewed. An experienced foster carer then talked to us for twenty minutes, giving us a down-to-earth, experienced-based account of her fostering, which was very interesting. We broke for coffee and had a chance to chat to the other couples present, all of whom, like John and me, had never previously fostered and had come to the meeting to learn more. After coffee the foster carer who had spoken to us before the break was available to answer our questions. Her candid responses and the little details of family life in her fostering family were riveting and also invaluable in helping us reach a decision on whether to proceed. By the time we came out, an hour later, I was enthusiastic again, and so was John. The descriptions we had heard of the children's sad lives and the reward of being in a position to help a little had won us over.

'We could have the second bedroom for the foster child,' I said. 'Which leaves the third bedroom for the nursery, as we planned.' John agreed.

We had been told at the meeting that we should think about what we had learned and if we were still interested to phone the duty social worker and 'someone' would get back to us.

When I think of the vetting process that prospective foster carers go through now, what happened then seems risible and also potentially negligent for the safety of the child in foster care.

I made the phone call the following week and was duly sent an application form, which we had to complete jointly. Apart from our contact details, date and place of birth, and employment history, there was a blank box for us to describe in fifty words why we wanted to foster. We spent some time drafting and re-drafting those fifty words, and eventually decided on something to the effect that we felt we could offer a child a loving home but were aware that the child would eventually be returning to live with his or her own family — we had understood from the introductory evening that it was important to include this. I mailed the application form, and a month or so later a social worker phoned and arranged to visit us one evening at home for an interview. Her name was Susan and once we had settled in the lounge with coffee, she went through our application form, and asked us to expand on why we felt we had what it took to look after a child who wasn't ours. John and I said that we wanted to be parents and in our hearts already were; that we knew how to parent from the fine examples our own parents had given us; and that when we eventually had a baby of our own we would still foster.

Susan seemed happy with our responses, smiling and nodding as we spoke. She asked us about our own families, and what impact we felt a newborn baby would have on a foster child. We were honest in our replies and answered as best we could, saying what we instinctively felt. We were also asked to think about the impact the foster child might have on our lives. Susan's first visit lasted about two hours; then she visited us again a couple of weeks later for an hour when she had written her report. We weren't allowed to read the report, as prospective foster carers are now, but she gave us the gist of what it contained, and said that she would be recommending our application and that it would have to be approved – by whom wasn't stated.

Another month passed before we received a phone call from Susan who was pleased to tell us that our application had been approved. Susan also said that we would have to attend an information evening before we could start to foster. Because we hadn't had experience of babies or very young children we would only be allowed to foster children from five years upwards. Perhaps whoever had approved our application felt that our naïve and clumsy efforts might be less damaging to older children – I don't know, but John and I were ecstatic that we had passed and were actually going to foster, albeit not a child of Mary's age.

At that point we told our parents that we were going to foster, and had a mixed response. John's mother said, 'Oh, I thought you wanted one of your own.' To which John replied, 'We do. This is as well as.' My mother said, 'That's very nice of you dear, but you don't know anything about children.' I said, 'Does anyone before they actually have children? And I think we shall be learning very quickly.' Never was a truer word spoken!

After a two-hour information evening, where we met other couples who had been approved for fostering and spent some time role playing various situations that could arise in the fostering home, we were ready to receive our first child. Susan phoned me two days later and said that she would be bringing Jack to us that evening.

'He's fifteen,' she said. 'He goes to school, so you will be able to work out your notice. A month, isn't it?'

'Er, yes,' I said, hesitantly. 'He's a teenager, then?'

'Yes. Most of the children we are placing now are. We have a shortage of teen carers, not helped by one of our teenage units closing. Don't worry,' Susan added. 'Jack won't give you any trouble.'

And that was the first indication that children in care (for reasons that weren't their fault) could cause 'trouble', and big time.

Chapter Two

False Sense of Security

Jack had been with us for three months when I started to feel sick. Not sick as in having eaten something which had disagreed with me, but a vague and persistent nausea which was worse first thing in the morning. Hardly daring to hope, and without John knowing, I bought a pregnancy testing kit and only told John when I had the result.

'Amazing! Fantastic! Yippee!' John cried. Usually he had a better command of the English language; indeed he has a degree. 'Let's celebrate! Tonight! Fetch Jack and we'll go out for a meal. No, on second thoughts, you sit down and put your feet up and I'll go up and get Jack.'

I laughed as John tore up the stairs to retrieve Jack from the all-consuming rapping music that accompanied him whenever he was in his bedroom. An hour later the three of us were seated at a corner table in our favourite Italian restaurant in town, with John proposing a toast. 'To Cathy: well done and congratulations. And to Jack, for doing so well at school.'

I smiled at Jack as we raised our champagne glasses. Jack's glass was only a quarter full, which at his age seemed appropriate — a few mouthfuls wasn't going to hurt him and it was important he felt included.

'I'm expecting a baby,' I said quietly to Jack, who hadn't the least idea why John had knocked on his bedroom door and, unable to contain his excitement, told him to get changed into his good gear as we were all going out to celebrate.

Jack smiled, a bit embarrassed, and took a sip from his glass. 'What's champagne made from?' he said, grimacing at the taste.

'Grapes, the same as wine,' John said. 'But it's a particular type of grape, and the fermentation process is different.'

'Not keen,' Jack said. 'Can I have a bottle of beer instead?'

'No,' John and I chorused. 'You're too young,' I added. 'Have your Coke if you don't like the champagne.'

Looking after Jack was all about making compromises, and John and I made decisions about what Jack could or could not do based on common sense. We'd had no training on how to deal with teenagers and, without the experience of having had our own teenagers, we relied on what we thought was appropriate for a lad of fifteen. So if Jack went out with his mates in the evening he had to be in at 9.00 p.m. on a school night and 10.00 p.m. on a Friday or Saturday. Jack had been used to hanging out with his mates a lot, and John and I had reduced it to twice a week, as he had important school exams at the end of the year. We had insisted Jack told us where he was going and gave us a contact number if he was at a friend's house. Jack hadn't bucked against our 'rules' and indeed had seemed to respond positively to the boundaries we had put in place, understanding they were for his well-being.

Susan's assertion that Jack would not give us any trouble had proved true. Apart from having to persuade him to shower each day rather than the once a week he was used to, we'd had little in the way of opposition. Because Jack was fifteen, John and I treated him as another adult in many respects, rather than a child in need of a mummy and daddy, and our confidence had grown from the positive results. Jack had easily fitted into our household, and his school work had improved dramatically. We only saw Jack's social worker once (when he had brought Jack to us), and since then he'd phoned once to ask if Jack was OK. Jack was going to live with his dad, Sam, as soon as his dad had found somewhere suitable for the two of them to live. Jack had left his mother and her new partner after escalating rows, which had culminated in Jack's stepfather punching Jack and Jack appearing at school the following day with a broken nose. We had met Sam briefly when he had come to the house shortly after Jack had moved in. Sam, a carpenter by trade, clearly thought a lot of his son, and had confided in John that he wished he'd taken Jack with him when he had left his mother. He now lived in a bed-sit and was looking forward to making a home for him and his son as soon as he found a two-bedroom flat at a rent he could afford.

'I think my mum might be pregnant,' Jack said towards the end of the celebratory meal. 'The last time I saw her she was fat.'

I looked at him. 'Oh yes? And how do you feel about your mum having a baby?'

Jack shrugged. 'Not fussed. I guess I'll visit her when I'm at my dad's.' Understandably Jack was hurt that his mother had chosen a partner who had abused him, and

Jack blamed her for not stepping in and protecting him. He had seen her only a couple of times since he'd left.

'You'll probably all get along a lot better once you're living at your dad's and just visiting your mum.' I said.

'I guess,' he said. 'It's up to her. She's the adult. I think she should make the first move.'

John and I exchanged a knowing glance. Jack was an intelligent and sensitive lad, and it was a great pity his mother hadn't given more thought to her son's feelings when he had been at home.

'Adults make mistakes too,' I said smiling at Jack. 'And sometimes it can take a while before they realise it.'

Jack moved in with his dad five months later, when I was seven and a half months pregnant. We met Jack's social worker for the second time when he collected Jack to take him to his father's. We had offered to take Jack but apparently the social worker had to move the child when he or she was officially in care. As we said goodbye to Jack, we wished him luck, and told him we had enjoyed having him stay, and to keep up with his school work.

'Thanks for everything.' Jack said with a small wave. 'You're both pretty cool as parents,' which we took as a compliment. We had enjoyed looking after Jack and the experience had given us confidence in our ability to foster.

It was strange suddenly having the house to ourselves again, but also something of a relief, if I was honest. I was feeling quite tired towards the end of the pregnancy, and not having Jack meant that I could relax more in the evenings and weekends. It also meant that I didn't have to be up at 7.00 a.m. during the week to get Jack off to school. We told the social services that we wouldn't foster again until after I'd had the baby, and John and I then concentrated on us, and making sure we had everything ready for the big day. At nine months and five days' gestation I went into labour and gave birth to a baby boy, 8lbs 3ozs – Adrian.

Our lives obviously changed with the arrival of the baby, although not as dramatically as it does for some couples when the woman has only recently given up work and suddenly has to adjust to being at home and looking after the baby. I had already given up work nearly a year before and had been looking after Jack. And although the needs of a baby are obviously very different from those of a fourteen-year-old, I was already in the caring/mothering role. In short, John and I took to parenthood like ducks to water. Life was running pretty smoothly, and we were feeling rather smug that we had adapted so easily. Perhaps we were too smug, because had we been struggling in our roles as new parents, we wouldn't have entertained fostering another child again so quickly.

Adrian was only four months old when I answered the phone one morning to a social worker, Ruth.

'I understand you have room for a teenager?' she asked. I was on the sofa in the lounge, breastfeeding Adrian, and was balancing Adrian against me with one hand and the phone against my ear with the other.

'Er, yes, well, no, not really,' I said, taken completely by surprise. 'I mean we do foster, but we've taken a break because I've had a baby.'

'But you haven't any foster children at present?' Ruth asked.

'Well, no.'

'Good, so you could take Dawn. She's thirteen, and at the teenage unit. I need to move her quickly. She's too young to be at the unit, and she's got herself into a bit of trouble.' I didn't know what to say. 'Can I bring her to you this evening?' Ruth asked.

I still didn't know what to say. 'I'll have to speak to my husband first. We hadn't planned ...'

'Could you phone him now, please, and I'll phone you back in half an hour. It is important I get things moving.'

I could hear the urgency in Ruth's voice and, ignoring her abruptness agreed to phone John – part of me was already caught up in the urgency of Ruth's request.

John was in his office and surprised to hear from me. He was doubly surprised when I told him the nature of Ruth's phone call.

'It's up to you,' he said. 'You're the one who will have do most of the looking after during the week. Won't it be too much for you with the baby as well?'

Lulled into a false sense of security by our experience of caring for Jack, I said, 'No, I don't think so. After all, she'll be in school most of the week. I think we should.'

Chapter Three

Stranger in the Room

D awn arrived with Ruth, her social worker, that evening at seven o'clock. John answered the door and showed them through to the lounge, where I was again feeding Adrian. Adrian was a big baby and seemed to be continually hungry – I spent most of the day in a state of undress.

'Hi,' I said to Dawn and Ruth, glancing up. 'Don't mind me. Do sit down.'

They both threw me a brief smile and sat on the sofa. Dawn was small for her age, slightly built, with fair, chin-length hair. She had grey-blue eyes and a light skin, and her features were pleasantly open, although she looked rather pale. She wore jeans and a black leather jacket, zipped up to the neck. It was the middle of February and cold outside, and although the heating was up high for Adrian she didn't take off her jacket. Indeed she pulled her jacket further around her and gave a little shiver.

'Would you like a hot drink?' I offered.

'No, thanks,' she said politely.

'Ruth, would you?'

'No, I need to be off soon.' Ruth was in her mid-forties, a large lady in a large pair of black trousers and beige jumper. She had slipped off her coat as she had entered the room and draped it over the sofa. We all looked at each other for a moment in uncomfortable silence. I had the feeling that Ruth and Dawn had had a disagreement before coming in: they sat at either end of the sofa, turned away from each other, and didn't make eye contact.

'How are you?' I asked Dawn, breaking the silence. 'How's school?'

'OK,' she said convivially, throwing me another smile.

'It would be if she went to school,' Ruth said sharply. I glanced at John, and we both looked at Ruth. 'Dawn hasn't been attending school,' Ruth said bluntly. 'She seems to think it is a part-time occupation, and that she can just pop in when she feels like it. Her non-attendance has got her mother in a lot of trouble, hasn't it, Dawn?'

Ruth now turned to look at Dawn for the first time, although her look was more of a glare. John and I looked at Dawn too.

'I don't like school,' Dawn said flatly.

'Why?' I asked, feeling that her social worker could have been a bit more sympathetic, and aware that there were a number of reasons which could turn a child against school – for example bullying.

'I don't like the teachers,' Dawn said. 'And they don't like me.'

Ruth sighed. 'Oh, come off it, Dawn, they've bent over backwards to accommodate you. I don't see how they could have done any more. You're not the only child in that school, although from the way you behave clearly you think you are.'

Dawn shrugged dismissively, and I knew that my initial surmise that they had had an argument (presumably about school) was true.

'Jack, the boy who stayed with us before, had problems with school,' I said positively. 'But he's fine now. Perhaps I can help sort out your problems at school, Dawn?'

Ruth snorted. 'Perhaps. Dawn's mother certainly couldn't.'

Dawn didn't say anything and I felt sorry for her – Ruth was being so brusque in her manner, and Dawn seemed so small and almost fragile beside her. And I wondered what exactly had been going on at school to make Dawn so against it. Ruth glanced at her watch.

'I'm going to set up a meeting with Dawn's mother,' Ruth said in a hurry. 'And we'll draw up a contract of good behaviour at the same time. We use contracts with teenagers so that all parties have an understanding of the expectations. It has no legal binding but a moral one. Hopefully Dawn will stick to it.'

Dawn looked up at me and smiled.

'I'm sure she will,' I said. 'Is this contract a new idea? We didn't have one with Jack.'

'Yes, very new. It's been tried by other social services, so we thought we'd give it a go.' I nodded. 'Dawn is an only child,' Ruth continued, clearly wanting to say what she had to, and then leave. 'She has been living partly with her mum and partly with her dad. And, as I said on the phone, Dawn has been in the teenage unit since she came into care three days ago, but she's too young – it was only an emergency measure.' Ruth glanced at her watch again. 'OK, well, I'll leave you to it then. Dawn's bag is in the hall. There isn't much. I'll ask her mother for some more of her clothes when I set up the meeting.' She stood.

John stood as well, ready to see Ruth out, as I winded Adrian. Ruth hesitated and glanced down at Dawn. 'Is there anything you want to ask while I'm here,' she said almost as an afterthought.

'What time do I have to be in?' Dawn said and looked at me. Ruth looked at me too.

'You are thirteen, so I wouldn't want you out on the streets after dark,' I said. 'I'm sure your mother wouldn't want it either.' John nodded.

Ruth looked pointedly at Dawn who lowered her eyes. 'No,' Ruth said. 'I agree. But that doesn't stop Dawn. When she sets her mind on doing something she does it regardless. Her mother isn't able to control her, and that's one of the reasons she's in care – lack of parental control. So we'll put coming in times in the contract, Dawn.'

Dawn shrugged, and that was it from Ruth. She called a brief goodbye to Dawn and me as she left the room with John. A few seconds later we heard John say goodbye, and the front door close. I continued massaging Adrian's back and he obligingly let out a loud burp. Dawn laughed. Leaving the sofa, she came over and knelt beside my armchair for a closer look at Adrian.

John stuck his head round the lounge door. 'I'm going to make a pot of tea. Does anyone want one?'

'Please,' I said. 'And your dinner is in the oven.'

'Yes, please, John.' Dawn said, and began cooing at Adrian. Now that Ruth had left, Dawn was quickly thawing. 'What a lovely baby,' she said. 'What's his name?'

'Adrian.'

'That's a nice name. How old is he?'

'Four months.'

'He's so lovely. Aren't you, Adrian? Aren't you a lovely baby?' Adrian was holding Dawn's forefinger and waving it to and fro. 'Look! He's smiling at me,' Dawn cried in delight. 'I like babies. I'd like one of my own.'

'They're hard work,' I said, feeling a bit overwhelmed (as Adrian must have been) by all this sudden and close attention.

'But once you get them in a routine, it gets easier, doesn't it?' she asked.

'I wouldn't know,' I laughed. 'I haven't done that yet.'

'My dad and his girlfriend have a baby but they won't let me play with her. I think dad's girlfriend is jealous. She's only six years older than me and she says I don't know how to hold a baby. But they won't show me how to hold a baby, so how am I supposed to know?' I looked at Dawn as she continued cooing at Adrian, besotted with him. I knew what was coming next.

'Can I hold Adrian, please?' Dawn said. 'I'll be very careful. You can show me how to hold him. Please.' She quickly manoeuvred herself to sit cross-legged on the floor, and cradled her arms ready to receive him. I slipped from the chair and, squatting down beside her, carefully placed Adrian in her arms. While she rocked him and then began kissing his forehead, I supported his head, aware that my precious son was in the arms of a thirteen-year-old who had just walked through the door and whom I knew virtually nothing about.

'What's your name?' Dawn suddenly asked, glancing up at me.

'Cathy. Didn't Ruth tell you?'

'No. She was too busy nagging me. John told me his name at the front door but I didn't know yours.' Even then, with my lack of fostering experience, I thought it was pretty bad of the social worker to leave a child with someone whose name she didn't even know. And while I knew Dawn's first name I realised that I didn't know her surname, date of birth or any details, other than those Ruth had just told me. At least Jack's social worker had written the basic details on a sheet of paper.

'What's your surname, Dawn?' I asked.

'Jennings.'

I nodded. 'And when's your birthday?'

'January the sixth.'

'So you're only just thirteen?'

'Yes.'

Dawn's rocking of Adrian had increased, and I was becoming concerned that it was a little too boisterous – more like a child playing with a doll than the careful soothing required for a fragile little being. 'Very gently,' I said, still supporting Adrian's head and placing my free hand on her arm. 'Babies' backs aren't very strong at this age.' Fortunately at that moment John rescued Adrian by coming into the lounge carrying a tray containing his dinner and three mugs of tea, giving me an excuse to retrieve Adrian from Dawn's arms.

'Help yourself to a mug,' I said. 'Do you want something to eat?'

'Only a biscuit. I had dinner at the teenage unit.'

John was about to go into the kitchen again to fetch the biscuits, but I said, 'You have your dinner. Dawn and I can get the biscuits.'

'Do you want me to carry Adrian?' Dawn asked, immediately standing beside me and stretching out her arms ready to receive Adrian.

'No thanks, love, I can manage. You can carry the biscuit tin.' I led the way into the kitchen and pointed out the biscuit tin on the shelf. Dawn looked around the kitchen before taking down the tin. 'You've got a nice place here. It looks new.'

I smiled. 'John and I have been doing up the house. We've more or less finished now. I'll show you your room later. I hope you like it.'

'I'm sure I will. That teenage unit was horrible. There were three of us crammed in one room, and the other two were up all night. I couldn't sleep. And when I stay at Mum or Dad's I don't really have a room of my own. Their flats are too small.'

'So where did you sleep and keep all your belongings?' I asked surprised and again feeling sorry for Dawn.

'On the sofa. I haven't got much stuff. I've got a few clothes at both flats, and there's some in my bag.'

'All right, love. We'll take your bag up to your room later and sort out your things.'

Dawn and I returned to the lounge, where we chatted with John as he ate his dinner and Dawn ate most of the contents of the biscuit tin. I thought that in future I would make sure she ate proper meals, for I now wondered if she had had dinner at the teenage unit. She was slightly built and couldn't afford to skip meals and then make up for it with biscuits. I sat with Adrian in my lap; he was contentedly gurgling, occasionally yawning and waving his arms. Dawn appeared to have lost her immediate interest in Adrian and had returned to sit on the sofa. John and I asked her about school, which according to her she did attend, but not regularly. I asked her if she found the work difficult or had problems with friends, but she said, 'No, not really.' So John and I assumed her non-attendance was more due to a lack of routine and parental guidance than school itself. From what Dawn said she appeared to have been shunted back and forth between her mum's flat and her dad and his girlfriend's, with neither parent actually taking charge of her or assuming responsibility. It seemed that she had fallen between the two of them and had just been left to get on with it, with both parents being too busy with their own lives and relationships to give Dawn the time and attention she needed.

I told Dawn that I would take her to school the following day in the car, and after that she could go on the bus as she had been doing, if she wanted to. The secondary school she went to, St James's, was only a fifteen-minute bus journey away on the edge of the town. But I wanted to make myself known at the school and find out what I needed to do to help Dawn. I had done the same at Jack's school with very positive results. Dawn accepted my suggestion quite affably, as indeed she accepted all our suggestions, including her bedtime, arrangements for seeing her friends (at their house or ours, not on the street), and that homework took priority over television. She appeared to be a good-humoured and sensible girl, who was immediately likeable and clearly wanted to get along with us and fit into our routine.

As 8.30 p.m. approached, the time we had said was a reasonable one for her to get ready for bed, Dawn stood, without being asked, and said, 'I'll say goodnight now, then.'

I was pleasantly surprised, as was John. Jack had needed reminders all the time he had been with us – to switch off his music or television, or stop whatever he was doing and get ready for bed.

'I'm sure you two would like some time alone now,' Dawn added, and I guessed that had probably come from staying with her dad and his girlfriend.

'OK, love,' I said, also standing. 'I'll come up and show you where everything is.'

'Thanks, Cathy. Goodnight, John. Can I give you a kiss?' John looked momentarily surprised but quickly recovered. 'Yes, of course.' Dawn went over and kissed John on top of the head. ''Night,' he said.

I lay Adrian in John's arms – they always spent time together in the evening once we had eaten – and went with Dawn into the hall. I picked up her one piece of luggage, a zip-up weekend holdall, and then led the way upstairs and to the second bedroom. I had given the room a good clean after Jack's departure and it had stood empty since.

'This is lovely,' Dawn said looking round her bedroom.

'I'm glad you like it. You'll feel more at home when you have your things around you.' John and I had kept the colours in the room neutral when we had decorated so that it would suit a boy or a girl. Adrian was still sleeping in his cot in our bedroom, but the third bedroom was ready for him as soon we felt he was old enough.

I placed Dawn's bag on the bed and unzipped it. 'You can hang your clothes in the wardrobe,' I said. 'And there are shelves for your books and CDs.'

It didn't take long to unpack and Dawn didn't need the wardrobe or shelving. The holdall contained a pair of jeans, a jumper, three pairs of pants, a pair of pyjamas and a wash bag.

'What have you been wearing since you came into care?' I asked, looking in horror at her few clothes.

'This,' she said, referring to what she wore.

'And where's your school uniform?'

'I've got a skirt at Mum's and a jumper at Dad's. I never had a PE kit. They go on at me at school because I'm not in uniform.' I wondered if this was one of the reasons Dawn was so against school – not wearing a uniform would get her into trouble with the staff and also single her out from her friends.

'I think I'd better buy you another set,' I said. 'Hopefully your social worker can get the skirt and jumper when she speaks to your mum and dad. They'll do as spares. And I'll wash those clothes you're wearing. You will have to wear your other pair of jeans and the jumper for school tomorrow. Don't worry, I'll come in and explain.'

'Thanks, Cathy,' Dawn said with a smile. 'I get fed up with being told off. If it's not me mum or dad going on at me, it's the school.'

I unzipped the wash bag, which contained a flannel, toothbrush and tube of toothpaste, which Dawn said had been given to her at the teenage unit. 'When do you usually have your bath or shower?' I asked. 'In the morning or evening?'

'I don't mind,' she said agreeably.

'It's probably best in the evening – about eight o'clock. John showers in the morning and I usually have my bath before I go to bed.' I thought that as Dawn had had no routine she would appreciate having one established; it was also practical, as clearly all three of us had to use the bathroom.

'That's fine, Cathy,' she said, and again smiled openly.

I took a towel from the airing cupboard and showed Dawn through to the bathroom, where I made sure she had everything she needed. I went downstairs briefly, and then returned when I heard the bathroom door open. Dawn was ready and had changed into her pyjamas. It was nine o'clock, and I said I thought she should get straight off to sleep now, as she had to be up early for school. As with everything John or I had so far suggested, she readily agreed. I drew her bedroom curtains as she climbed into bed; then I said goodnight.

'Will you give me a kiss?' she asked, as she had done John.

'Yes, of course, love.'

She snuggled her head into the pillow and I leant over and kissed her cheek. 'Did your mum and dad always kiss you goodnight?'

'No, they were always too busy.' Her face fell.

'I'd better make up for it, then,' I said, and leaning over, I gave her a second kiss on the cheek.

She smiled. 'Thanks, Cathy. 'Night.'

''Night, love. Sleep tight.'

I came out and closed her bedroom door. Although Dawn was thirteen she was like a much younger child in many respects, and my heart went out to her.

Downstairs, John and I sat together on the sofa with Adrian lying contentedly in the crook of his arm. 'She seems a good kid,' John said. 'Very eager to please and fit in.'

'Yes,' I said thoughtfully, 'she does – almost a bit too eager.' John glanced sideways at me. 'I mean Jack was good, but do you remember all those debates we had about coming in time and not hanging around the streets, and doing his homework, not to mention hygiene?' John nodded. 'Dawn has accepted everything we've said. Don't you think she's a bit too compliant? It seems odd, particularly when her social worker is clearly exasperated by her behaviour.'

'It's early days yet,' John said. 'But she is probably just grateful to have a home at last. It doesn't sound like she's had much of one before, from either parent.'

'No, you're probably right. I'll have to buy her some clothes tomorrow, and a whole new school uniform. She's got nothing with her, and doesn't seem to have much at her parents' flats either.'

'Have you got enough money?' John asked, mindful his salary wouldn't go into our joint account for another week.

'I'll write cheques. By the time they clear, they'll be covered.' With only John's wage and the expense of the house and the baby, we had to be careful with money. Now most social services make an initial payment towards the cost of clothes for foster children, in addition to a weekly allowance. Then, foster carers received occasional payments, which barely covered the cost of the child's food, let alone anything else, and many often received nothing at all.

I fed Adrian again, as usual, at 10.30 p.m.; then John winded him and settled him in his cot while I had my bath. All was quiet in Dawn's room and I silently opened her bedroom door to check she was all right. She was curled on her side and fast asleep. I came out, quietly closing the door behind me. Aware that Adrian would be waking at about 3.00 a.m. for a feed, John and I were both in bed and asleep by eleven o'clock. But when I woke, it wasn't to Adrian's cry.

Chapter Four

Apparition

The room was dark, save for the faintest glimmer of light coming through a crack in the curtains from the streetlamp. Assuming I had woken because I had heard Adrian waking for his feed, I stayed where I was, nestled in the small of John's back, listening for Adrian's next cry. Then I heard a noise, one I couldn't place. I turned to look at the bedside clock and, as I did, I screamed. Across the room, beside Adrian's cot, was a shadow.

I sat bolt upright. 'My God! What are you doing here?'

I switched on the bedside lamp as I got out of bed. John was immediately awake, out of bed, and switching on the main light.

'Dawn?' he said as we crossed to her. 'What are you doing?'

My scream and the light had woken Adrian and he let out a sharp cry. I picked him up and looked at Dawn, my heart thumping wildly and my mouth dry. She was in her pyjamas, eyes open and staring at me. But something in her look said that she wasn't seeing me: her eyes were glazed and unfocused, and her face was set and expressionless.

'Dawn?' I said, and looked at John. He was pale from the shock of suddenly waking to find someone in our room. 'Dawn?' I tried again. But there was nothing – no movement of her face or body, not even a blink. Nothing to say she could hear or see me, or that she was even aware of our presence.

I cradled Adrian close to my chest and glanced at the bedside clock. It was 1.30 a.m. Dawn remained standing perfectly still and staring straight ahead. She could have been made of stone for all her lack of movement and her fixed staring eyes.

'Dawn?' John said. Then he moved his hand slowly up and down in front of her face. She didn't blink or move a muscle but remained staring, unfocused. I felt my stomach tighten.

'Is she sleepwalking?' John said quietly.

'I don't know.' His expression mirrored mine in fright and concern.

We both looked at Dawn, into her face and eyes. To have someone standing in front of you, apparently awake, but not seeing or hearing, not outwardly functioning at all, was the most chilling experience I have ever had. She was like a breathing statue, or a ghost. Devoid of all expression and movement, she was like the walking dead.

Adrian was still close to my chest, and the comfort of being held had sent him back to sleep. I could have returned him to his cot but I still held him protectively; something told me I needed to protect him – from what I couldn't have said.

'What shall we do?' I asked John. I continued to gaze, mesmerised, into Dawn's lifeless eyes.

'Take her back to her bed?' John suggested.

'I suppose so, but how?'

I had never personally seen, known or heard of anyone sleepwalking, although I had seen it portrayed in horror films and psychological thrillers. Whether it was from those, or something I had once read, I didn't know, but I thought that it could be harmful to abruptly wake a person when they were sleepwalking.

'Dawn?' I said very quietly. 'Dawn, can you hear me?'

There was nothing, just the same lifeless stare.

'Dawn, I think you should go back to bed,' John said softly, as impotent as I was to know what to do next.

There was still nothing from Dawn – no response or indication that she could hear, or that any of her senses were working. 'She must have been able to see to have walked round the landing and come into our bedroom,' I whispered to John.

He nodded. 'Dawn, go back to bed,' he said, lightly touching her arm. That touch, the feel of John's hand on her arm, appeared to reach Dawn and kick-start her into action. Still not blinking or showing any facial expression, and standing very upright, she gradually began to turn.

John and I watched with a mixture of awe and horror as, very slowly and like a robot, she completed the turn so that she was facing away from the cot. Taking regular and mechanical steps she began to cross the bedroom towards the door. John and I followed in silence a couple of steps behind, Adrian still nestled in my arms, asleep.

We followed Dawn out of our bedroom and on to the landing. I watched, dumbfounded, as Dawn navigated the right turn on the landing, and then paused at the top of the stairs. For a moment I thought she was going to try to go downstairs, and my breath caught in my throat. But after a brief hesitation she continued the few steps into her bedroom. John and I stood at her bedroom door and watched as she slowly crossed her room without bumping into anything and then got into bed. The room was at the back of the house and, without any glow from the street lamps outside, very dark. We could see her profile as she sat upright in bed for a few seconds and, then pulling up the duvet, lay down.

'Just a minute,' John whispered to me, and he went on to the landing and switched on the light. There was now enough light for us to see most of her room, including the bed. Gingerly, I followed John across the room, half expecting Dawn to sit up and stare at me with those life-less, glazed eyes. But she was lying flat on her back with her eyes closed and breathing evenly, apparently asleep. John and I stood by her bed for a moment looking down at her; then, moving away, we crept out of her room. John closed her door and we returned to our bedroom.

'Christ!' John said as we entered. 'Whatever was that all about?'

I shook my head and shivered, but not from cold. I lay Adrian in his cot and tucked him in. He murmured and waved his little fist in the air but stayed asleep. I kissed him goodnight and returned to bed. John closed our bedroom door and joined me. We lay side by side, propped up on our pillows, for a few minutes without saying anything. There was no way I could go back to sleep. I could still feel my heart thudding from the shock I'd had, and I guessed John felt the same.

'Whatever was that all about?' John said again after a moment, rubbing his hand over his forehead.

'Do you think she *was* sleepwalking?' I asked, glancing at the bedroom door. 'I hope she doesn't do it again.'

'The social worker didn't say she had done it before, did she?' he asked at length.

'No, but she didn't say much at all. Perhaps it's the first time. Perhaps Dawn is worried by her first night somewhere new. Sleepwalking is caused by anxiety, isn't it?'

John shook his head. 'I've no idea. I don't know anything about it.'

'Neither do I.'

We didn't really know what to say to each other. The episode was completely outside anything we had experience or knowledge of, as I am sure it is for most people. 'I don't suppose she will do it again,' I offered, as much for my own benefit as John's.

Eventually, in the soothing half light, my eyes began to close. But no sooner was I asleep than I heard Adrian cry for his 3.00 a.m. feed. As I woke my gaze immediately went to the bedroom door. It was still shut, and I breathed an audible sigh of relief. I looked at John, still propped up on his pillow and asleep. Careful to wake him, I got out of bed and, collecting Adrian from his cot, returned to bed to feed him. Sometimes John heard Adrian cry and other times he didn't, depending on how deep a sleep he was in and how tired he was. Now he was exhausted, not only from his day at work but from a broken night's sleep. I felt pretty exhausted too, and the worry of what had happened stayed with me.

As Adrian suckled contentedly, blissfully unaware of the previous drama, I allowed my head to rest back on the cushioned headboard, and my eyes closed. Five minutes later I felt Adrian stop suckling, and I put him on the other breast. Again, my head slowly inched back as I began to doze.

Suddenly I was awake again, and my heart started pounding. I thought I heard a noise. With Adrian still feeding, I watched the door, my ears straining for any noise that suggested Dawn was out of bed, but no sound came from the carpeted landing. Then I jumped as the door handle slowly began to lower.

'John,' I said, and shook his arm. He was immediately awake. 'Look! The door.' He sat upright and we both stared, horrified, at the door. The handle moved down as far as it would go and then the door slowly opened.

Dawn appeared, her head held upright and her open eyes staring straight ahead. Her face was expressionless, as it had been before, and she looked even paler in the half light coming from the lamp. John and I sat motionless in bed, as Adrian continued to feed. We watched, transfixed, waiting to see what she was going to do next.

Dawn stood still for a moment, almost as though she was getting her bearings, although her eyes didn't move. Then slowly, with the same mechanical robot-like steps, she began to cross the room. She navigated her way round the end of our bed and stopped in front of Adrian's empty cot.

I consider myself level headed and not easily spooked, but at that moment, tired from lack of sleep and seeing Dawn's ghost-like figure in the half light, I reacted emotionally. 'She's come to get my baby!' I cried.

'Stay there,' John said firmly to me. He got out of bed and went to Dawn. She was now standing in exactly the same position as she had been before – in front of the cot, expressionless and very still.

'Dawn,' John said. 'Go back to your bed.' There was no reaction. He placed a hand lightly on each of her shoulders, and slowly began to turn her away from the cot. She didn't resist. Once turned, and facing towards the door, she began to walk of her own accord. John followed a step or two behind, and I watched as she went out of the door and on to the landing.

'No, into your bedroom,' I heard John say a moment later, so I thought she must have paused at the top of the stairs, as she had done before. A minute passed, when I assumed Dawn was getting into bed, then I heard John close her bedroom door. He reappeared, and shut our door firmly.

'She went straight to sleep again,' he said with a sigh, and climbing into bed. 'This is ridiculous! We can't have this at night. I don't feel safe in my own home.'

I looked at him. His brow was creased with worry. And although I couldn't have said why, I didn't feel safe either. We knew very little about Dawn, and nothing about sleepwalking. To have a stranger, albeit a girl of thirteen, come into your bedroom like a zombie in the middle of the night and go to your baby's cot was neither safe nor normal.

Adrian had finished feeding, and I changed his nappy and tucked him into his cot. John was propped up on his pillows, deep in anxious thought. I returned to bed, and lay down beside him. Neither of us spoke. Exhausted, and beside ourselves with worry, we remained on guard, listening for the slightest sound coming from the landing. I saw 4.00 a.m. come and go, and then at some point we must have both fallen asleep.

When I woke I did so with a start, and my eyes went straight to the bedroom door. It was still shut. I turned to look at the bedside clock. It was 7.30 a.m. We had over-slept!

'John,' I said rubbing his arm. 'It's seven thirty. John, wake up.'

'Damn!' he said, dragging himself up. 'I've got a meeting at eight thirty.' He heaved himself out of bed and went straight into the bathroom to shower.

I pulled back the duvet and hauling my feet to the ground, staggered to Adrian's cot. He was awake, chuntering, and wondering where his 7.00 a.m. feed had got to. He grinned when he saw me.

'Hello, my little man,' I said, and picking him up, I gave him a hug. 'Time for breakfast.'

Following my usual routine, although half an hour late, I took him into bed and fed him. As he suckled, I could have easily gone back to sleep. I felt absolutely exhausted, and the anxiety of the night hadn't left me. It was quiet in Dawn's room, so I guessed she was still asleep – hardly surprising, given the amount of time she had spent wandering around. Again I wondered why she had done it and whether she had done it before. Was it because she was in a strange house? Why she had gone to Adrian's cot I had no idea, and it still unsettled me. However, now that it was morning and the winter sun was making a brave attempt to light up the room, things somehow didn't seem quite as bad as they had done during the night.

John reappeared from his shower and quickly began to dress. 'I should just make it,' he said buttoning up a clean shirt and then opening the wardrobe for his suit. 'I'll grab a coffee before I go into the meeting. I'm knackered! What a night! Will you be all right alone today? I'll phone as soon as I come out of the meeting.'

'Yes, don't worry about me,' I said. 'I'll be fine. I'm going to take Dawn to school.'

Had I known what lay in wait for us in the months ahead, I would have answered 'No, I won't be all right, and neither is Dawn.'

Chapter Five

A Warning

I finished feeding Adrian and then changed his nappy, dressed him in a clean Babygro and resettled him in his cot while I washed and dressed. There was still no sound coming from Dawn's bedroom to suggest she was awake, and it was now 7.50 a.m. We needed to leave the house by 8.30 if she was to arrive at school on time. I had anticipated waking Dawn at seven on a weekday, which would give her plenty of time to wash and have breakfast, but with the broken night and oversleeping, that routine would have to be postponed until the following day.

I could have woken Dawn before I went into the bathroom, but I knew I was putting off facing her. Although the happenings of the night seemed less sinister now it was a new day, I still felt some unease and also trepidation. I didn't know what to expect, and what I was going to say to her? Would she remember what had happened? Did sleepwalkers remember their nocturnal wanderings? I'd no idea.

As I washed, I briefly wondered if we should have a lock fitted to our bedroom door to stop Dawn if she tried to come in again. Then I caught myself. Don't be so silly, I told myself; Dawn is a thirteen-year-old girl who became unsettled by spending her first night in a strange room, not something we had to lock out.

Washed, dressed, and as refreshed as I was going to be after the disturbed night, I collected Adrian from his cot and went to Dawn's room. The door was still shut, and there was no sound of movement coming from the other side. I knew teenagers liked their sleep: Jack would have slept away entire weekends had John or I not woken him. Now it was nearly eight o'clock and I knew I had to wake Dawn. I still hesitated. I hadn't yet worked out what I was going to say to her or how to approach what had happened. Would she look or behave any differently? Admonishing myself again, I knocked on the door and slowly opened it.

The room was lit by the early morning light and Dawn was in her bed, on her side, and fast asleep. Relieved to find she was still sleeping, I crossed to her bed. I didn't know what I had expected, but in sleep she looked so peaceful and serene that all my previous anxieties vanished.

'Dawn?' I said gently. 'Dawn, love, it's time to get up. It's nearly eight o'clock.'

She didn't stir; her breathing continued deep and uninterrupted. The poor kid was tired out and making up for lost sleep.

'Dawn, love,' I said again, a little louder. 'It's Cathy. Time to wake up.' I placed my hand lightly on her shoulder and gently rocked her. Her eyes slowly opened and, still on her side, she looked at me. 'Hi, love. It's morning,' I said. 'Do you remember where you are?' Whenever I was away from home, on holiday, I woke on the first morning wondering where I was.

She looked at me, blinked, and then smiled. 'Hi, Cathy,' she said brightly. 'Hi, Adrian, how are you?' She sat up in bed and, reaching out, lightly stroked his arm. I chided myself for entertaining the fears I had about seeing her again.

'Dawn, I'm sorry, love,' I said. 'But we've overslept. You'll have to wash and dress very quickly – otherwise we'll be late.'

'No problems,' she said, throwing back the duvet and getting out of bed (a lot quicker than Jack ever had).

'I'll fix your breakfast while you're in the bathroom,' I said. 'What would you like?'

She shrugged. 'I don't usually have breakfast, just a drink.'

In her pyjamas I could see just how slim she was – too slim I thought. 'I'd like you to have something,' I said. 'It's good to have some breakfast, even if it's just a slice of toast and a drink.'

'OK, toast. Thanks.'

'Good girl. What would you like on your toast? Jam, marmalade, honey – or Jack used to have peanut butter?' She pulled a face. 'No, I agree,' I said with a laugh. 'I couldn't stomach peanut butter either first thing in the morning. How about toast and honey?'

'Yes, but only one slice please.'

I smiled, 'Sure.' I opened the curtains and then reminded her to wear her clean jeans and jumper for school. 'I'll explain to the Head,' I said. 'And we'll go shopping after school and buy you some new underwear and clothes.'

'Are you coming to collect me from school?' she asked.

'Yes, for today. Then you can come home on the bus, if you like.'

'That's fine,' she said amicably. Dawn was the same cooperative and pleasant child she had been the evening before, and I again chided myself for thinking she would be any different – she was only a girl who had been sleep-walking, not some malevolent changeling.

I hesitated before going out of the room, and looked at her as she gathered up her clean clothes. 'Did you sleep well, Dawn?'

'Yes thanks. Did you?'

'Not really. John and I were up twice in the night.' I watched her for any sign that she could remember.

'What, with Adrian?' she asked, meeting my gaze. 'Babies have to be fed in the night, don't they?'

'Yes,' I said, still looking at her. 'I'm glad you slept all right because sometimes it can be a bit unsettling sleeping somewhere different. But you were OK?'

'Yes, fine. It's a very comfortable bed.'

'Great,' I said brightly, and left her to get ready.

Going downstairs, I decided that Dawn had no idea she had been sleepwalking, and I saw no point in telling her. It could have been very embarrassing for her to learn that she had been wandering around in her pyja-mas in the middle of the night, with no knowledge of, or control over, what she had been doing. Telling her was likely to make her even more anxious. I came to the conclusion therefore that just as some people grind their teeth or talk in their sleep when anxious, Dawn had been sleepwalking because she'd become unsettled by spending her first night in a strange room. Perhaps she had drawn comfort from coming into our bedroom and 'seeing' us, and Adrian. Clearly the experience, and whatever had brought her to us in the middle of the

night, was in her subconscious, where I thought it
should stay.

In the kitchen, I sat Adrian in his recliner so that he
could see me, and I dropped a couple of slices of bread in
the toaster and set about making myself a cup of coffee. I
now felt a lot happier, having seen Dawn, and also very
positive. Dawn was a lovely kid, and although I remained a
little concerned about her being too compliant, my
worries about her sleepwalking had now gone. I was looking forward to getting to know Dawn and, supporting and
helping her in any way I could. I was also looking forward
to having another female in the house – at present I was
outnumbered by John and Adrian – and I envisaged Dawn
and myself chatting like mother and daughter. How long
Dawn would be staying with us, I'd no idea. But from what
I knew of her previous behaviour, I suspected her parents
hadn't provided much in the way of parenting. I felt sorry
for Dawn. At thirteen, with all the changes and conflicting
emotions that accompanies being a teenager, when
support, understanding and reassurance is most needed,
Dawn had just been left to get on with it.

Five minutes later Dawn appeared, washed and dressed.
'I'm sorry to be a nuisance, Cathy,' she said, hesitantly, 'but
I haven't got a hairbrush. Have you got a spare one,
please?'

'Yes, I think I so. You sit down and have your toast and
juice while I pop upstairs and try to find it.'

'Thanks,' she said, and she smiled at Adrian.

I gave Dawn her toast and juice and left her eating at
the table in the dining area of the kitchen, with Adrian
watching her from his recliner, while I went upstairs. I
knew I had a spare hairbrush somewhere – it had been

part of a set given to me by an aunt at Christmas – but I spent some minutes rummaging through the drawers in my bedroom, not sure where I had put it. Eventually I discovered it at the bottom of my underwear drawer and I quickly returned downstairs.

'Oh!' I said with a start as I entered the kitchen. Dawn had taken Adrian out of his recliner and had him sitting on her lap at the table. 'Be careful he doesn't fall,' I said, going straight to the table.

'I am careful,' Dawn said, lightly bouncing Adrian on her lap. 'He's having a bit of breakfast.' I looked at Adrian and saw he had something in his mouth, which he was trying to spit out. I quickly lifted him off Dawn's lap and opened his mouth. A large lump of toast was lodged at the back of his mouth and I hooked it out with my forefinger.

'Dawn, love,' I said, 'you can't give him toast! He's only sixteen weeks old. He hasn't any teeth. He can't chew it. He would choke.' I checked his mouth to make sure it was empty.

'I'm sorry, Cathy, I didn't realise.'

'No, OK. But don't give him anything again, will you, love? And also I would rather you left him in his recliner. You can hold him by all means, but please wait until I'm with you. He's very precious, all right?'

She nodded agreeably. As she was unaware of the danger of giving a baby something hard to eat, or what could happen if a baby fell from a lap, I could hardly tell her off. But it was a warning to me that I should not assume a girl of thirteen would know such things – I'm sure I didn't at her age – and I needed to be more vigilant.

Chapter Six

No Homework

St James's School was a medium-sized comprehensive, catering for boys and girls from the ages of twelve to eighteen. I had driven past it on a number of occasions but had never been in. I knew it had a good reputation and was generally held by parents to be better than the other secondary school in the area. Jack's school had been further away, on the edge of the county, near where his parents lived; he had continued going there when he had stayed with us to avoid disrupting his education. The building was about fifty years old and fronted the road. Its playing fields were at the rear, together with a large extension, which had been recently added to accommodate the ever-increasing local school population.

I parked in a side road and reached into the back of the car for my large shoulder bag, which had become my constant companion since I'd had Adrian. It contained clean nappies, baby wipes, a small bottle of boiled water, and a rattle and a dummy in case he became restless. Then I carefully lifted Adrian out from his baby seat.

'Shall I carry him?' Dawn immediately asked. Already standing on the pavement, she stretched out her arms ready to receive him. 'You're with me, and I won't drop him.'

I looked at the hard concrete pavement. 'No, it's all right, thanks, love. I can manage.' She wasn't offended by my refusal, and I recognised she only wanted to help but, again, I could see the dangers where a thirteen-year-old could not. I briefly wondered if her enthusiasm for helping with Adrian was going to cause a problem.

Dawn and I joined the other pupils who were heading towards the main entrance, and followed a couple of boys up the stone steps and through the open double doors. Reception was immediately on the right and the sliding glass partition doors were closed. Repositioning Adrian in my arms, I pressed the bell for attention. Dawn hadn't said anything since leaving the car, not even to Adrian, to whom she had chatted constantly during the journey.

'Are you all right?' I asked her, as we waited for the reception bell to be answered. Dawn nodded but didn't say anything.

Pupils streamed along the corridor behind us and then a siren signalling the start of school suddenly went off over our heads. Adrian nearly leapt out of my arms with fright and I held him close and rocked him. 'That was loud,' I said to Dawn when the noise had stopped.

'I have to go to my lessons now. I can't be late.'

'All right. You join your class while I see someone here. If your teacher asks why you're not in uniform, explain I am seeing the Head.'

She nodded, and kissed Adrian's cheek, and then mine.

'Have a good day,' I said. 'I'll wait for you outside. Three fifteen, isn't it?'

'It'll take me five minutes to get out.'

'OK, love. See you later.'

She gave Adrian another kiss and then disappeared down the corridor with the other students. I pressed the buzzer again at reception and a woman finally appeared behind the glass partition and slid open one of the doors.

'Yes?' she asked, brusquely.

'My name is Cathy Glass. Dawn Jennings is staying with me. I'm her foster carer.'

'Dawn Jennings? Which class is she in?'

I hadn't thought to ask Dawn. 'I'm not sure. She's thirteen.'

'That's the second year.' She paused. 'Oh yes, Dawn Jennings. She hasn't been here long, has she?'

'I really don't know. I'd like to speak to someone about Dawn. Is the Head available? Or the Deputy?'

'At this time of day? You must be joking! They're busy. And her teacher will be with her in the classroom for registration. Can't you come back later?'

'I could,' I said, not appreciating her manner. 'But Dawn isn't in school uniform, and I wanted to explain the reason to someone. And also have a chat about Dawn.'

She hesitated. 'Stay there.' She closed the glass partition and went to a desk behind her, where she picked up a phone. As the noise level in the corridor rose with the last of the pupils running in to avoid being late, I rocked Adrian. I saw the receptionist put down the phone, and then the glass door slid open again.

'You're in luck,' she said. 'The Head of Year can see you for a few minutes. Wait over there.' She pointed across the corridor to an open door.

'Thank you,' I said.

I went over to the waiting room, where there were four wooden chairs and a small table displaying copies of the school prospectus. I sat down and resettled Adrian on my lap. He was busy looking around, although there wasn't much to see. The walls were light grey and blank, except for a couple of road safety posters warning children about the hazards of crossing a road. I slid my bag from my shoulder and took out Adrian's rattle, which I tucked into his hand. He grinned, waved it around and threw it on the floor. I picked it up and tucked it into his hand again, and he threw it straight down. 'I think you're having a game with me,' I said as I bent to retrieve it. He giggled and kicked his feet in the air. I tucked the rattle into my coat pocket in case he needed it later.

'Mrs Glass?' A smartly dressed woman in her mid-thirties appeared through the doorway. 'I'm Jane Matthews, Dawn's Head of Year.' I shook her hand and she smiled at Adrian. 'I thought Dawn was in a teenage residential home?' she asked, sitting in the adjacent chair.

'She was for three days. But she came to me yesterday evening. I wanted to introduce myself, and also to let you know that Dawn hasn't got her school uniform with her. I'll be buying a replacement this afternoon. I didn't want her to get in trouble.'

Jane Matthews looked at me carefully. 'To be honest, Dawn is rarely in school uniform anyway, and come to that she's rarely in school.'

'That will change now,' I said. 'She seems to have been very unsettled at home, and to have spent most of her time going between her mum and dad's.'

'They're divorced, aren't they?'

'So I believe.'

'Let me make a note of your contact details. I'll get some paper.' She disappeared across the corridor and into

the reception office, reappearing with a sheet of paper and
a biro. Jane Matthews seemed efficient yet approachable,
and I was hoping to learn more about Dawn's background. Sitting down beside me again, she headed the
paper 'Dawn Jennings' and wrote my name beneath it. I
gave her my address and telephone number.

'Which shop do I buy her uniform from?' I asked, aware
that different schools had different supply outlets.

'Gray's, in town. Do you know it?'

'Yes, it's in the High Street, isn't it?' She nodded. 'I
want to give Dawn any help I can with her school work,'
I said.

'Good. If Dawn comes to school regularly it will help.
Her attendance has been appalling. We've sent numerous
letters to mum, asking her to come in and talk to us but
she hasn't taken up any of the appointments. We've tried
phoning, but she's never there, and we don't have a phone
number for dad.'

I nodded. 'Dawn doesn't seem to like school. I don't
know why. Can you think of a reason?'

'Not really, other than that she hasn't been here long
enough to make friends. She only started at this school in
September, and since then she's missed more days than
she's put in. She does the work set in class but as far as I'm
aware has never handed in a piece of homework."

'Oh,' I said. 'I didn't realise it was that bad. I know very
little about Dawn's background. Can you tell me anything?'

'Unfortunately not. Dawn's notes are very thin. She
attended a school in Manchester for a while and also one
in Gatesby. I think she's been a poor school attender from
the beginning. How long will she be staying with you?'

'I don't know,' I said. 'I'm hoping her social worker will let me know what's happening.'

'Hopefully she will let us know too. We can't support a child if we're not kept informed.' I nodded in agreement. 'Dawn is quite an able child,' Jane Matthews continued, 'but she is well behind in her education. Hopefully she will start to catch up now. She seems likeable enough; there haven't been any incidents. But as I said, she's hardly been here, so I don't really know her.' She leant forward and smiled at Adrian. 'He's a real cutie, is he your first?'

I smiled. 'Yes. Does it show?'

'No, I just wondered. My husband and I have been trying for a baby for some time, but the years are passing.'

I know the feeling, I thought. 'Well, I wish you luck,' I said. 'And thanks for seeing me.'

'You're welcome.'

We said goodbye and I left, passing a couple of very late students going in. Although I hadn't learned any more about Dawn's background, I had at least made contact with the school, and they now knew I wanted to help Dawn with her school work.

I returned home, fed Adrian and while he had his nap, did the housework. Then I sat on the sofa with my lunch and soon found I was beginning to doze. The phone rang. It was John, making a quick call between meetings.

'How are you all?' he asked.

'OK, apart from being tired. Dawn doesn't remember a thing about last night and when I asked her, she said she'd slept well. I took her to school and met the Head of Year.'

'Good. And how's Adrian?'

'Asleep.'

'Well, when he wakes, tell him his daddy sends his love.'

'I will. Are you home at the normal time tonight?'

'Should be. See you later then. Love you.'

'And you.'

I collected Dawn as arranged at the end of school and took her shopping. We bought a new school uniform and a pair of school shoes first, then some casual clothes – joggers, a pair of jeans, a skirt, two jumpers, T-shirts and underwear. I wrote the cheques but didn't dare add up the accumulated amount. If Dawn's social worker didn't produce any more clothes from Dawn's mum or dad, I would have to add to Dawn's wardrobe gradually. But for now Dawn had three changes of casual clothes and a complete school uniform. Dawn thanked me profusely as I bought each item and I was really touched. Adrian was in his stroller as we shopped and Dawn pushed him for most of the time. I had fed him before I had left home and he had his boiled water in the shops.

When we arrived home, Dawn hung her new clothes in her wardrobe while I fed Adrian. I settled Adrian in his recliner in the kitchen while I made dinner. Dawn helped me prepare the vegetables and then watched television in the lounge until John came home. The three of us, watched by Adrian, ate together at the table. John asked Dawn about her day at school, as I had done, and she gave the same reply: 'It was good, thanks.' He also asked, as I had done, if she had any homework and received the same reply: 'No.'

We accepted this as the truth; having made contact with the school I assumed they would let me know if homework wasn't done, or was handed in late.

Dawn had a bath at 8.00 p.m. and then came downstairs to say goodnight. Half an hour later when I went up to check on her she was fast asleep – on her side and looking very peaceful. I bathed Adrian and then, following our usual routine, I fed him and John settled him in his cot while I had my bath. After so little sleep the night before, we were both grateful to be in bed at 10.30 p.m., but while neither of us said so, I think we were both feeling pretty apprehensive about what the night might have in store.

'I'm sure she'll sleep well tonight,' I said as we drifted off to sleep. 'She's as exhausted as we are.'

'Hmm,' said John, 'I hope so.' And followed it with a snore.

At 2.45 p.m., when Adrian woke for his feed, my eyes went straight to our bedroom door, and it was still shut. Likewise when the alarm went off it was still closed. I finally put the incident of the night before behind us. Clearly, I thought, Dawn had been unsettled by her first night in a strange bed and, having now got used it was now going to be fine.

Chapter Seven

Deceived

Two weeks passed and Dawn appeared to be settling in. I saw her off at the front door to catch the bus to school at eight o'clock each morning, and welcomed her home at 3.45 each afternoon. She had a drink and a snack when she first got in, and then spent some time playing with Adrian under my (not conspicuous) supervision, before going to her room to do her homework. Each night John, Dawn and I ate together. John and I always asked Dawn about her day at school, and if she needed any help with her homework, which she never did. She said she found the work 'quite easy' now she had 'got down to it'.

On the Thursday morning of her third week with us, I was doing my usual tidying up when the phone rang. It was Jane Matthews, the Head of Year.

'Is Dawn ill?' she asked.

'No,' I said, surprised. 'Why? Is she saying she is feeling unwell?'

'I don't know, Mrs Glass. Dawn isn't here to ask. She hasn't been in school all week.'

'What? Are you sure?' I gasped.

'I'm absolutely positive. The last time Dawn was in school was on Friday morning. We haven't seen her since.'

I paused in disbelief. 'And you don't know where she is?'

'No. And I take it you don't either?'

I was silent as I grappled with what I was being told, and my thoughts raced over the preceding week. 'But Dawn has been leaving the house to catch the bus to school each morning, and returning at the end of school. She's even been doing her homework!'

I heard a small cynical laugh. 'Then the only thing she hasn't been doing is attending school! I wonder if she's been setting the homework herself – ten out of ten for inventiveness if she has!'

Now I came to think of it, John and I hadn't actually seen Dawn doing her homework. We had trusted her when she had gone to her room each evening and then reappeared later saying she had done it. Accepting her word, we had never asked to see the completed work. But I realised that if I told Jane Matthews this she would think me very naïve. 'She's been lying to us then,' I said in dismay.

'It certainly sounds like it. And I am now wondering about the dental appointment she had last Friday.'

'What dental appointment?'

There was another cynical snort. 'I needn't wonder any longer! Dawn came into school last Friday morning with a letter from you saying she had to leave school at twelve o'clock for a dental appointment, and wouldn't be returning in the afternoon. Can I now assume it was a forgery?'

My heart sunk further. 'Yes. I didn't write it. There was no dental appointment,' I confirmed in disbelief. Then immediately began to add worry to my feelings of incredulity and bitter disappointment. 'I hope Dawn is all right. Where do you think she could be?'

'I've no idea, but I'm sure she can take care of herself. My guess is she'll stroll in at her usual time as if she has just returned home from school.'

My thoughts flashed to the previous afternoons when she had done just that – smiling sweetly, and answering my questions as to whether she'd had a good day. She had replied positively, and with details of her day at school, all of which I now knew she had made up. For a second I wondered if there was a rational explanation, for I still couldn't believe Dawn would have lied to me so extensively and with such conviction. But what explanation could there be?

'Thank you for telling me,' I said lamely. 'I'll speak to Dawn as soon as she comes home.'

'Can we expect to see Dawn in school tomorrow?'

'Yes, most definitely, even if I have to bring her myself.'

'And in future if Dawn is genuinely absent could you phone the school secretary and let us know? I've put a note on her file that if she doesn't arrive then the school secretary is to phone you. That way we won't be duped again.'

'Yes, I will.'

'I'll notify Dawn's social worker,' Jane Matthews finished by saying. 'And I'll look forward to Dawn gracing us with her presence tomorrow.'

'Yes. Thank you. Goodbye.'

I assumed Jane had to tell Ruth, but I felt as if I was being reported for doing something wrong, which in a way I was – for unwittingly allowing Dawn to play truant.

Jane Matthews had been light and almost flippant in her approach to Dawn's behaviour, presumably from years of being a teacher and having to deal with similar situations;

perhaps it was a coping mechanism. However, as I put down the phone, I was still reeling from the shock. How could Dawn have lied to us all week, and so convincingly? And forge a note from me! Clearly I had been too naïve and trusting, but the little details Dawn had given me of her day at school and the new friends she had made had been so plausible. I hadn't for one moment doubted her. Why should I? There had been no reason. I had even suggested to Dawn that she might like to invite her new friend, Mandy, home to dinner one evening. Was there a Mandy? Did she even exist? And what had Dawn been doing in her bedroom for the two hours each evening when she had said she was doing her homework? There was no television in her room, and her music hadn't been on.

I returned to the lounge, where Adrian was dozing in his recliner. I sat on the sofa, staring into space and thinking. I considered phoning John and telling him, but I didn't like to disturb him at work. He was highly committed and had a lot of responsibility, and I only ever phoned if it was an emergency – the last time had been when I had gone into labour. Sometimes he phoned me in his lunch hour and I dearly hoped he would do so today. I really needed to offload what had happened, my sadness that Dawn had abused my trust and my concern for her safety.

The afternoon passed with my heart heavy, and my thoughts chasing in all directions. I worried about what Dawn had been doing all week when she should have been in school, and what she was doing now. Where could she be? A day can be a long time if you aren't gainfully occupied. Was she wandering the streets? Sitting in the library or a coffee shop? Or had she gone somewhere, or met someone I didn't know about? It was the middle of winter and bitterly cold, and I worried if she was managing to keep warm, and whether she'd had anything to eat. I had given her money for school dinner, but £1.50 wouldn't buy much outside the subsidised school canteen.

At 2.15 p.m. the phone rang and I quickly snatched it up, hoping it was Dawn, confessing all and asking me to collect her, or even John phoning late. But it was Ruth, Dawn's social worker.

'Has she appeared yet?' she asked bluntly.

My sense of responsibility and guilt for Dawn's absence soared. 'No, she hasn't. Do you know where she could be?'

'No. We never do.'

'She's vanished for a whole day before, then?' I asked. Ruth and Jane Matthews had said Dawn had missed school but neither had given any details.

'When she was with her mother. It seems she's up to her old tricks again. It's a pity – I thought she might have settled with you.'

'She has settled,' I said defensively. 'Dawn is very settled at home. I'm sure there's an explanation. There must be.'

Ruth said nothing, but her silence said it all. She clearly thought me naïve, and my confidence in Dawn misplaced. 'We can but hope,' Ruth added dryly. 'Doubtless she'll stroll in when it suits her with a very good explanation. Whether it's true or not I'll leave it to your judgement. Have you given her pocket money?'

'Yes.'

'All of it?'

'Yes. Was that wrong?'

'It might be better in future if you gave her a little at the end of each day, as part of a reward system. We'll discuss it. I've set up a meeting for next Tuesday so that you and your husband can meet Dawn's mother. Bring Dawn with you and we can draw up a contract of good behaviour.'

'All right, next Tuesday,' I said, more concerned with Dawn's safety than a meeting.

'It's at the teenage unit at seven o'clock.'

'We'll be there,' I confirmed. 'Shall I phone you when Dawn comes home?'

'Only if there's a problem. Otherwise we'll discuss it at the meeting.'

We said goodbye and I hung up. I took my diary from my handbag and made a note of the meeting. I couldn't settle to anything for the rest of the afternoon. I watched the clock, wondered where on earth Dawn could be, and rehearsed what I was going to say to her when she did come home. It crossed my mind that possibly I should leave confronting her until John came home so that I had his moral support, but I dismissed the idea. I couldn't carry on as normal, chatting to Dawn as though nothing had happened, knowing what I did. Although of course that was exactly what Dawn had done – carried on as normal and pretending she had been in school all week.

Adrian was unsettled too. I was so preoccupied that I hadn't played with him as much as I usually did and neither had I taken him out for our usual 'breath of fresh air'. By 3.30 p.m. I was pacing the room with Adrian in my arms and waiting for Dawn to return. At 3.45, dead on time, the front door bell rang, and my stomach churned. I braced myself as I went to the front door. I still hadn't formulated what I was going to say, but I knew I would be saying it sooner rather than later.

Cut

I opened the door. 'Hello, Dawn, come in. It's freezing out there.' I gave a brief tight smile.

'I know,' she said, shivering. 'I'm so cold.' As usual she gave Adrian a kiss on the cheek.

I closed the door and looked at her. She was perfectly relaxed and at ease, as if she had just returned from a normal day at school. She dropped her school bag in the hall and then unzipped her jacket and looped it over the hall stand. Normally I asked her how her day had been, but today I didn't. I couldn't set her up for another lie, for doubtless she would have said, as she had been saying, 'Good, Cathy,' and then added some detail, which now I knew would be a lie.

'Dawn,' I said sombrely. 'When you've got yourself a drink and a biscuit, I need to talk to you.' I felt my anxiety level rise.

She looked at me, apparently completely innocent and without any hint of guilt. 'Is everything OK, Cathy?' she asked concerned. 'You look serious.'

'Yes, it is serious, Dawn. I've had some rather bad news. Get yourself a drink and then come into the lounge, please.'

'I don't want a drink. I'll come in now.' She headed towards the lounge, and as I followed with Adrian in my arms, I clung to the last unrealistic hope that there was a plausible explanation.

She sat in the armchair and I sat on the sofa with Adrian in my lap.

'You look unhappy,' Dawn said. 'I hope it's nothing I've done?'

I met her gaze. 'Dawn, Mrs Matthews phoned me today. I think you can guess what she told me.'

For a moment her face registered astonishment and she looked as though she was about to say 'No', but then thought about it and, looking down, said a quiet 'Yes.'

'You haven't been going to school all week, have you?'

She shook her head. 'I'm sorry, Cathy. You have been so good to me. I've let you down badly, haven't I?'

'Yes, you have. And not only because you haven't been going to school. It's the lying and deceit that I find most hurtful. And that letter you wrote on Friday pretending it was from me, saying you were going to the dentist – that was very dishonest. Why haven't you been going to school?'

She raised her head and looked at me, her face sad and her eyes filling. 'I'm sorry, Cathy. Really I am, but school is a bad place for me. I hate it. I can't make any friends. I feel so alone.'

I immediately felt a stab of sympathy. 'Is that why you haven't been going – because of not having any friends?' I continued to look at her.

She nodded, and then sniffed.

'There's no need to cry. We just have to get this sorted and find a way forward.'

She rubbed the back of her hand over her eyes. 'I haven't been at that school long, and everyone already has their own friends. No one wants to let me into their group. I've tried to be friends but no one wants to know. I feel so alone when everyone is laughing and talking at breaktime. I think they're laughing at me – Johnny-no-mates. I nearly told you, Cathy, but I couldn't. I thought you would think me silly.'

'I would never think you silly, Dawn. I'm just sorry you didn't feel you could tell me.' I was so relieved that there was a genuine reason, and one that was understandable, that I could have forgiven Dawn anything at that point. I also felt very sorry for her, and sad that she had been suffering all this time in silence. 'Thank you for telling me,' I said at last. 'But if you had told me sooner I could have helped you.'

'How?' she said. 'You can't force other kids to be my friend.'

'No, but I can speak to your Head of Year and make her aware of the problem. I'm sure she will be able to offer something. At present she just thinks you're playing truant. And, Dawn, it's so important to talk about your problems. You know what they say – a problem shared is a problem halved.' She nodded. 'I'm always here to listen to you and help in any way I can. But Dawn, love, you won't make friends if you don't go to school, will you?' She nodded and sniffed again. 'Now dry your eyes and come over here and give me a hug.'

She took a tissue from the sleeve of her school jumper and wiped her eyes, then came over and sat beside me on the sofa. With Adrian on my lap I put my arm around Dawn's shoulders and gave her a big hug. 'I know making friends can be difficult, especially when you're new to the school. But running away from a problem never helps. At some point it has to be confronted and dealt with.'

'I know, Cathy. Thank you for being so understanding. Will you speak to the school and explain?'

'Yes. Tomorrow I'll come in with you and see Mrs Matthews. I'm sure she'll be able to help.'

'Thanks,' she said again. 'You're so kind. My mum didn't care a toss.'

'Didn't she?'

Dawn shook her head sadly but clearly didn't want to say any more.

'So you promise you won't miss school again?' I said, easing my arm from her shoulders to resettle Adrian on my lap.

'I promise,' she said.

'And one last thing, Dawn, before we put all this behind us.'

'Yes?'

'Where have you been going when you haven't been in school?'

She shrugged. 'Just wandering around. In and out of the shops, McDonald's, anywhere that was warm. It was horrible. I really wanted to come home to you, but I daren't.'

'OK, love. Thanks for telling me. Now let's get you that hot drink and a snack. I take it you won't be going to your bedroom to do your homework tonight?'

She met my gaze and returned my smile. 'No, I'm sorry. I hated deceiving you and John. And it was so boring sat up there alone.'

'All right, we'll say no more about it.' Before I got up from the sofa Dawn planted a big kiss on my cheek.

'Thanks, Cathy. You're great! I love being here.'

When John arrived home from work, at his usual time of 6.30 p.m., it was to a calm and happy household. Adrian was in his recliner in the kitchen being entertained by Dawn, while I put the finishing touches to the dinner. The three of us chatted as we ate, mainly about the liquidised food I was now introducing into Adrian's diet in the hope that he would start to sleep through the night. I waited until Dawn had gone up for her bath before I told John what had happened. And because the matter had been dealt with, it wasn't a big issue: just something else we discussed in the evening when we swapped details of our day.

The following morning I took Dawn into school and, while she joined her class for registration, I saw Jane Matthews.

'I've got just the answer,' Jane said helpfully after I'd explained Dawn's problem with making friends. 'We've got a new girl arriving in school on Monday, Natasha, and she will be in Dawn's class. I'll speak to Dawn today and I'll ask her if she'd like to be Natasha's "buddy". We usually team up anyone new with another student for the first few weeks. The buddy shows them around, sits next to them in lessons and generally helps them settle in. They often remain good friends.'

'That sounds terrific,' I said. 'I'm sure it will help. Thank you so much.'

'You're welcome. Let's hope it has the desired effect. Dawn can't afford to miss any more school.'

'She won't.' I said confidently. 'I'm sure of it.'

When Dawn came home from school that Friday afternoon, the first thing she told me was that she was going to be a 'buddy' for a new girl starting on Monday. I understood from what she said that it was quite a privilege to be asked, and buddy status was much coveted by the other students.

Friday evening passed with John, Dawn and me relaxing at the end of the school/working week, together with the maths homework Dawn produced, which John helped her with. The three of us then watched a television movie, and Dawn went up to bed when it had finished at 10.30 p.m.

With Adrian now on solids, and it being the weekend, I was hoping for a lie-in. But at 2.00 a.m. I was suddenly awake. In the small light coming from the street lamp, I saw Dawn in her pyjamas, enter our bedroom and cross to Adrian's cot. As before, she moved mechanically, with her eyes wide and staring. I was just waking John, when Dawn leant forward over the cot, about to pick up Adrian.

'No, Dawn!' I cried, and leapt out of bed.

Chapter Eight

Womanhood

She must have heard my voice, because she froze.

John was beside me at the cot; Adrian's eyes flickered open and closed again. Dawn remained where she was, leaning over Adrian's cot. Very slowly she began to straighten, and turning, she 'looked' at me. But as before when she had been sleepwalking, her eyes were glazed, and I was sure, sightless. She didn't blink, and seemed to be staring through me rather than looking at me.

'Dawn,' I said. 'Go back to your bed.' I felt my heart pounding with the shock of waking suddenly to find her in our room.

'Dawn go to your own bed,' John repeated, more firmly. He put his hands on her shoulder to turn her in the right direction. But as his hands made contact she suddenly took a step back, as though she had felt his touch and recoiled. John and I started as she spoke.

'No,' she said in a slow, heavy voice. 'No, it wasn't me. I wouldn't do that.' She stopped, and still staring straight through me, raised her arms and began making a 'chopping' motion with the edge of her right hand on her left wrist.

We watched, transfixed in the half light, as Dawn continued to 'chop' her wrist; then, as though satisfied, she lowered her arms to her sides. She slowly turned to face the door and began to cross the room. John and I followed; Adrian had returned to sleep. We went out of our bedroom and along the landing. When Dawn reached the top of the stairs she paused, as she had done before, and then continued into her bedroom. We waited at her bedroom door, watching the dim outline of her shadow as she approached the bed. Slowly lifting back the duvet, she climbed in. She sat upright for a moment, staring straight ahead, then lay down and pulled the duvet up around her.

We came out, quietly closed the door and returned to our bedroom. I checked on Adrian, who was still sleeping, and then got into bed beside John.

'We're going to have to say something to her,' John said, flopping back on the pillows, exhausted. 'This isn't normal. Perhaps if we tell her it will help.'

'Do you think she is worrying about school?' I suggested. 'When she said "No, it wasn't me," it sounded as though she was being blamed for something. Do you think she's in trouble at school?'

'I've no idea.' John sighed. 'But why would she come to Adrian's cot if it was to do with school? If it happens again, I'll put a lock on our bedroom door. At least then we'll know Adrian's safe.'

'I'm sure she wouldn't harm Adrian,' I said with a start. 'I think she just wants to cuddle him like she does during the day.' But even as I said it I knew that picking up Adrian while sleepwalking could easily have resulted in her harming him, even though Dawn wouldn't have intended it.

'We'll raise the subject with her mother and social worker when we see them on Tuesday,' John said. 'Perhaps they can throw some light on it. It's very disturbing.'

* * *

Dawn came into our room again half an hour later. We were still awake, and we steered her straight back to bed, where she remained until morning. John and I spent the rest of the night tossing and turning, and each time I woke my eyes immediately went to the bedroom door to check it was still closed. Adrian didn't wake for a feed again until 5.00 a.m. I fed and changed him and he went straight back to sleep. As it was Saturday, John and I were able to doze until 7.30, when Adrian woke again, and we brought him into our bed.

We had breakfast together just before nine o'clock; Dawn was still asleep. John ate his breakfast with Adrian on his lap, with Adrian making repeated little attempts to grab John's spoon on the way to his mouth, and giggling when he missed it.

'I *will* say something to Dawn,' I said to John as we ate. We had been talking about Dawn and her sleepwalking on and off since waking. 'But I won't actually tell her the details of what she did. It could make her even more anxious. And I'll try to find out what's worrying her.' John and I had agreed that we thought Dawn's sleepwalking, together with her comment 'No, it wasn't me', must be caused by worrying.

When Dawn finally came downstairs at just gone ten o'clock she was washed, dressed and very relaxed. John was playing with Adrian in the lounge, having some quality time, and a father-to-son 'conversation' in which Adrian answered by babbling. I made Dawn the toast she asked for and then sat at the table with my mug of coffee while she ate.

'Did you sleep all right?' I asked her after a moment.

'Yes, thanks. I always do.'

I hesitated, looked down at my coffee, and then summoned up the courage to say what I had rehearsed in my head, which I hoped was tactful and wouldn't make her anxious. 'Actually, love, you were quite restless last night. You got out of your bed, and I had to resettle you.'

'Oh, I'm sorry. Did I wake you?' she asked, surprised and embarrassed.

'Yes, but that doesn't matter. I am more concerned that something could be worrying you. You were talking in your sleep.'

She looked at me anxiously. 'Was I? What did I say?'

'It sounded as though you were being blamed for something you didn't do. You said, "No, it wasn't me."' The words seemed to register with Dawn and she looked away, almost guiltily.

'Is there something worrying you?' I asked. 'Remember what we said about sharing worries?'

She brought her gaze back to mine. 'No, Cathy. There isn't, really. I don't know what I was talking about. I did it at my mum's and she said I was sleepwalking, but I don't remember. I hope I haven't been sleepwalking here.'

I didn't know what to say. As sure as I was that Dawn was worrying about something, although she had denied it, I was now equally sure she had no idea that she had been sleepwalking. If I told her, wouldn't it make her even more anxious? I decided not to. 'You were very restless,' I said. 'Are you sure there's nothing bothering you? Often worries can play on our minds at night.'

'No,' she said, leaving the rest of her toast. 'I would tell you if there was. I'm so sorry I woke you and John. I hope I don't do it again.'

* * *

Dawn and I had a pleasant day on Saturday. Leaving Adrian with John, I took Dawn clothes shopping and, among other things, bought her a new winter coat, which she loved and was also warmer than the leather jacket she had been wearing. In the afternoon she helped me with some housework and seemed to enjoy chatting as we worked together. That evening John, Dawn and I had a Chinese take-away, which Dawn thoroughly enjoyed; then we watched a video together, and she went up to bed at 10.30 p.m.

However, at 2 a.m., John and I, either sensing her presence or hearing our bedroom door open, woke to find Dawn entering our room. We immediately got out of bed. As before, Dawn went to Adrian's cot, but this time she didn't lean over to try to pick him up. She stood beside the cot, slightly turned away, staring straight ahead with her eyes glazed and unfocused. After a moment she raised her arms and began making the same chopping motion she had done the night before, with the side of her right hand coming down on to her left wrist. Only now it was harder, more insistent, as though she was punishing herself. As she 'chopped' she grimaced, as if she was inflicting and experiencing pain, although of course the soft flesh of one hand striking the other couldn't have caused her real damage or pain. She continued this chopping for about half a minute; then, as though she had finished what she had set out to do, she turned and left our room, and we saw her back to bed.

On Sunday morning, after John and I had spent another sleepless night, and had become beside ourselves with worry, John went to the large hardware store on the edge of town and bought a lock. While he fitted it on our bedroom door, I took Dawn out for a walk with Adrian in his stroller so that she wouldn't know what we were doing. John and I both felt guilty about locking Dawn out of our bedroom, but what else could we do? We were both exhausted, and if we were honest, we no longer felt safe in our own bed. We were also worried that the next time it happened we might not hear Dawn enter; visions of her taking Adrian from his cot and then dropping him while we slept on haunted me.

When Dawn and I returned home, John nodded to me that the job was done, and the next time I went upstairs I had a look. The key was in the lock on the inside of the door and only a small hole was visible on the outside. I was immensely relieved, but also still uncomfortable that we were having to use a lock at all. I had decided, while strolling in the park, that on Monday, when Dawn was at school, I would visit the library and try to find out more about sleepwalking and how to deal with it. If we could stop Dawn from sleepwalking, the lock wouldn't be needed.

That night John locked our bedroom door before he got into bed and we slept soundly, only waking when Adrian cried for a feed at 4.00 a.m. In the morning John was up first and said that Dawn's bedroom door was still closed, so we assumed that she hadn't been sleepwalking and therefore hadn't attempted to enter our room. I was doubly relieved, for what had started to worry me was that if Dawn did sleepwalk, where would she go now our door was locked? Would she simply try the door and, unable to get in, return to her own bed? Or would she sleepwalk somewhere else and put herself in danger? Downstairs possibly, with all the hazards that entailed. We could only wait and see what happened.

For now I had to concentrate on the day ahead – it was Monday and the start of a new week.

Once John had gone to work, I fell into the weekday routine – feeding and changing Adrian, washing and dressing myself, then waking Dawn. She had her usual toast and honey, and although I had offered to take her in the car to school and see her in, she wanted to catch the bus. I had to trust her to go to school, and I didn't envisage a problem because she was looking forward to meeting Natasha, the new girl she was going to buddy. Checking Dawn had her dinner money and bus pass, I wished her luck, told her how smart she looked in her new coat and said I would be thinking about her. She gave me a kiss and I saw her off at the door. Adrian had an appointment for a routine check-up at the baby clinic that afternoon, so after a quick tidy-up in the kitchen and putting the washing machine on, I drove into town and to the library to research 'sleepwalking'. This was in the days before homes had Internet access – now I would have simply googled 'sleepwalking'.

I pushed Adrian in his stroller up the ramp and, with my ever-present bag of baby paraphernalia over my shoulder, entered the too-quiet library. I had Adrian's dummy in my coat pocket, and bottle of boiled water in the bag in case he became unsettled while I searched for what I wanted. Silently crossing the carpeted floor I went to the non-fiction section and began scanning the shelves. I have always found the Dewey system of classification confusing, even after having had it explained to me as a student, although I'm sure it makes good sense to all the librarians who use it daily. I'd no idea which category 'sleepwalking' would come under and I tried psychology, but it wasn't there. Eventually I wheeled Adrian over to the information desk and asked the librarian where I could find information on sleepwalking. She checked on her computer and found it was listed under 'Health', sub-category 'sleep disorders', Dewey number 616.84. I went to the relevant section and, parking Adrian's stroller so he was looking out over the main body of the library and could see what was going on, I began scanning the shelves.

I found four books on sleeping disorders and, taking them down one at a time, had a quick look at the chapter headings and what looked like relevant pages. Two of the books were highly academic, detailing research that had been compiled for doctorates, but the other two appeared more aimed at the general public. Fishing my library card out of my purse, I wheeled Adrian over to the desk where the librarian checked out the two books. I had entertained a brief idea about a coffee in the library coffee shop but Adrian was becoming restless and refusing his dummy, so I went back to the car and returned home.

Once I had fed Adrian and had settled him for his lunchtime nap, I made myself a sandwich and mug of tea, and took these through to the lounge, where I began reading the first book. It was entitled *Relief from Sleep Disorders*.

I quickly learned that sleepwalking was more common than John or I had thought, and tended to affect children and young people. 'Sleepwalking is a disorder charac-terised by walking or other activity while seemingly still asleep,' the book said, which obviously described what Dawn had been doing. It said that sleepwalkers often performed tasks like eating, washing, dressing, or even going to the toilet or having sex while asleep.

'Sleepwalkers do not walk around with their eyes closed
and arms outstretched as portrayed in films,' it stressed,
but have their eyes open, although they often appear
glazed or 'empty'. If the sleepwalker speaks, it said, their
voice is often slower than usual, which had been true of
Dawn. I read that 'contrary to popular belief it is not
dangerous to wake a sleepwalker', although it would make
them confused and disorientated, and it was better to steer
them back to bed than wake them. More worryingly, I
then read that it was another misconception that sleepwalkers couldn't harm themselves – 'they can', the book
stated categorically. It continued to say there were also
cases of sleepwalkers harming others, some even committing murder. This was referenced to some actual court
cases where sleepwalking had been used as a defence and
the defendants had been found not guilty on the grounds
that they were not responsible for their actions. However,
the author said that it was unusual for a sleepwalker to
harm others, and that they were more likely to acciden-
tally hurt themselves. One man had crashed his car while
driving while sleepwalking, having driven over thirty
miles from his home in his sleep.

When sleepwalkers wake they don't remember sleepwalking, the book confirmed, and I gathered that the
causes of sleepwalking remained largely unknown.
However, research suggested that sleepwalking could be
triggered by 'extreme fatigue, stress, anxiety, drugs
(prescription and illegal substances), alcohol, and psychiatric disorders' – i.e. mental illness. There was a whole
chapter on 'dealing' with sleepwalkers and the conclusion
was that they should be directed back to bed before they
injured themselves, 'though the person,' it continued, 'will

often keep getting up again until they have accomplished the task they set out to do.' This appeared to be what Dawn had been doing. It said that sleepwalkers were in a 'highly suggestive state' and that it was all right to talk to them, and talk them through whatever they had got up to do, and then direct them back to bed.

I considered this. I thought about Dawn going to Adrian's cot. John and I had handled Dawn correctly in sending her back to bed, but according to the book I should have calmly talked to her and said things like: 'It's OK, Dawn, Adrian is fine. You have given him a cuddle and now you can go back to bed.' Would it work? Was it worth a try, instead of locking Dawn out of our bedroom, in the hope she wouldn't sleepwalk again? The book didn't say if talking a sleepwalker through an action and out of it stopped it from happening again, and this would have been difficult for us as we didn't actually know what Dawn was trying to do.

Interestingly, I read that because sleepwalkers were unaware of their surroundings they were more likely 'to divulge information that they wouldn't otherwise give'. They could also exhibit behaviour that could be very embarrassing if they knew about it, like urinating in inappropriate places or having sex. I breathed a sigh of relief that Dawn's behaviour was pretty mild compared to what some sleepwalkers did. The general consensus of the advice was that there was no point in telling the sleepwalker of their behaviour, as they had no control over it, and being told was likely to make them very embarrassed and more anxious. I gave myself a mental pat on the back for getting that right. I finished by reading that episodes of sleepwalking could last anything from a few seconds to hours, and that usually the child grew out of it. In cases where it was prolonged, medical advice should be sought, as psychological factors or a personality disorder could be involved.

Setting this book to one side, I quickly flipped through the second, which seemed to contain similar information and advice; I would look at it again later. I had been reading for over an hour and a half, and I had mixed feelings. I was reassured to know that John and I had instinctively been handling Dawn's sleepwalking correctly by directing her back to bed, but I was concerned that sleepwalkers could harm themselves, and others, and that the causes were generally unknown and the condition untreatable.

That afternoon I took Adrian to the baby clinic to be weighed, and found he had put on another 6oz and now weighed 14lbs 1oz. I hadn't received a phone call from the secretary at Dawn's school that morning, so I knew Dawn had arrived. But my thoughts kept returning to her during the day and I fervently hoped and worried that she was getting on all right.

When she came home at 3.45 p.m., I could tell immediately that she'd had a really good day. She was smiling, her voice was light and she talked non-stop about Natasha – how she had sat next to her in lessons, taken her to the school canteen, and generally looked after her and helped her settle in. To say I was relieved was an understatement. I thought I would give Jane Matthews, the Head of Year, a ring the following day to thank her – her strategy really had worked wonders.

Dawn had an English essay to write for homework, and also some dates to learn for a history test the following day. She got down to her homework as soon as she'd had a drink and a snack on coming in. When John came home from work we ate dinner together, and then afterwards Dawn asked me if I could check her English essay for spelling and grammar.

We sat together on the sofa as I read the essay; it was a piece of creative writing entitled 'Five Again'. The class had been asked to write from the perspective of being five years old. They could use their own experiences of childhood or make it up if they preferred. I smiled as I read the idyllic world Dawn's five-year-old had inhabited, where she played endlessly in 'green parks' with 'bright yellow daffodils', and had 'red jelly and strawberry ice-cream' for tea every evening, and where there were no worries beyond that of choosing which sweets she would buy with her pocket money. Considering Dawn had missed a lot of schooling, her essay was pretty good. She had used plenty of adjectives, as her teacher had told the class they should, and there weren't that many spelling mistakes. Dawn made the necessary corrections as we went along and I continually praised her essay.

When I came to the end, I said, 'That's excellent, Dawn, really good. It sounds as though you had a great time when you were five years old.'

'I made it all up,' she said dismissively. 'I can't remember when I was five.'

I smiled. 'Well, it's very good. You've got a good imagination, but I'm sure if you thought carefully you could remember some things from when you were five. I can, and I'm a lot older than you.'

'No,' she said adamantly. 'Not a thing. I did try and think back, because it would have been easier than making it up. But my first memory is when I was eight and I started school.'

I looked at her, puzzled. 'You would have started school three years before then,' I said. 'That memory must have been from when you changed schools, which can be very traumatic.'

She shook her head. 'No, it was my very first day at school, and I was eight. I remember how scared I was, and I can't remember anything before then.'

I let the subject drop, for clearly Dawn was mistaken. She must have started school by the time she was five years old: it was a legal requirement. I decided she was confusing being five with being eight and it didn't really matter. John and I were meeting her mother and social worker the following evening, when hopefully the conversation would turn to Dawn's past. It would be helpful for me to have some background information and it would also probably jog Dawn's memory.

'Well, Dawn, made up or not, it's very good,' I finished by saying. 'I'm sure your teacher will be very pleased. I am.'

She glowed from the praise, and carefully folding the A4 sheets of writing paper, placed them in her school bag, ready for the following day. She then set about learning the dates for history, and I tested her on them. Later that evening, as John and I sat in the lounge, Dawn went to get ready for bed.

She came downstairs again almost immediately, and standing in the hall outside the lounge, called me quietly. 'Cathy, can I speak to you in private?'

Exchanging a quizzical glance with John, I left him with Adrian and went into the hall. Dawn was only half changed, with her pyjama top on but still in her joggers.

'Cathy,' she whispered, glancing anxiously at the open lounge door. 'I've started my first period. I haven't got any sanitary towels.'

'Oh, right, love,' I said, understanding her need for privacy. 'Don't worry. Come with me. I'll get you some of mine.'

I took Dawn upstairs, gave her a pack of sanitary towels and then waited while she finished in the toilet. When she came out she gave me her stained clothes, and I reassured her that it wasn't a problem and I would put them in the wash. I felt I should talk to Dawn about periods as a mother would do, and as my mother had done with me. We went into her bedroom and sat side by side on the bed, where I explained what was happening to her body, and reassured her that the stomach cramps she was experiencing were quite normal, and that I could give her some pain relief if necessary. I told her about the need for good hygiene at this time, that she must change her sanitary towel regularly and how to dispose of them – at home and at school. She nodded as I spoke, and when I came to the end I asked her if she had any questions.

'Does it mean I can have a baby now?' she said.

'In theory your body is able to, yes. But you wouldn't, not at your age, and without a partner.' I hesitated, and wondered if I should talk to her about relationships and boys, as a mother would. 'Dawn, do you know anything about boys and sex?'

She grinned. 'Yes, of course. I'm thirteen.'

'Is there anything you want to ask me?' I didn't want to embarrass her, but possibly I was the only one Dawn could ask.

'What age can you do it?'

'What, have sexual intercourse, you mean?' She nodded. 'Legally not until you are sixteen, but you wouldn't want to unless you were in a committed relationship anyway. I think that sexual intercourse, or making love as it's some-times called, should be part of a loving relationship, don't you? I mean it's easy enough to have sex, and boys will want you to, but it's so much nicer to wait until you have found someone you love.' I thought I was sounding like my own mother, although attitudes had changed a lot in the intervening years. My mother's advice (read warning) had been 'don't until you are married.' I recognised that for most people that view was now very dated, and felt my save-it-until-you-are-in-love was more appropriate, and indeed what I had done.

'Cathy,' Dawn said looking worried. 'You won't tell John, will you?'

'That you have started your periods?' She nodded. 'No love.'

I smiled as I remembered asking my mother the same question about my father when I had started my periods, and she had given me the same reply. It had been embar-rassing enough that my body was being subjected to this monthly intimate indignity, without my father (and brother) being made aware of it.

After I had kissed Dawn goodnight, and loaded her washing into the machine, I returned to the lounge. 'Is everything all right?' John asked, concerned. I had been upstairs with Dawn for over half an hour.

'Yes, fine,' I said. 'I've just had a little chat with Dawn. About women's matters,' I added pointedly.

He nodded, guessing. 'Oh, I see. I've been looking at these books,' he said, referring to the library books on sleepwalking. 'I found them behind the cushion on the sofa.'

I laughed. 'Yes, Dawn came in with her homework while I was reading them. I thought it was better she didn't see them.'

I sat on the sofa beside John and I told him what I had learned from my reading. I mentioned the author's suggestion of talking the sleepwalker through their activity. But as John pointed out, this would necessitate us leaving our bedroom door unlocked, then spending every night listening for Dawn until she did it again, with the worry that we might fall asleep and not hear her. We decided to leave trying that strategy for now in the hope that if the next time Dawn sleepwalked she found our bedroom door locked she might not bother again, and stop sleepwalking completely.

It was a hope that was soon to be dashed.

Chapter Nine

Cutter

The teenage unit was a large rambling Victorian house, converted and modernised to accommodate eight teenagers and two staff. The large oak door was ajar. Dawn pushed it fully open and we went into the poorly lit but very large reception hall. A couple of girls were going up the stairs leading off to the right.

'Hi,' Dawn called. They paused and looked back, gave a little wave and continued. 'They're sisters,' Dawn said to John and me. 'They were here when I was.'

I nodded, more intent on Adrian, who was in my arms and, having had his usual evening routine disrupted for this meeting, was now becoming slightly fractious.

'Shall I take him?' Dawn asked, always eager to help me with Adrian.

'Don't worry,' I said. 'He'll be OK. He's just wondering where we are.'

We were hovering in the hall with no idea where we should go, and expecting someone to come and greet us. Other than the fact that we were meeting Dawn's social worker and mother here at 7.00 p.m., I had received no details from Ruth. John had left work early to attend the meeting, and was still in his suit, having only had time to eat dinner, but not change, before we'd left the house.

'Is there an office?' John asked Dawn.

'Sort of,' she said. 'It's one of the bedrooms upstairs.' The three of us looked at the old Victorian winding stair-case, which still retained the original wooden balustrades and dado rail on the wall. 'Shall I go up and find some-one?' Dawn asked helpfully.

'It might be a good idea,' John said, and I nodded.

Dawn disappeared up the staircase while John and I waited in the hall. The hall was cold; the single radiator was no match for the draught coming from the ill-fitting front door. I moved Adrian from one arm to the other and then John took him. Presently we heard footsteps at the top of the stairs and we both looked up. A lad of about fifteen, dressed in jeans, caterpillar boots and a denim jacket clumped down the uncarpeted stairs, passed us with a nod, and then went out of the front door.

Another five minutes went by, during which John paci-fied Adrian by rocking him over his shoulder. It wasn't the best time for a meeting – I should have been bathing Adrian, and John would have preferred to be at home, unwinding after a day's work. Eventually more footsteps sounded from the top of the stairs and John and I again looked up. Dawn appeared first, followed by Ruth, dressed in jeans and a large baggy jumper, and another woman whom I took to be Dawn's mother. They reached the bottom of the stairs before anyone spoke.

'We've been trying to find a room for us to use,' Ruth said, unapologetically. 'This is Barbara, Dawn's mother. Barbara, this is John and Cathy.' I smiled at Barbara and she returned a small half smile. She was a petite woman, neatly dressed in a skirt and blouse, with bobbed fair hair, and I could see a strong resemblance to Dawn. I guessed

Barbara was only in her mid-thirties, so she must have had
Dawn quite young. John stepped forward and offered his
hand for shaking, and Barbara looked most embarrassed as
she took it.

'Pleased to meet you,' John said. Barbara smiled.

'Dawn's father won't be coming,' Ruth said. I nodded,
although I hadn't been aware he was even expected. 'We
can use the sitting room,' she continued. 'There are only
two girls in the house tonight and they're in their
bedrooms.'

Ruth led the way through a heavily panelled fire door at
the end of the reception hall, and along a wide corridor.
Our shoes clipped noisily over the tiled Victorian floor.
The hall still had the original Anaglypta wallpaper below
the dado rail, but the gloss grey paintwork was badly
scarred and could have done with redecorating.

We turned right into a room which, while warmer than
the hall, was as dingy and uninviting, and reeked of stale
cigarette smoke. The pale lilac painted walls were grubby,
chipped, and graffitied with coloured felt tips. Most of the
comments were unintelligible, apart from *shit* and *dick
head*, together with a few vague attempts at drawing
cartoon characters. In the centre of the room were two
badly stained and faded red sofas opposite each other,
either side of a long low coffee table, which was in no
better condition than the sofas. At one end of the table was
an overflowing ashtray and a couple of mugs containing
the remnants of cold congealed coffee. There was no
carpet on the floor and no curtains at the windows.
Discarded crisp packets and biscuit wrappers littered the
badly worn linoleum. The room was disgusting and while
I recognised it was probably the teenager residents who

were responsible for the state of it I thought that the staff could have at least organised a cleaning party.

Dawn immediately flopped on to one of the sofas and put her feet up on the coffee table, seeming quite at home. John and I glanced at each other and then at Dawn's mother. Dawn wouldn't have been allowed to put her feet on our coffee table at home; indeed I doubt it would have crossed her mind to do so. Barbara didn't say anything and I felt uncomfortable about telling Dawn to put her feet down with her mother present. Barbara didn't sit next to her daughter but perched tentatively on the sofa opposite. Ruth had crossed to the windows and was now struggling to lower one of the upper sashes.

'Here, let me,' John said, passing Adrian to me and going to her assistance. He gave the window a good wrench and it graunched down an inch. Although the night air was cold, the draft was preferable to the stench of stale smoke, and a damn site healthier for Adrian, I thought.

Ruth took the full ashtray and placed it on the floor by the door. John and I sat on the sofa next to Dawn, and Ruth sat next to Barbara. I felt it was odd that Barbara hadn't wanted to sit next to her daughter, given that she hadn't seen her for over a month. I also felt that the seating arrangement, with us on opposite sides of the coffee table, was almost confrontational.

'Barbara wanted to meet you,' Ruth began. I nodded and smiled at Barbara. 'She was very concerned that Dawn arrived on her doorstep last week when she should have been in school.' The smile faded from my lips.

'Did she?' I asked, dumbfounded. John glanced at me. I looked from Barbara to Dawn. 'Did you?' I asked Dawn.

Cut

'I'm not making it up,' Barbara said evenly.

'No,' I said quickly. 'I'm not for one moment suggesting you are. I'm surprised – shocked really. I knew that Dawn hadn't been in school and I've dealt with it. But Dawn didn't say she had been to your house.' We were all looking at Dawn now. She still had her feet on the table and was leaning back on the sofa with her arms folded into her chest with an almost bemused smile on her face. 'Why didn't you tell me, Dawn?' I said. 'I asked you where you'd been.'

'You surely didn't think she was going to tell you?' Barbara asked sceptically. 'She never used to tell me where she was or what she had been up to, and I'm her mother.' Barbara spoke calmly and rationally, and I felt stupid that I had been unaware of where Dawn had been. 'All those days and weeks,' Barbara continued, 'when I sent her to school and she never arrived. I didn't ever know where she was. And when she was out all evening and didn't come home until the early hours, sometimes not until the following morning; she never once told me where she was. I have to work; I can't be her keeper.' I glanced from Barbara to Dawn as Barbara spoke. Dawn remained passive and apparently unperturbed. 'The police and school blamed me,' Barbara said. 'But what was I supposed to do? I mean I can't physically make her go to school, or prevent her from leaving the house in the evening, can I?' She stopped.

John and I looked at each other, amazed by the picture Barbara had just painted of her daughter. 'But Dawn has never even asked to go out since she has been with us,' I said, at a complete loss. 'Let alone stayed out all night.'

There was silence, and I saw Dawn, Barbara and Ruth exchange what I took to be a pointed glance, as though there was something John and I didn't know.

'Going out is something we need to discuss,' Ruth said
tersely. 'Dawn wants to go out but hasn't liked to ask
you.'

I looked again at Dawn and wondered why she hadn't
asked me. She had been relaxed enough in my company to
tell me when she had started her periods; surely she could
have asked about going out? It made John and me appear
like ogres.

'Going out, and coming-in times are things we can
include in the contract of good behaviour,' Ruth said. 'And
a clothing allowance. Dawn would like a clothing
allowance, and I think at her age it is appropriate.'

I felt John shift uncomfortably on the sofa beside me
and I guessed he was thinking the same as me: that this
meeting appeared to be a forum in which to air Barbara's
and Dawn's grievances. Dawn had said nothing to us
about a clothing allowance, but clearly she had raised it at
some point with her mother or social worker. Although
where this 'clothing allowance' was supposed to come
from I didn't know.

'I've been giving Dawn pocket money,' I said looking at
Ruth. 'A little each day, as you suggested. And I've bought
Dawn new clothes.'

Ruth nodded. 'In your fostering allowance is an amount
for clothing. A child of Dawn's age would normally be
given the money to choose her own clothes. Although I
appreciate the allowance isn't much and you will have to
add to it.' Which I thought was choice.

'We haven't had an allowance at all yet,' I said bluntly. I
didn't want to discuss money in front of Dawn, but as
Ruth had raised the matter I felt it was appropriate to set
the record straight.

'No,' Ruth agreed. 'It takes a few months to go on the system before it's paid. But you will get it, and Dawn would appreciate having it to buy her own clothes.'

'As long as it doesn't go on drink or fags,' Barbara added.

Again, John and I stared in amazement at Barbara and her portrayal of Dawn. 'She got in with a bad lot before,' Barbara qualified. 'Older kids who showed Dawn all kinds of new tricks.'

I glanced sideways at Dawn, who remained impassive: arms folded, feet up and, if I was being unkind, almost revelling in her dubious achievements and being the centre of attention.

'I'm sure she won't now,' I said, feeling the need to say something positive. 'Dawn's made a nice new friend at school – Natasha. She's just started at the school and Dawn has been looking after her and helping her to settle in.'

Dawn nodded. Ruth and Barbara looked at Dawn but didn't say anything. I didn't know what to make of Barbara. At one level she was sensible and level headed, not aggressive or loud. But she was quick to point out Dawn's wrongdoings, and there appeared to be an emotional distance between her and her daughter – a void, even – and little warmth or respect between them.

There were a few moments of uncomfortable silence before John spoke. 'Barbara, is there anything you can tell us about Dawn that would help us to look after her? I think that would be useful.'

Barbara looked sideways at Ruth and then at us. 'I'm not sure what else I can tell you. I tried with Dawn but I don't understand her. If you can get her to go to school and come home on time, that would be something. And keep her away from the knives. She's a cutter, you know.'

'A cutter?' I asked. 'I'm sorry, I don't understand; what do you mean.'

'She cuts herself,' Barbara said, again glancing pointedly at Ruth. 'Haven't you seen the scars on her arms?'

I stared at Barbara, amazed. John was staring too. 'No,' I said. 'I haven't. What scars?'

'Show her what you've done, Dawn,' Barbara said.

The three of us looked at Dawn as she slowly unfolded her arms and then pulled up the sleeve of the jumper on her left arm. I gasped. There were a dozen or so pink scar lines, an inch or more long, evenly spaced and running from her wrist to her elbow on the upper side of her arm. Some were more recent than others.

'I'm surprised you haven't seen them,' Barbara said, as John and I continued to stare, horrified, at Dawn's arm, struggling to understand what we were being told.

'Did you do that to yourself, Dawn?' I asked after a moment. She nodded. 'With what?'

'Kitchen knives, pen knives, broken bottles,' Barbara said. 'Anything she can get her hands on.'

I felt my pulse rise and my stomach churn as my gaze remained on Dawn's scarred arm. 'But why?' I asked at length. 'Why do you want to hurt yourself, love?'

Dawn shrugged, and then began running her forefinger along the scar lines, toying with and examining them.

'There's research going on in the field of self-harm,' Ruth said, quite matter-of-factly. 'There are different theories but no one knows for sure. One line of thought says it could be attention seeking. It rarely leads to suicide.'

Dawn pulled her sleeve down to cover her arm and I
looked at John, who was clearly as shaken as I was. It was
a bit of a drastic way to gain attention, I thought.

'I take it she hasn't done it with you yet?' Barbara said.

'No, she hasn't,' I said adamantly.

'We would have known, obviously,' John added.

'Not necessarily,' Barbara said. 'Cutters can be very
good at hiding it, and you hadn't seen the scars, had you?'

Which was true, and I then realised that I hadn't seen
the scars was because I had never seen Dawn's arms.
Obviously at her age she bathed and changed in private,
and with it being winter she was in long-sleeved day
clothes and nightclothes.

'That's why she doesn't do PE at school,' Barbara said.
And I remembered that Dawn hadn't done PE the previous week because it was timetabled on one of the days she
had played truant. 'Her school know about her cutting,'
Barbara added. 'Her dad phoned and told them.'

Dawn pulled a face.

Clearly Ruth was aware of all this and I thought that
she should have told us. If I had discovered the scars or,
heaven forbid, had walked in on Dawn cutting herself,
I would have been horrified, and probably would have
panicked. Now I knew, although I really couldn't get my
mind round anyone deliberately harming themselves, I
would obviously be careful that Dawn didn't have access to
anything sharp, and I would also try to talk to her – something must be making her want to hurt herself so badly,
and I doubted she was doing it purely for attention.
Then with a jolt I remembered the chopping motion that
Dawn had made on her arm while sleepwalking. Could
Dawn have been re-enacting her self-harming while

sleepwalking? Following the advice in the books – that it would make the person more anxious to be told of their sleepwalking – John and I had decided not to mention Dawn's sleepwalking at the meeting unless Barbara or Ruth did, so I didn't say anything; and in the light of what we had just learned, Dawn's sleepwalking seemed the least of our worries.

'How long has Dawn been harming herself?' John asked, slowly recovering.

'About two years,' Barbara said. 'One of the older kids she got in with showed her how to cut. It became a regular Friday night activity, didn't it, Dawn?'

Dawn grinned sheepishly and looked embarrassed, but I viewed what Barbara had said in a positive light. If the cutting was something Dawn had been doing simply to be in with an older group (albeit quite a disturbed one by the sound of it), then it was hopeful that when removed from that influence Dawn would stop it. The alternative was that her need to harm herself was because of psychological illness, which would be far more difficult to deal with, and more worrying.

'Is there anything else we should know?' John asked Barbara hesitantly.

Barbara again glanced at Ruth before speaking, as though seeking her permission. 'Hide your matches, or lighters if you smoke. Dawn was playing with matches and caused a fire.'

There seemed to be no end to the horrors Barbara was now disclosing about her daughter. John and I looked to Barbara and Ruth for further explanation.

'It was nothing much,' Ruth said dismissively. 'Dawn was with a friend and the two of them were playing with matches and caused a fire. Dawn now understands how dangerous it is to play with matches and has learned her lesson.'

I noticed that Barbara and Dawn both watched Ruth intently as she spoke, as though they were waiting to see exactly what she said – or admitted to, maybe? Was there more? Were details being omitted that only they were party to? I wasn't sure, but I had the feeling there might be. How or what to ask I'd no idea.

'So, let's draw up the contract of good behaviour,' Ruth said, changing the subject. 'It's getting late and I'm sure we would all rather be at home than in this meeting.' I glanced at Adrian, who had now fallen asleep on John's lap, as Ruth delved into her bag and took out a journalistic writing pad and a pen. John and I were still quiet, shocked and coming to terms with what we had learned.

Dawn, on the other hand, now suddenly found a new enthusiasm. Finally taking her feet off the table and unfolding her arms, she leant forward. 'I'd like to go out on Friday and Saturday evenings, please,' she said, and the three of them looked at John and me.

We were silent for a moment. Then John slowly said, 'Yes. But you are only thirteen. Where would you be going?'

Dawn shrugged.

'You can always bring friends home for the evening,' I suggested.

'She'd rather be out,' Barbara said. Ruth nodded.

'Out where?' John asked again.

'Just out,' Dawn said.

'I don't think it's a good idea to be hanging around the streets,' I said.

'You can't curtail all Dawn's movements,' Ruth said. 'She's used to leading her own life.'

I felt there were some peculiar group dynamics going on in the room in which John and I weren't included. Clearly there had been a previous conversation between Dawn, Ruth and Barbara; and Dawn's mother and social worker seemed to be in quiet collusion. We were all supposed to be working together for the good of Dawn, yet Ruth now seemed to be suggesting we perpetuate some of Dawn's previous unsafe behaviour – the very behaviour that had brought her into care.

'We are not suggesting we curtail all Dawn's movements,' John said decisively. 'But I wouldn't have a daughter of mine out on the streets. At a friend's house, yes, or going to the cinema – we could drop Dawn off and pick her up.' I nodded.

Ruth sat forward a little, and poising her pen over her pad began to write. 'Let's say that Dawn can go out on Friday and Saturday evenings, assuming she has been going to school, but she has to be in by nine-thirty.' Clearly this decision was a fait accompli, and nothing John and I could have said would have made any difference.

'Can we make it ten o'clock?' Dawn asked.

'No,' Ruth said. 'Nine-thirty is late enough.' Dawn pulled a face. John and I glanced at each other.

'I think nine-thirty is too late,' John said.

''We'll try it and see how it goes,' Ruth said, dismissing any discussion. 'Now, contact with mum,' Ruth continued. 'Obviously Dawn wants to see her mother regularly. And the best evening for Barbara is Sunday.'

'Wouldn't during the day be more convenient?' I queried. I remembered that Jack had gone to his father's for Sunday lunch and stayed the afternoon, which had worked very well.

'I spend time with my partner, Mike, during the day on Sunday,' Barbara said. 'Dawn can come to me at six.'

My suggestions again dismissed, my sympathy flared for Dawn, who had just heard her mother effectively say that she would rather spend time with her partner than her.

'Dawn has caused problems in the past between Mike and me,' Barbara added. 'Mike doesn't want to see her. He'll be gone by the time she arrives.'

My initial surge of empathy for Dawn was heightened, but I could hardly tell Barbara that I thought her loyalties were misplaced. Dawn seemed unmoved by her mother's rejection and I guessed she was already well aware of her mother's partner's hostility towards her. Ruth's pen was on her notepad again. 'So shall we say six o'clock to nine, then?' she said, writing as she spoke.

'Six to eight,' Barbara said. 'I have to be up early for work the following morning.'

I again glanced at Dawn, who appeared to accept this without upset, although obviously I didn't know what she was thinking.

'And what about Dawn's father?' John asked. 'Will Dawn be seeing him?'

'No,' Ruth and Barbara said together.

'I've spoken to Dawn's father,' Ruth clarified. 'And he doesn't want contact at present. Dawn is aware of the reasons.'

There was a moment's silence before John asked, 'Are we to know the reasons?'

Ruth shook her head without looking up from her notepad. 'No, there are confidentiality issues which I'm not at liberty to discuss.'

I felt the collusion in the room rise to a new level as Dawn and her mother both looked at the floor and Ruth concentrated on her notepad. John shifted uneasily beside me on the sofa.

'Do you want us to bring Dawn to you for the visit and then collect her?' I asked Barbara.

Barbara and Ruth looked at Dawn, who shook her head.

'No,' Ruth said. 'Dawn can use the bus, but make sure she has enough money for the return bus fare. We don't want her using lack of a bus fare as an excuse for not returning.' Ruth glanced up from her notepad at John and me. 'Is there anything else that needs to go into the contract of good behaviour?' she asked.

'I can't think of anything,' I said quietly.

'Keeping her bedroom tidy?' Ruth suggested.

'Dawn does that already,' I confirmed.

'Good. Well, I'll just add that Dawn undertakes to attend school every day,' Ruth said. Which to my ears made school attendance sound like an option rather than a legal requirement.

Ruth finished writing and, quickly closing her notepad, returned it to her bag. 'I'll type this up and give everyone a copy for signing,' she said. 'Thanks for coming.' She immediately stood.

Barbara also stood. 'I must go. I have work tomorrow.' She threw John and me a small smile. As she passed Dawn she said simply, 'Goodbye, Dawn. See you on Sunday.' And without attempting to kiss or hug her daughter she left the room. We heard her footsteps receding down the tiled floor of the corridor.

John and I stood. Adrian stirred in John's arms but didn't wake. Ruth was by the door, holding it open, and

Dawn went out first. John followed. As I passed Ruth she touched my shoulder and I held back.

'Just wanted to say that mum has problems showing affection to Dawn,' Ruth said, 'but I'm sure she cares for her.' I nodded. 'Dawn lived with both her parents from birth to the age of four, when they divorced. Then there was a gap of five years. Since the age of nine Dawn has lived partly with her mum, and partly with her dad and his partners. But it hasn't worked out. Neither of Dawn's parents has a strong relationship with her, although I think they have tried their best.'

I shook my head sadly. 'I see. But when you say there was a gap, what do you mean?'

'No one knows where Dawn was between the ages of five and nine. Mum says she was living with dad, and dad says she was with mum. Social services weren't involved until Dawn was nine and started getting into trouble with petty thieving.'

I glanced down the corridor to where John and Dawn were standing. Dawn was peering into John's arms at Adrian, who was apparently awake. 'Won't Dawn miss seeing her dad and his baby?' I asked. 'She seems very fond of her half-sister.'

Ruth closed the door to the sitting room behind us and made a move down the hall. I knew instinctively that the conversation was at an end, and that nothing more would be forthcoming. 'It's not appropriate for Dawn to see her father and his new family,' she said curtly; then she went ahead to join John and Dawn.

Adrian was wide awake now and grinning widely.

'Nice baby,' Ruth said as I caught up.

'I help look after him,' Dawn said, coochi-cooing at Adrian.

'Well, just you be careful,' Ruth warned. 'Babies are delicate. They don't bounce.' Ruth continued to lead the way out of the reception hall and into the car park, where we said goodbye.

John strapped Adrian into his car seat and Dawn climbed into the back beside Adrian. I turned in the passenger seat to look at her. 'Dawn, you do know you have to be careful with babies, don't you?' I said, for something in Ruth's warning to Dawn had unsettled me.

Dawn smiled and nodded. 'I wouldn't hurt a baby. It was an accident.'

'What was?' I asked, with a start. 'What accident, Dawn?

'Nothing.' She shrugged.

I returned my gaze to the front as John started the engine. He pulled out of the car park and drove us home while Dawn kept Adrian amused.

Chapter Ten

A Different Person

'Are we talking about the same child?' John said to me as soon as we were alone. We had driven home with the only sound being that of Dawn talking to Adrian in the rear of the car. Dawn was now in bed, as was Adrian. John and I were sitting in the lounge with a mug of tea each, finally able to voice our concerns, of which there were plenty. 'Do you think there's another side to Dawn that we haven't seen yet?' John asked.

'Yes, I suppose there must be. Although I think she's changed since she's been with us and is far more settled and happier now. But those scars! Imagine her cutting into her arm like that! It's horrendous. And I felt such a fool for not seeing them.'

'I don't think either of her parents had much time for Dawn,' he said.

'No. And Ruth told me that there is a big gap in Dawn's history, between the ages of five and nine, when no one seems to know where she was!'

'What?' John frowned, puzzled. I told him what Ruth had told me of Dawn's past, and his frown deepened. 'Did Ruth tell you anything else? She wasn't very forthcoming at the meeting.'

'Only that Barbara couldn't show her daughter affection, and that neither of her parents have a close relationship with Dawn.'

'That was pretty obvious,' John sighed. 'But even so, drinking, smoking, staying out all night, truanting and slashing her arm. I can't believe it's the same girl.'

'No,' I agreed. 'I'm sure she's different now.'

We both sat quietly for some moments, contemplating what we had learned that evening. It was after ten o'clock and normally I would have been in the bath by now, but I felt exhausted and I was finding it difficult to drag myself from the sofa and go upstairs.

'Why do you think Dawn's father doesn't want to see her?' John asked, leaning forward to place his empty mug on the coffee table.

'I don't know, but I hope it's nothing to do with Dawn's treatment of their baby.'

John's gaze immediately darted to mine. 'What do you mean?'

'Something Dawn said as we were getting in the car tonight. Didn't you hear her?' He shook his head. 'She said she wouldn't hurt a baby, that it was an accident.'

'What was an accident?'

'That's what I asked her, but she didn't answer. Perhaps she's a bit over-enthusiastic with her dad's new baby, as she can be with Adrian, and perhaps her stepmother doesn't like it? Or maybe Dawn's sleepwalking put them on edge? I mean it's pretty scary. It's a pity we didn't have a chance to discuss it in private with Ruth or Barbara.'

'Even if we had,' John said dryly. 'I doubt Ruth would have told us much. It would have been another "confidentiality issue". I must say I didn't find her attitude very helpful.'

'No,' I agreed.

When I finally hauled myself upstairs to bed, I fell into an immediate and deep sleep. Adrian obligingly didn't wake until 4.30 a.m., and as I fed him by the light of my bedside lamp, John stirred, then got up and, unlocking our door, went along to the toilet. A second later he called out and I could hear the anxiety in his voice, and also the edge of protection.

'Dawn's bedroom door is open and she's not in bed! Stay there, I'm going downstairs.'

The landing light went on and John's footsteps sounded on the stairs. I felt my tension rise as I remained propped up on my pillow, feeding Adrian, and straining my ears for any sound. Then I heard John's voice again, coming from the hallway below.

'This way to bed, Dawn. Come on, up you go,' he encouraged.

I listened as two sets of footsteps slowly came up the stairs and then turned on to the landing. A silence followed, and I guessed John was steering Dawn into her bed. I heard her bedroom door close. Then John went to the toilet, the landing light went off and he reappeared.

'I found her sitting on the bottom stair,' he sighed as he climbed back into bed.

'I wonder if she tried our bedroom door first before going downstairs? I didn't hear her.'

'No, but at least we know she can safely navigate the stairs,' he said.

'It's very worrying, though. I mean she could have easily tripped and fallen.'

'But what are we supposed to do? We can't lock her in her room!'

'Perhaps she'll stop sleepwalking if she tried our door and found she couldn't get in,' I offered.

'Hopefully,' John said.

It was an optimism we had expressed before and, as before, it was soon to prove unfounded.

The following night when Adrian woke at 4.30 a.m. for his feed, John woke too and immediately went to check on Dawn.

'She's gone again!' he called, and once more he found her sitting on the bottom stair. While I fed Adrian, John steered Dawn back to bed and she slept through until morning. We didn't, though. We both slept fitfully, listening out for any sound of Dawn, and the following morning we were again exhausted.

'I really think I'm going to have to do what the books suggest and try to talk Dawn through whatever it is she's getting up to do.' I said to John as he dressed for work. 'It's almost as if she has some unfinished business. Perhaps once she's been reassured, or done whatever it is she has set out to do, she'll stop sleepwalking.'

'Fine,' John said a little sharply, tetchy from lack of sleep. 'We'll try it next time. But I'm not leaving our bedroom door unlocked. It's too risky. Particularly as it seems Dawn's unfinished business has something to do with Adrian.'

'OK, next time, if there is a next time, I'll get up and try to talk to her. That book said sleepwalkers often divulge things while sleepwalking that they wouldn't normally do. If I can find out what's bothering her, then maybe I can help.'

With so little background information on Dawn, John and I were trying to deal with her sleepwalking in any way we could, using common sense and what we had read. Had Dawn's social worker been more proactive and forthcoming we would have raised the matter with her, and hopefully would have found out what was worrying Dawn. And even had some advice. As it was, with virtually no involvement from Ruth, we felt that Dawn was solely our responsibility and her problems were ours to deal with. We were treating Dawn, and dealing with her, as parents, and I wondered what I would have done if Dawn had been my own daughter. Spoken to my doctor, I thought, which is what I decided to do if Dawn continued sleepwalking for much longer.

Dawn completed a full week at school and therefore, according to Ruth's instructions, was allowed out on Friday and Saturday evenings, and as the contract of good behaviour stated, she had to be home by 9.30 p.m. John and I didn't know where Dawn went or who she was with, and it wasn't an arrangement either of us approved of, or was happy with. As John had said at the meeting (and I completely agreed with him), we wouldn't have allowed our own daughter to simply go out without us knowing where she was going or who she was with. And although it was now April and the days were growing longer, it was still pitch black by 8.00 p.m.

Before Dawn went out she spent some time upstairs getting ready, washing her hair and changing into fresh clothes, then came down to say goodbye. We asked her where she was going, and who she was going to meet, but she said she 'hadn't plans'. John again offered to give her a lift in the car but she said, politely, 'No thanks, no need. I'll be fine.'

This was in the days when only a few business people owned mobile phones and neither John, Dawn nor I had one. Once Dawn left the house, therefore, we had no way of contacting her to make sure she was all right. I told her if she got stranded and needed a lift home to phone us from a call box, and to this end I made sure she had some twenty-pence pieces for a public phone. However, this was small comfort, and on both Friday and Saturday evenings John and I sat in the lounge, ostensibly watching television, while most of our attention was focused on the hands of the carriage clock.

When the bell rang at dead on 9.30 p.m., I immediately answered the door, and we were both extremely relieved to see Dawn back safely. I praised her for getting home on time, and also asked her if she had had a good evening.

'Yes, thanks,' she said, but she offered nothing else.

She sat with us in the lounge for half an hour and then went up to bed at ten o'clock.

On Saturday night when she came home John and I thought we could smell smoke on her clothes, and I took the opportunity to say a few words to her about smoking in general.

'It's better never to start,' I said. 'It can easily become a habit, and before you know it you're addicted.' I was speaking from experience, for I had smoked, albeit only a few a day, before having Adrian. I'd given up as soon as I'd found out I was pregnant, and I didn't intend starting again.

Dawn nodded and said she wouldn't start smoking, and I accepted what she said. Perhaps she hadn't been smoking; perhaps she'd been in a smoky environment or with someone who had been smoking. I knew that to confront or lecture her wouldn't do any good and would probably put her on the defensive.

On Sunday we went to my parents for lunch and as usual our visit was very pleasant and relaxing. Once we had started fostering both our parents had quickly become as enthusiastic and committed as we were. My parents always made such a fuss of us, and we all enjoyed Mum's cooking, particularly her homemade apple pie, which I promised to try to make when I had time. They went out of their way to chat to Dawn and make her feel welcome, as they had done with Jack. Unfortunately we had to leave early, as Dawn was seeing her mother in the evening.

Again, we offered Dawn a lift to her mother's, but Dawn politely refused. I gave her the return bus fare, plus some extra for emergencies. I had already given her a £5 weekly clothing allowance. She thanked me, and I said I'd see her at about nine o'clock – Dawn would be leaving her mother's at eight and it was about fifty minutes on the bus.

I was less worried about Dawn going to her mother's than I had been on Friday and Saturday, when I hadn't known where she was. Although I still wasn't happy with a thirteen-year-old girl travelling alone on the bus after dark, there was nothing I could do about it. Ruth had made the decision.

* * *

Dawn arrived home early from seeing her mother – it was only 8.30 p.m. I answered the door and asked her if she'd had a nice time and if her mum was OK.

Dawn shrugged. 'Mike was there. They were still eating, and I had to go to my bedroom until they'd finished. He came back again at seven thirty, so I left.'

I was astounded. Barbara was only seeing her daughter for two hours a week. Couldn't she have arranged her Sunday evening better? What a rejection – to send Dawn to her room, while Mike finished eating, I thought! Clearly Mike's relationship with Dawn was far worse than we had been led to believe, and I wondered why.

'That was a disappointment,' I said as Dawn hung her coat on the hall stand.

'Not fussed,' Dawn said, and she changed the subject.

Clearly Dawn didn't want to talk about it, and she came through and sat in the lounge with John and me for half an hour. Then, with school the following morning, she went up to the bathroom and to bed.

When I went up to say goodnight at 9.30 p.m. she was already asleep. The sleeve of her pyjama top on her left arm had ridden up and the scar lines from her cutting were visible. I hadn't broached the subject of her self-harming with her yet, clutching to the hope, that like the rest of the behaviour her mother had described, it was a thing of the past. If Dawn mentioned it, I would obviously talk to her and listen, for I suspected that her cutting had probably been a cry for help, and listening to her worries might be all that was needed.

I switched off Dawn's light and came out, closing her bedroom door. John and I were in bed at 10.30 p.m. and hoped to have an unbroken night's sleep. With Adrian now on three small meals a day, he needed less breast milk, and on Saturday had slept until nearly 6.00 a.m. I knew the time was fast approaching when he would stop needing me for this purpose, and the nurse at the clinic had said I should start introducing cow's milk into his trainer beaker and gradually wean him.

If John and I were looking forward to an unbroken night, it was a lame hope. At 2.00 a.m. we were both wide awake, staring into the darkness and listening. Something had woken us and it wasn't Adrian – he was still fast asleep in his cot.

'Is Dawn out of bed?' I whispered to John.

'Not sure. I'd better take a look.' Quietly unlocking our bedroom door, he went out on to the landing. He returned a few seconds later. 'She's sitting on the bottom stair again,' he whispered. 'I'll take her back to bed.'

'Let me try talking to her,' I said quietly. 'See if I can find out what's bothering her.' For while I didn't relish the thought of leaving the warmth and comfort of my bed after only three hours' sleep, if I could find out what was worrying Dawn and stop her from sleepwalking, this small discomfort would be a good investment.

'I'll come too,' John said.

He unhooked our dressing gowns from the back of the door and passed mine to me. We padded along the landing and John put the landing light on so that there was enough light to see Dawn but not to startle her. We went down the stairs and stepped round her, then with John standing to one side in the hall, I squatted down on my heels so that I was at eye level. Her hands were in her lap and she was staring straight ahead, her eyes fixed and glazed, as though staring through me.

'Dawn?' I said quietly. 'Dawn, it's Cathy. What's the matter, love? Is there something worrying you?'

There was no movement, no blink of the eyes or facial expression to suggest she could even hear me.

'Dawn?' I said again. 'It's Cathy. I want to help you. Can you tell me what's worrying you?'

John was standing motionless in the hall behind me and we both concentrated on Dawn, watching for the slightest sign that she had heard me or was receptive to my words. But there was nothing.

'We may as well take her back to bed,' John whispered after a while.

I continued to look into Dawn's unseeing eyes, waiting, almost willing her to hear me so I could help. Then I placed my hand lightly on top of hers.

'Dawn?' I tried again. 'Can you tell me what's worrying you, love? Can you show me, Dawn? Where do you want to go? Show me what you want to do, and perhaps I can help.' The books said that sleepwalkers could talk and answer questions but there was no indication that Dawn could even hear me, let alone have a conversation. 'Dawn?' I said again, lightly encircling her hand in mine. 'Show me what it is you want and I can help you find it.'

Suddenly she moved. I started and nearly fell back off my heels. Slowly taking her hands from her lap, she placed them either side of her on the stair, and pushed herself up into a standing position. I was also standing now, and John and I took a step back to give her room. She stood still for a few moments, her arms hanging loosely at her sides, as though she was getting her bearings. The staircase was behind her and she was staring straight in front. I think we both expected her to turn and go upstairs, for we were sure that Dawn's 'unfinished business' or anxiety lay with Adrian, and that was where she would go. She remained impassive for a moment; then she took a step forward and slowly began to turn, but away from the stairs.

She was now facing the length of the hall, towards the back of the house. She took another faltering step, then another, and began walking slowly down the hall. John and I followed in absolute silence, the only sound coming from my thumping heart and the faint stir of the material of our nightclothes. Dawn reached the end of the hall, paused for a moment, then turned ninety degrees and went into the kitchen. It was dark in the kitchen – the light from the landing above didn't reach this far. I didn't want to put the kitchen light on for fear of startling her, but we needed to see what she was doing.

'Can you put the lounge light on?' I whispered to John, who was just behind me.

He went out of the kitchen and switched the lounge light on. With the lounge and kitchen doors open there was just enough glow to allow us to see. Dawn had come to a halt in the centre of the kitchen and was now standing, arms at her sides, staring straight ahead.

John returned to my side. 'What does she want in here?' he whispered, voicing my thoughts.

'I hope she's not planning on cooking a roast,' I quipped with a small nervous laugh.

John smiled and touched my arm. 'Try talking to her again. It might help.'

I quietly stepped forward, and lightly placed my hand on her arm. 'Dawn, love, what do you want in the kitchen? Tell me and I'll try to help you find it.'

It crossed my mind that perhaps she wanted to prepare a bottle of milk or some food for Adrian; perhaps her sleepwalking was caused by some anxiety that she needed to look after him and was in some way failing. 'Adrian's been fed. He's not hungry,' I said, following the book's advice about reassuring the sleepwalker. 'Are you looking for food for Adrian?'

There was a pause, and then Dawn answered. In a deep voice, heavy with sleep, she said, 'No.'

I glanced at John. 'What do you want then, love?' I persisted quietly. 'Tell me, and I can find it for you so that you can go back to bed.'

Dawn didn't answer but moved slowly to the kitchen cabinets, and the drawers under the work surface. Stopping at one drawer, she pulled it open, and slowly lowered her head and looked down, as though she was actually seeing into the drawer. She stood still again; then her hands left the edge of the drawer and she began steadily searching the contents, as though she was looking for something specific. Her movements were slow and slightly cumbersome, and I wasn't sure if she could actually see what she was doing or if she was using touch to guide her. The drawer contained an assortment of miscellaneous items, including clean tea towels, oven gloves, a packet of candles from when we'd had a series of electricity cuts and a large box of matches for lighting them.

I was so engrossed in watching Dawn in the half-light that it took me a moment to realise that I hadn't removed the box of matches after Barbara's warning, and that Dawn was now taking the box of matches from the drawer. Even when I realised, I was so mesmerised that I didn't immediately stop her.

It was John who intervened. 'You can't have those,' he said, stepping forward and taking the box of matches from her hand. 'They're dangerous.'

Dawn didn't move. She remained where she was, statue-like, standing beside the open drawer, with her left hand cupped where the box of matches had been. Then slowly she raised her head, turned from the drawer, and moved to the centre of the room. Standing still again, with her feet slightly apart, quite bizarrely she began to mime opening the box of matches as though the box was still in her hand and taking one out. John and I watched, transfixed, as she closed the non-existent box, and then taking the imaginary match in her right hand began to strike it.

Chapter Eleven

Cry for Help

Once, twice – Dawn struck the 'match' on the side of the box and then appeared to watch it flare. Her eyes seemed to focus on the imaginary flame. Then her face began to crumple into a mixture of pain and fear, as though she was remembering something dreadful. She stared at the 'match' for a moment, and then suddenly flicked her wrist and 'threw' it away. I watched, horrified, as she buckled to the floor, clasped her knees and began rocking, back and forth. Her eyes were still and open and her face was steeped in pain; then she began to cry, and I couldn't simply watch her any longer.

I went forward to comfort her, but as I did her expression suddenly changed from pain to anger, and I stopped. She threw out her left arm; then, yanking up the sleeve of her pyjama, and using the edge of her right hand, she began chopping along the scar lines.

'You wicked, wicked, girl,' she hissed under her breath. 'You evil bitch! You're not human! You're evil. An evil, evil child.' Her jaw was clamped and she gritted her teeth as she chopped at the scars. There was no doubt in my mind that Dawn was punishing herself – for what, I didn't know.

I went over and squatted beside her and encircled her with my arms. 'It's all right, love,' I soothed. 'It's OK. You're all right now.'

Suddenly she stopped all movement and gave a small cry of alarm. 'Cathy?' she asked, raising her head to look at me. Her eyes focused on me and I knew she was awake and really seeing me. 'Cathy? Where am I?' She stared around, anxious and confused.

'It's all right, love. You've had a bad dream. Now let's get you back to bed.' I looked to John to help me, and he came over.

'Cathy?' she said again, searching my face, disorientated and anxious. 'John?' she said, gazing at him and around the kitchen.

'Yes, we're both here,' I reassured her again. 'You've had a bad dream. Let's get you back to bed.'

John took one arm and I took the other, and together we helped Dawn to her feet. Although she was awake and no longer sleepwalking, she was so dazed and disorientated that it took both of us to steer her out of the kitchen and along the hall. I talked to her calmly as we went. 'It's all right now, love. There's nothing for you to worry about. We're taking you back to bed.'

At the foot of the stairs, John went up first, and Dawn followed, with me gently steering her from behind. She seemed less co-ordinated and less able to navigate things now that she had suddenly woken than she had been when sleepwalking. It was almost as if she was in a twilight world, somewhere between waking and sleeping, and her senses were caught between the two and not fully functioning. At the top of the stairs John led the way into her room and I steered her to the bed.

'In you get, love,' I said gently, holding back the duvet. She climbed in and lay down. 'You go back to sleep now,' I soothed. 'Everything is fine.' She didn't speak, but turned on to her side and immediately closed her eyes.

John and I waited for a few minutes to make sure she was properly asleep, then came out and quietly closed her bedroom door. We hovered on the landing for a few moments, looking at each other, and I could see John was as shaken as I was. My heart was still pounding from the shock of it all and my knees felt weak. 'I'm going back to bed,' I said quietly. John nodded, switching off the landing light, and we returned to bed.

We lay side by side as our eyes adjusted to the dark and the small glow coming from the street lamp. It was some time before I felt my body slowly start to relax, and longer before either of us spoke.

'Jesus!' John sighed eventually. 'Whatever was that all about?'

I shook my head. 'I've no idea, but supposing we hadn't woken and she had found the matches?' My stomach churned at the very thought – Dawn playing with matches in the kitchen and possibly setting fire to the house while we slept on upstairs with Adrian in his cot. The implications were too horrendous to contemplate. 'Do you think she wanted the match to light the hob and try to cook?' I asked at length. 'I mean, I know the burners light automatically but Dawn might not have realised that.'

'It didn't look like it to me,' John said. 'She was nowhere near the stove, and what about the expression on her face? You don't normally show pain and anger when you are cooking. And why was she punishing herself? She was definitely trying to hurt herself for something she'd done.'

'I know,' I agreed reluctantly. 'I know.' I paused. 'I was thinking I might go to the doctor tomorrow when Dawn is at school, and discuss her sleepwalking with him.'

'Good idea,' John said. 'I also think we need to tell her social worker and ask her what she knows about it.'

'And if Dawn remembers what happened tonight,' I said, 'which she might do, as she was awake, I could try to talk to her about it. At least it will be out in the open then, and it might help her.'

Utterly exhausted the following day, Monday, we hauled ourselves into the weekday routine. When I woke Dawn at 7.00 a.m. to tell her it was time to get ready for school, she was in a very deep sleep and it took me some time to raise her. When she finally came down to breakfast I had already eaten mine and was spoonfeeding Adrian his baby porridge. I watched Dawn as she took her place at the table. She was obviously very tired and looked almost hung over, with dark circles round her eyes, but she managed to say good morning and smile. I continued to watch her as she began eating her toast, half expecting her to say something about the previous night, but she didn't. She carried on eating and sipping her juice; then she yawned, and I seized the opportunity.

'Are you still tired, love?' I asked, giving Adrian his last spoonful of porridge.

'Yes,' she said, and yawned again.

'You didn't sleep well. You had a really bad dream. Do you remember?'

Dawn looked at me puzzled and nearly yawned again. 'Not really. Was I talking in my sleep?'

I nodded. 'You seemed really worried about something. Don't you remember John and me resettling you?'

She shook her head. 'I hope I didn't say anything rude or embarrassing.' She gave a small nervous laugh.

'No, nothing like that.'

She shrugged and returned to her toast. Despite waking from her sleepwalking, clearly Dawn had no idea what she had been doing. I saw no point in telling her – she couldn't add anything if she didn't remember, and being confronted by what she had done was likely to have caused her more anxiety. I lifted Adrian from his high chair, sat him on my lap and gave him a teaspoon to play with, which he tapped on the table.

'Dawn,' I said looking at her seriously. 'Is there anything worrying you? You've had a few restless nights since you've been with us. Is there anything troubling you? If there is, maybe I can help.'

She briefly met my gaze and then looked away, and I knew in that look that there *was* something worrying her. I also knew that she wasn't about to tell me. Her usual open expression closed. 'No,' she said. 'I'm sorry if I woke you. I'd better go and do my teeth now. I don't want to be late for school.' Quickly finishing the last of her juice, she left the table and went upstairs to get ready. Five minutes later she reappeared and I saw her off at the door.

As soon as she had gone, I changed Adrian's nappy, made up a bottle of boiled water, put Adrian in his stroller and left the house. It was about a twenty-minute walk to the doctor's surgery, on the High Street, and I was pleased to be walking; it was a lovely spring morning, and I hoped the air might clear my head, which was still thick from lack of sleep, despite two cups of strong coffee.

The front gardens of the houses I passed were all coming to life with green buds shooting from the brown twigs of the shrubs, and late spring flowers replacing the daffodils and tulips. Birds were nest building and singing in the trees and Adrian was joining in with a song of his own. The air smelt fresh and clean, and I had a certain optimism. Though it saddened me that Dawn didn't feel able to confide in me, I was relieved that I had decided to unburden my worries about her to the doctor. As well as telling him that I thought Dawn was concealing big problems, and asking him if these could be responsible for her sleepwalking, I had decided I was also going to talk to him about her self-harming, for although she hadn't actually done it since she'd been with us, she had re-enacted it three times now. After I had seen the doctor I intended to go to the library and see if I could find any books on self-harming. Looking after Dawn was proving to be something of an education, a sharp learning curve, but on subjects I would rather not have known about.

The doctor's surgery was full with the accumulated ailments of the weekend. I gave my name to the receptionist and said I was happy to see any doctor – the one with the shortest queue; it didn't have to be my own doctor. In the waiting room I took one of the last two empty seats, between a badly overweight woman on my left who wheezed and coughed continuously, and a child of about three on my right who was seated on his mother's lap and also had a bad cough. I hoped Adrian wouldn't catch anything. Fortunately Adrian was usually very healthy and we rarely came to the doctor's.

By the time it was my turn, an hour had passed, and Adrian had drunk his bottle of boiled water and had exhausted playing with the contents of my large bag. I went through to 'consulting room two,' where Dr Roman waited. He was fairly new to the practice, which was probably the reason why his queue was the shortest – patients tend to opt for what had been tried and tested. I sat in the chair opposite his desk with Adrian on my lap. Dr Roman was quite young, and I thought it was likely he was only recently qualified, but he was very approachable. I explained that I had come not about me, but about the girl I was fostering, Dawn Jennings.

'Have you registered her with this practice?' he asked.

'Yes, when she first arrived.'

'Just a moment and I'll send through for her notes. I only have yours here.'

'Sorry,' I said. 'I should have explained at reception.'

He pressed the intercom button on his desk phone and asked the receptionist to bring through Dawn's medical records. 'You realise confidentiality stops me from disclosing what's in her notes,' he said to me. 'But it might be useful for me to refer to them. What exactly is the matter with Dawn?'

Good question, I thought; I wish I knew. I began outlining Dawn's behaviour.

His phone buzzed and he picked it up. 'OK, thanks,' he said, and replaced the receiver. 'Dawn's notes haven't arrived yet, which is nothing unusual. It can take months to transfer them.'

I nodded, and continued with the résumé of Dawn's background (what I knew of it), and then her sleepwalking and previous self-harming. I finished with a description of her behaviour in the kitchen the night before. 'I am obviously very worried, Doctor,' I said. 'And really I don't know what to do to help her.'

'And she's not telling you anything about her problems, or what could have caused this?'

'No. Nothing. She's always very polite and wants to please.'

He had listened carefully as I was speaking, occasionally nodding, and taking my concerns seriously. Now he sat back and thought for a moment before speaking.

'Not knowing Dawn or having her medical records it is difficult for me to say. But in my opinion she is exhibiting signs of very disturbed behaviour, presumably as a result of something that has happened in her past. It sounds as though she's had a very unsettled time between her parents, and you say that according to her social worker there is a gap in her history that no one can account for – indeed no one seems to know where she was?'

'Yes, between the ages of five and nine.'

'I'll know more once I have her notes, but I think it would be my recommendation that she has counselling. I could make a referral under the NHS for her to see a psychologist. However, I would need to see Dawn in person – I can't do anything unless she comes in and asks for help. I would also need the consent of either her parents or social worker before I made a referral, as she's a minor.'

'I see,' I said reflectively. 'I'm going to speak to her social worker later today. I'll tell her what you said.'

Dr Roman nodded. 'That would be the first step. In the meantime my advice is to try to talk to Dawn again;

perhaps eventually she will start to confide in you. You're handling her sleepwalking correctly, and sleepwalking is more common than you think, though not to this extent, I agree. I appreciate it can be very distressing to watch, but just keep her safe, and put anything she could use to harm herself with out of reach. If it was an adult who was sleepwalking regularly I might prescribe a sedative. I could for Dawn, but again I would need to see her first and obtain the permission of a parent or social worker.'

I realised that Dr Roman couldn't add or do anything more without Dawn, and aware there was still a waiting room full of patients, I thanked him for his time and left the surgery. I didn't feel it had been a waste of time – he had taken my concerns seriously, and his suggestion of counselling sounded a very positive one, although of course Dawn would have to be made aware of and recognise she had a problem first, which realistically meant me telling her.

In the library, I returned the two books on sleep disturbances, and then scanned the non-fiction section for books on self-harming. I was no more adept at navigating the Dewey classification system now than I had been before, and eventually I went to the desk and asked the librarian. At least I had the subject matter named correctly this time – self-harming – and the librarian checked on her computer and found there was one book listed. She led me to the shelf and took down the book. It was entitled *Self-harming and Adolescents: The Therapy*. Before she passed it to me she briefly flicked through it.

'I'm not sure this is what you want,' she said. 'It seems to be about teenagers.'

'It's not for me,' I said quickly, 'but someone I know.'
Thanking her, I took the book to be checked out and then
headed for home.

Once I had given Adrian his lunch and settled him for his
nap, I phoned the social services and asked to speak to
Dawn's social worker. A colleague answered and said that
Ruth was on annual leave and wouldn't be back for
another two weeks. I asked if there was anyone else I
could speak to who might know Dawn's case. 'Not really,'
the woman said. 'If it's an emergency you can speak to the
duty social worker, but otherwise it's best to wait until
Ruth returns.' I didn't think it constituted an emergency,
so I left a message to ask that Ruth phone me on her
return.

While Adrian slept, I read the book. It was really aimed
at therapists working with adolescents who self-harmed
and was full of psychologist's jargon. However, it contained a lot of in-depth information, and cited research
based on case studies of young people who had deliberately hurt themselves. What I read in no way lightened my
concerns: it was truly horrendous.

There were black-and-white photographs of the injuries
that adolescents (and it seemed to be mainly teenagers
who self-harmed) had inflicted on their arms, legs and
sometimes their bodies, some of which had required hospi-
talisation. I quickly learned that self-harmers, or 'cutters'
as they are colloquially referred to, are very good at hiding
their injuries, and the cutting is usually a secret activity.
Cutting was described as a 'coping mechanism', born of
anger and self-loathing, and was often a punishment for
how the young person perceived themselves. In many

cases the cutting continued for years undiscovered and, even once diagnosed, the cutting often continued, despite therapy. Reasons why young people harmed themselves included: lack of love; physical, sexual and emotional abuse; acute bullying; low self-esteem; and depression. 'Cutting makes the blood take away the bad feelings,' one young person was quoted as saying. 'I feel so guilty, I punish myself,' another admitted. The author added that if someone was feeling 'numb', then the pain of cutting could make them feel 'alive'. In some cases the cutting escalated and led to death – intentional or otherwise. Cutting was not simply a failed suicide bid, though, the book explained: it was an act in itself, although some professionals viewed it as a cry for help. I learned that cutting wasn't the only means by which self-harmers hurt themselves: they also took overdoses; punched themselves; threw themselves against walls; pulled out their hair and eyelashes; burnt, scratched, picked and tore at their skin – in fact anything that vented punishment or gave relief from their inner turmoil.

It was very harrowing reading, and the general con-sensus of opinion among the psychologists was that self-harmers were disturbed and could be suffering from any number of psychological illnesses. However, nowhere did I read about anyone re-enacting their cutting while sleep-walking, as Dawn had done, and I'd no idea if this was significant or not.

When Dawn returned from school I asked her, as I always did, if she'd had a good day. She said she had, although she added that she'd been so tired she had nearly fallen asleep in the English lesson. I said she'd have to have an early

night. I then said I'd like to talk to her before she started
on her homework. She fetched a drink from the kitchen, as
she usually did on returning home, and joined me in the
lounge. During the afternoon I had carefully thought
about what I was going to say and had come up with a
way of broaching the subject without actually having to
tell Dawn of her disturbed behaviour.

'What is it?' she asked sipping her milk. 'You look
worried. Have I done something wrong?'

I smiled. 'No, Dawn, you haven't done anything wrong,
but I am worried. Come and sit down.' I patted the sofa and
she sat beside me. 'John and I are both worried about something your mother said when we all met the other evening.'

'Oh, her,' she said dismissively. 'You don't want to
believe what she says. She doesn't like me and never has
time for me. In fact she'd rather I wasn't around at all.'

I was taken aback to hear Dawn say that, although it
appeared to be the truth. 'I understand, love, but what I
want to talk to you about is not something your mother
made up, but the scarring on your arms. I'm very worried
that you felt the need to hurt yourself, and I was wondering if you would like to talk to someone who may be able
to help. Someone called a counsellor, who is trained and
used to listening to people who have problems, and can
give advice.'

'I'm not cutting now,' Dawn put in quickly.

I looked at her. 'No, but you must have been very upset
and hurting inside to want to harm yourself like that. And
some of the scars are quite recent, aren't they?'

'But I haven't done it here,' she said defensively.

'I know, love. But to have done it at all makes me think
you were very upset about something, and might still be.'

She glanced away, and absently rubbed the sleeve of the jumper on her scarred arm, as though remembering.

'You know you can always talk to me, Dawn, but sometimes it's easier to talk to someone outside the family. Someone who knows about these things, who has experience in dealing with other people who have self-harmed and can offer help. It would mean going to see the doctor, but I could come with you, and we would need the consent of your social worker or mother.'

She stopped rubbing her arm. 'But I'm OK now, aren't I? I mean I'm not doing it now, and if I don't do it again I don't have to go to the doctor, do I?' She was making it sound like a penance.

'No, love, and you don't *have* to go at all if you don't want to. I just thought it might help to talk to someone if you have problems that you can't tell me. John and I care for you and it makes me sad to think that you might be hurting and wanting to punish yourself.'

The word 'punish' seemed to register with Dawn and she sat upright and looked at me. 'I haven't done wrong,' she said again, defensively. 'And I won't, not here.'

I met her gaze. 'It's not that you've done anything wrong, love. It's more that it's worrying.' I paused, realising I wasn't getting very far. 'Well, it's obviously your decision whether you see the doctor or not, but will you think about it? I'm sure it could help.'

She nodded. 'OK, Cathy, I'll think about it. Can I go and do my homework now.'

'Of course.' I hesitated again. 'And Dawn, it's only you I'm thinking of. I want you to be happy. I don't have an ulterior motive.' For something in her manner suggested

she thought I could be part of a conspiracy that was gang-
ing up against her.

'OK,' she said amicably, and, standing, left the room.

I leant back on the sofa and sighed. I felt I had handled
it all wrongly. Not only was Dawn refusing to go to the
doctor but it seemed I had unintentionally put her on the
defensive. But at least I had made her aware that help was
available if she felt she needed it.

That evening after Dawn had gone to bed I told John
about my day: what the doctor had said, my visit to the
library, phoning the social worker and leaving a message,
and my non-productive talk with Dawn. I showed him the
library book on self-harming, and pointed out some of the
relevant sections. John grimaced as he read, and looked at
the photographs of lacerated arms, legs, and bodies; as
shocked as I had been. By the time we had finished dis-
cussing what we had learned his concerns for Dawn had
deepened considerably, as had mine.

Dawn slept soundly that night, and so too did John and I;
all three of us were exhausted from the previous night. The
following morning after John had gone to work and Dawn
had left for school, and with my mood somewhat lighter
after a good night's sleep, I set about some overdue housework. It was another beautiful April day and I had the
French windows open in the lounge; I was busy vacuuming
and dusting the corners that weren't included in the usual
weekly clean. Adrian was on the carpet in the centre of the
room and practising getting into a crawling position. I
thought it wouldn't be long before he was off, and then I'd
have to move from the floor everything that might topple
over if he grabbed it, like the large leafy plants he'd been

eyeing for ages. The phone rang, and keeping an eye on Adrian, I picked up the extension on the corner unit.

'Mrs Glass?' a female voice asked.

'Speaking.'

'It's the school secretary at St James's. Dawn's Head of Year has asked me to phone you. Dawn isn't in school and we were wondering if she was ill?'

My heart fell. 'No, she isn't ill. And she left for school this morning at the normal time.'

'Well, she hasn't arrived. I take it you don't know where she is?'

'No, I don't.'

'I'll have to mark it as an unauthorised absence. Hopefully she'll be in tomorrow.'

'Yes,' I said. 'Thank you for telling me.' And I hung up.

I stood still, staring over the half-cleaned room, the previous lightness in my mood gone. On top of the worry about all Dawn's other behaviour I now had the worry of her truanting. It was only 10 a.m. and the hours to when Dawn would reappear at the end of the school day stretched before me with gnawing anxiety. I had no way of contacting her or of knowing where she was, and with her social worker away I couldn't even tell her. There was little to be gained from phoning John at work – he had enough to contend with, without this. I guessed there was a chance Dawn had gone to her mother's, as she had done before, although why she sought refuge with her when they had such a low opinion of each other, I didn't understand. I didn't have Barbara's telephone number, so I couldn't phone her to check.

Apart from the worry of not knowing where Dawn was, or what she was up to, I felt she had badly let me down. I had placed my trust in her and she had reassured me she wouldn't play truant again. Indeed she had been quite settled with her new friend, Natasha. I looked at Adrian, still on his stomach on the carpet, flapping his arm and legs excitedly, when suddenly I had a thought – one which I immediately chided myself for thinking, but didn't reject. Was there an address book or diary of Dawn's in her room? Or even a scrap of paper that would give me some clue as to where she had gone? I never normally went into Dawn's room when she wasn't there: I recognised that at her age she needed and deserved privacy. But if there was something there, some clue to her whereabouts, I could get in the car and go and find her. I felt her truanting, on top of everything else, could well be another cry for help. She knew that the school would phone me when she didn't arrive and that she would be found out. Was she testing me? Testing the boundaries to see if I cared? If I went to the trouble of finding her it could be proof to her that I worried, and cared for her very much.

With this in mind I scooped Adrian up from the floor and went upstairs. Opening Dawn's bedroom door, I went in, and what greeted me was certainly a cry for help, but not in any way I had anticipated. I gasped and stared in horror as my knees went weak. The pillow on Dawn's bed was caked in bright red blood.

Chapter Twelve

Missing Persons

I stood motionless just inside the room with Adrian in my arms, staring in horror and disbelief. My stomach churned and panic gripped me. I mechanically took a few steps further into the room and gradually approached the bed. My thoughts whirled, and I swallowed hard, not knowing what else I might find. Taking hold of the edge of the duvet, I slowly drew it back. To my small relief the rest of the bed was empty and unstained, but the blood on the pillowcase was fresh.

There was no doubt in my mind that it had come from Dawn cutting herself. There was no other explanation. But when? And why? It hadn't been there this morning when I'd woken her. 'My God!' I said out loud, as I realised the implications. Dawn must have cut herself after breakfast, when she'd come up to get ready for school. But she'd come down perfectly normal and had said a cheery goodbye; I'd seen her off at the door. 'Dear God,' I said again, and my head spun. She'd been wearing her long-sleeved school jumper when she'd left, so her arm hadn't been visible. Had she bandaged it? Or was the cut still seeping? How big was the cut? Did it need stitches? Should she be at the hospital?

I stood still, appalled and completely overwhelmed. Dawn had eaten her breakfast with Adrian and me, then

come upstairs, ostensibly to do her teeth and collect her
school books, and had cut herself! With what? I stared
around the room for any object that she could have used,
but there was nothing – nothing visible that was sharp
enough for her to have used. Then, with another stab of
horror, I wondered if I was to blame. Had my raising the
subject of her scars and her cutting yesterday produced
this? I thought it might have done, and I could have wept.
Possibly because of my clumsy attempts at trying to talk
to her, Dawn was out there somewhere, cut and bleeding.

I hurried out of her bedroom and, taking hold of the
handrail, went unsteadily downstairs. I continued through
to the lounge where, sitting Adrian on the floor with his
toys, I picked up the phone. At the same time I grabbed
my address book for the social services number.

'I want to speak to the duty social worker,' I said in an
uneven voice as the woman answered the switchboard.

'In connection with what?'

'The child I'm fostering – Dawn Jennings.'

'Your name?'

'Cathy Glass.'

There was a click; then her voice again. 'The line's busy.
Will you hold?'

'Yes, unless there is someone else I can talk to. It's an
emergency.'

'What sort of emergency?'

'Dawn has vanished, and I've found blood on her pillowcase. I think she has harmed herself.'

There was another pause. 'Who's her social worker?'

'Ruth Peters, but she's away.'

'How old is the girl?'

'Thirteen.'

'You need to speak to the duty social worker. I'll put you through when he's finished his present call.'

The line went dead and I waited. My knuckles clenched hard and white around the receiver as I thought of Dawn, out there, hurting and bleeding because of what I'd said. How I wished I'd left the subject alone!

When the duty social worker came on the line, my voice trembled, and I could barely get out what I had to say.

'She's only thirteen, and she's cut herself, and I don't know where she is. She left for school, but didn't arrive, and I've found blood all over her pillow.'

'The girl's name?' he asked, interrupting my ramblings.

'Dawn Jennings.'

'Has this happened before?'

'No – well, yes. I mean she's truanted before, and she's cut herself, but not since she has been with me.'

'And how long has she been with you?'

I thought. 'Three months.'

'And do you have any idea where she might be? Missing teenagers often return to the same place.'

'She might have gone to her mother's. She went there when she truanted before. But her mother works, and I don't have her number.'

'It'll be on our records. Was Dawn upset when she left you this morning?'

'No. Not at all.' I took a deep breath and swallowed hard, fighting back the tears. 'She seemed perfectly calm. I'd no idea she'd cut herself until I went to her room a few minutes ago.'

There was a pause. Although the duty social worker was obviously taking my concerns seriously, there wasn't the urgency or panic in his voice that there was in mine; it was as though he was used to dealing with missing teenagers, only of course this wasn't simply a missing teenager but one who had harmed herself and could do so again.

'OK,' he said after a moment. 'I'll see if I can find the case notes, and call Dawn's mother. I'll get her to phone you if Dawn is there and put your mind at rest. If Dawn hasn't returned by the end of school, give her a couple of hours and then do a missing persons.'

'Missing persons?' I asked, not understanding what he meant and assuming it was a social services procedure.

'Yes, with the police. If Dawn doesn't return this evening and mum hasn't called you to say she is with her, you will have to phone the police and report Dawn missing. But phone this number first, and say you are about to do a missing persons. The police will ask you if the social services have been informed.'

'I see,' I said, totally unfamiliar with the procedure, and the words 'police' and 'missing person' adding to my anxiety. 'And you'll ask Dawn's mother to phone me straightaway if she is there?"

'Yes, I will.'

I replaced the receiver and sat for a moment, staring into space. How long would it take the duty social worker to find Dawn's case notes and Barbara's telephone number, and then call her? Fifteen minutes? Half an hour? It couldn't take longer than that, surely? Aware I wouldn't hear the phone ringing with the vacuum cleaner on, I unplugged it, and slowly wound up the lead. I no longer had any enthusiasm for cleaning; in fact I had no enthusiasm for anything, beyond knowing Dawn was safe. I returned the vacuum cleaner and dusters to the kitchen and then sat on the floor with Adrian in the lounge. Deep in thought, I vaguely kept him amused with his toys. Fifteen minutes passed, then thirty, and the phone didn't ring. I wondered if that was because the duty social worker was still trying to find Dawn's case notes or if her mother wasn't at home; or even if he'd phoned Barbara and Dawn wasn't there. I wished I had asked him to phone me whatever the outcome – not knowing anything and being impotent to do anything was worse than knowing something bad.

An hour passed and I couldn't stand it any longer. I phoned the social services again and asked for the duty social worker. I gave my name again to the woman on the switchboard, and then again to the duty social worker, who recognised me.

'Mrs Jennings isn't at home,' he said. 'I'll try her again later.'

I thanked him and hung up. There was nothing else I could do but wait. John phoned at lunchtime to ask if I was going into town because he'd left a suit at the dry cleaner's and wanted me to collect it. I told him what had happened and he was obviously very concerned – for Dawn and me. 'Are you all right?' he asked more than once. 'Whatever made her do it?'

I now said that I thought I could have caused it by raising the subject. 'Don't be silly,' he said. 'Of course not. You were trying to help her, and we know she's done it before.' He paused. 'Cathy, I really think we need to consider our options and whether we can realistically continue to look after Dawn. I have big doubts after this. We've had nothing but worry since she came to live with us. I know it's not her fault, but we need to think about the effect all this is having on us, as a family, and you in particular.'

'I'm all right,' I said lamely.

John was unconvinced. 'We'll talk about it later. I'll see you at the usual time, and try not to worry. Dawn's done this before and survived. I'm sure she'll be all right. Give my love to Adrian.'

'I will.'

We said goodbye and I hung up. Although John was only voicing his concern and trying to reassure me, it didn't help. I was aware that Dawn had done it before – she had the scars to prove it. But it didn't mean she now suffered less; indeed each new cut seemed to make it worse and highlight her continuing inner turmoil and desperate need for help. Furthermore, she hadn't been in my care when she'd cut before, and I now felt responsible for her and negligent in allowing it to happen.

The afternoon passed; I didn't leave the house. I busied myself, mainly in looking after Adrian, while listening, hoping, that the phone would ring with some news. It rang once, just before two o'clock, and I leapt to answer it. But it was a double glazing salesman cold-calling for business, and I quickly got rid of him, wanting the line free. Three o'clock approached and my sprits began to lift slightly. I was hoping that Dawn might return home at the end of the school day, as she had done before when she'd played truant. But my hope was tempered by the knowledge that this time Dawn had cut herself and left the evidence for me to see.

At 3.30 p.m., with Adrian in my arms, I went through to the front room and stood behind the net curtains, where I would see the first sign of Dawn's approach. I waited, willing her to appear. Her usual coming-home time of 3.45 p.m. came and went; then the hands of the clock settled on four. I reminded myself that on a couple of occasions when the buses had been running late she had arrived just after 4.00 p.m. I wandered around the room, up and down the hall, and then returned to the window, but there was still no sign of Dawn.

At five o'clock I went through to the kitchen and began preparing dinner – Adrian would be hungry, even if I wasn't. By 5.30 p.m. I was forced to admit that Dawn wasn't coming home and I was sick with worry. I made one last trip to the front room window, hoping beyond hope that I would see her coming down the street, but she wasn't there. She was now nearly two hours late, and following the duty social worker's instructions, I phoned the social services.

'Out of hours response,' a female voice said tritely, and I said I needed to speak to the duty social worker. It was a different person on duty to the one I had spoken to previously, and I had to explain all over again what had happened, and that I'd been told to phone before I reported Dawn missing to the police. He asked me why Dawn had come into care and if she'd gone missing before. I repeated what little I knew.

'It's still early for doing a missing persons,' he said. 'We usually wait for at least two hours, and it's not dark yet. The police receive a lot of calls about missing teenagers, and the kids usually turn up at home later.'

'But she's never gone missing here before and she's hurt!' I blurted, frustrated, and losing patience with all the worry.

'No, but from what you've said, she often went missing when she was with her parents.'

'Yes, but what about the blood? She's cut herself and might need first aid.'

'Look, I'll log this call, so you needn't phone here again. Give it until six thirty; then if she still hasn't shown, phone the police and do the missing persons. If she does turn up in the meantime, ring this number so I can take it off the system.'

'Right,' I said, and curtly thanking him, hung up. Bloody system! I thought. He hadn't shown a shred of sympathy, and Dawn had appeared to be just another inconvenient statistic.

I gave Adrian his dinner, and plated up John's and left it in the oven. I had no appetite, and made do with a mug of tea and a biscuit. If Dawn did appear I could eat with her later, and I entertained the briefest picture of Dawn and me sitting down to dinner and talking. I gave Adrian his bath and got him into his pyjamas; then I returned to the lounge with him and waited. At exactly 6.30 p.m. I picked up the phone ready to call the police, then realised I didn't know the number. Missing person wasn't really a 999 call, I thought, so returning the phone to its cradle, I searched the directory until I found the number of our local police station. My head was thumping and I had a pain across my forehead from all the worry and anxiety. With the phone directory open on my lap, and Adrian on the sofa beside me, I keyed in the numbers. I was surprised and somewhat dismayed to hear a recorded announcement telling me I was being held in a queuing system and would be connected to an officer as soon as one was available. 'Shit,' I said out loud, feeling the tears well in my eyes. Adrian looked at me.

Ten minutes later I was finally speaking to a police officer. I had just told him I needed to report someone missing when I heard the front door open as John came in from work. 'Sorry,' I said to the officer, 'can you hold on a minute.' I put down the phone, picked up Adrian, and went down the hall. 'Can you look after him?' I said bluntly, and completely stressed out. 'I'm on the phone to the police. Dawn hasn't returned.' Before John had time to take off his coat, I'd dumped Adrian in his arms. 'Your dinner is in the oven,' I called before I retrieved the phone.

'Sorry,' I said again to the police officer. 'You asked for my name.'

'Yes,' he said patiently.

I gave it to him; then he asked for our address and telephone number. There was a pause while he wrote.

'And who is it that is missing?'

'Our foster daughter, Dawn Jennings.'

Another pause. 'Her date of birth please.'

I had to think. 'She's thirteen. Her birthday is the sixth of January.' I left him to calculate the year for it was more than my brain was capable of at that point, but I felt guilty for not knowing it off by heart as I obviously knew Adrian's.

'And she's your foster child?' he confirmed.

'Yes.'

'Have you told her social worker?'

'I've told the duty social worker. Dawn's social worker in on holiday.'

'Aren't they always?' he said dryly. 'And her social worker's name?'

'Ruth Peters.'

Another pause. 'When was the last time you saw Dawn?'

'This morning at eight fifteen.'

He asked for the circumstances of her leaving the house and I explained that she'd left to go to school but hadn't arrived, and how I had gone to her room and found the blood. I told him about the scars on her arm where she had previously cut herself, and what I knew of her past. He then asked for a description of Dawn and what she was wearing.

'She's small for her age, about five feet tall,' I said, speaking slowly and allowing him time to write. 'Slightly built, with fair chin-length hair and blue eyes. She was wearing her school uniform – a navy pleated skirt, black tights, light blue blouse under a navy sweater with the school's logo.'

'And her school is?'

'St James's.'

'Was she wearing a coat?'

'No. She didn't take it because of the warmer weather.'

'Is it possible Dawn could have taken clothes with her and changed out of her uniform?' he asked.

I thought. 'I don't think so. Her school bag isn't really big enough with all her books.'

'What about without her books? Could she have taken a change of clothes and left her books at home?'

'Well, yes, but I'm sure she wouldn't deceive me like that.' Yet as I said it I realised that Dawn had deceived me in not going to school. I so desperately wanted to believe and have faith in Dawn that I instinctively rushed to her defence. 'It's possible,' I added quietly.

'Have you checked her wardrobe for missing clothes?' he sensibly asked.

'No.'

'Would you do so, and tell the officers when they arrive if you find anything missing.'

'Officers?' I asked.

'The police officers who will come to your house later; it's part of the missing persons procedure.'

'Oh, I see,' I said, once again feeling completely ignorant, but how many people know the missing persons procedure unless they've had cause to implement it? 'Perhaps Dawn met someone on the way to school,' I offered as he wrote. 'Her mother said Dawn got in with a bad lot when she lived with her and went missing.'

'Quite possibly she met up with others,' the officer said with a certain resignation. 'These kids usually do. Do you have any of her friends' contact details or know places where Dawn might have gone to hang out with her mates?'

Again, I felt totally inadequate. 'No. She hasn't told us. She goes out on Friday and Saturday evenings and has to be home by nine thirty. But she never tells us where she's going.'

'Do you have her mother's address or phone number?'

'No,' I said again, thinking that perhaps we should have been given it by the social worker.

'I'll check our records. If Dawn has gone missing before or is known to the police we should have some details.'

'Thank you.' I said.

'And you say she has harmed herself in the past?'

'Yes, but not since she's been living with us. There are scars on her arms from before. This is the first time she has cut herself here, and I really don't know what made her do it. She wasn't upset.'

'I understand,' he said. 'Do any of her friends have cars?' But before I could answer, he added, 'I don't suppose you know?'

'No,' I agreed. 'I've no idea, but she is only thirteen, so I wouldn't think so.'

He didn't pass comment, but I recognised that my assumption might well be another example of my ignorance about Dawn and teenagers in general.

'Does she have a passport?' he asked.

'Not as far as I know.'

'How much money did Dawn have on her this morning when she left the house?'

'It's difficult to say. We give her pocket money and clothing allowance. If she hasn't spent any of it, which I don't think she has, it could be over £40.'

I heard him draw a sharp breath. 'It's not a good idea for persistent runaways to be given a lot of money. They can travel further.' It was the first hint of reproach I had heard in his voice, and I secretly agreed with him.

'Dawn's social worker said we had to give it to her,' I said, which I knew sounded pathetic.

There was another pause before he said. 'Mrs Glass, I'll put Dawn's details on our missing persons register. When the officers visit you, can you give them a recent photograph of Dawn, one that they can take with them, please?'

'I'm sorry,' I said, my anxiety rising. 'We haven't got one. We've taken family photographs that include Dawn, but they are still on the camera. I haven't had them developed yet.'

'Don't worry. We have a good description of her and we might still have a photo from the last time she ran away. But in future when you foster teenagers with a history of running away, it would help us if you could have a photo-graph to hand.'

'I'm sorry,' I said again, my feelings of inadequacy and ignorance escalating. 'This is all new to us. When will the officers visit?'

'I can't give you a time. We're very busy and short staffed. Hopefully later this evening. If Dawn comes home in the meantime, please phone us and we'll take her off the missing persons register to save wasting police time.'

'Yes, of course.' I hesitated, not wanting to show further ignorance but needing to know. 'Could you tell me what you actually do now, please? I mean how you try to find Dawn. I'm very worried. '

'I'm sure you are. Dawn's description will be circulated to all patrols so if she's out on the streets there's a good chance an officer will spot her. If she hasn't returned by tomorrow we'll put her details on the National Missing Persons Bureau, and check the hospitals.' My stomach tightened at the mention of hospital: I pictured Dawn lying alone in a hospital bed and having her wounds stitched, with no one there to comfort her. 'If we thought there was a chance of her leaving the country,' he con-tinued, 'we'd notify the airports and ports, but I don't think that is the case here.'

'No,' I quietly agreed. 'I wouldn't think so.'

'That's it, then, for now. I'm sure Dawn is safe and will come home soon.'

'I hope so. Thank you, you've been very helpful.'

By the time I put the phone down, John had eaten his dinner and had taken Adrian upstairs with him while he changed out of his work suit. I felt tired and strained, yet

peculiarly alert from all the adrenalin of the stress. I went
upstairs and into our bedroom, where I tried to raise a
smile for John's sake.

'Look!' John said before I had chance to say anything,
and he nodded towards Adrian. Adrian was on all fours,
making small sporadic movements across the carpeted
floor, and it took me a moment to realise that he was
crawling. The moment I had anticipated and had looked
forward to for weeks had happened in my absence, while I
had been on the phone reporting Dawn missing. And my
happiness was marred by disappointment that I had
missed this milestone, and the continual worry about
Dawn.

I crossed the bedroom, and sitting on the floor, a short
distance in front of Adrian, beckoned for him to come to
me. 'Come on, come to Mummy,' I said encouragingly,
lightly clapping my hands. Adrian grinned, gurgled, and
then with a sudden crab-like movement scampered the
small distance between us, and squatted in my lap. 'Well
done!' I cried. 'Who's a clever boy?' John clapped loudly. I
picked up Adrian, gave him a big kiss and then held him
up in the air, where he giggled. Bringing him down again,
I looked at John and sighed. 'Have you seen Dawn's bed?'

'Yes.' John said flatly.

'I've done the missing persons and the police will be
coming later. The police officer asked for a lot of details
about Dawn and I realised just how little we know. He said
we should have a photograph for next time, in case she
does it again.'

John gave a half nod of acknowledgement and continued changing from his suit. 'I'm not sure there will be
a next time,' he said. Adrian was now standing in my lap,

bouncing up and down, his chubby warm arms lightly brushing mine. I looked up at John. 'We can't go on like this with Dawn,' he said seriously. 'We're lurching from one crisis to another. I know you feel a lot for her, and feel sorry for her, and so do I, but the continual worry and lack of sleep is getting ridiculous. I'm going into work every morning exhausted and firing on only one cylinder. Even when Dawn doesn't sleepwalk, I'm still listening out for her. And now she's gone missing! I've got a very responsible job and I can't function like this, and neither can you. How are you managing to cope with Adrian? You look ill.'

'I've been worried sick all day, that's why,' I said defensively. 'And Adrian's fine. So what are we supposed to do? Tell the social worker that Dawn has to leave? That we've had enough, and she can be someone else's problem?'

'Yes, if necessary,' John said, his voice rising. 'I think Dawn needs more help than we can give her. We've done our best and it's not helping her. How many teenagers do you know who sleepwalk, go missing and slash their arms? How many parents do you know who have to lock their bedroom door to keep them and their baby safe? The doctor said she probably needs to see a psychiatrist, and that book said so too. I think they're right. Dawn's behaviour isn't normal and she needs help fast.'

John's voice had risen and so had mine. We stared at each other in emotionally charged silence. It was the nearest we had come to a full-scale argument in over four years of marriage. It didn't escape me that it was Dawn who was (inadvertently) responsible, and that she had caused problems between her parents and their partners.

'But what's it going to do to Dawn, if we send her away?' I said quietly after a moment. 'Her parents don't want her; she knows that. What's it going to do to Dawn if we now tell her we don't want her either?'

'Look,' John said more evenly. 'When Dawn returns, which I'm sure she will, let's sit her down and talk to her, and try to find out what's going on. If she's open and honest with us, perhaps we can find a way forward. She's always so polite, and seems to want to co-operate, perhaps she'll open up after all this. I also think that social worker needs to start being more forthcoming. Dawn's living in our house, and we are responsible for her. We should be entitled to know her background.'

I smiled, and John smiled back. 'Agreed,' I said.

'Come on, then. Let's get Adrian into bed, and go and sit in the lounge, and unwind.'

Relieved to have John's support again, I changed Adrian's nappy and then lay him in his cot. He looked up and grinned. John came over. "Night, 'night,' we both said, kissing him goodnight. 'It won't be long before he can go into his own room,' John said as we came out. 'He's old enough now.'

'Yes, and now he doesn't need a night-time feed it will be easier.'

Adrian's room had been ready since before his birth and, in truth, he could have moved in there sooner. But there was one thing stopping us, and I knew it hung unspoken in the air. If Adrian were in his own room, how safe would he be? Adrian's room was next to Dawn's, at the other end of the landing, and it was doubtful we would hear her if she sleepwalked in to find him. We couldn't lock Adrian in his bedroom any more than we could lock

Dawn in hers. Neither John nor I said it, but we both knew that Adrian would be staying in our bedroom until Dawn stopped sleepwalking and we felt it was safe for Adrian to be alone in the nursery.

Chapter Thirteen

Crime Scene

Keeping my gaze from Dawn's blood-stained pillow, I went into her room to check if any of her clothes were missing, as the police had asked. I opened the wardrobe doors first and flicked through the rails. Apart from the clothes Dawn had arrived in, virtually everything she owned I had bought her – she had never retrieved any of her belongings from either of her parents, and indeed I now doubted she had anything else – so I was reasonably familiar with what should be there, and I couldn't see anything obviously missing. Closing the wardrobe doors, I then searched the chest of drawers, and the bedside cabinet. I felt guilty looking through Dawn's belongings without her present, but I couldn't afford to be precious about this now that Dawn was officially missing and the police were involved. I returned everything I moved to its exact position – Dawn kept her room neat and tidy.

I couldn't find anything missing, and neither could I find an address book or diary that might have given some clue as to where Dawn had gone. I checked under the bed and then, steeling myself, I peeled off the bloodied pillow-case, with the intention of changing it for a fresh one. When Dawn eventually arrived home it wouldn't help her to be confronted with the evidence of her cutting and distress. However, when I removed the pillowcase, I found that the blood had seeped through to the pillow beneath, and I knew the lot would have to be thrown away. I found a spare pillow in the airing cupboard, and putting on a fresh case, I remade the bed, closed the curtains against the dark outside and, gathering up the pillow and case, went downstairs. I dumped the lot by the back door in the kitchen ready to take out to the dustbin the following morning.

I joined John in the lounge; he had just made a pot of tea and I gratefully accepted the mug he offered. It was now nearly 8.30 p.m., two hours since I had reported Dawn missing, and we sat on the sofa, waiting for the police and speculating on where Dawn could possibly be. At nine o'clock John switched on the television for the news, which offered some diversion for our thoughts. At 10.45, when the police still hadn't arrived and we were both exhausted and wanting to go to bed, John suggested he phoned the police station to find out what time we could expect them. I opened the telephone directory and read out the number of our local police station as John dialled. 'It's a recorded message,' he said a moment later, as surprised as I had been. 'I'm being held in a queue.'

The police station must have been even busier or more short-staffed than when I had phoned, for it was fifteen minutes before an officer finally answered. John gave his name and explained that I had reported our foster daughter missing and we were still waiting for the police to visit. He was asked for Dawn's name and our address; then he said, 'I see, all right, thanks, we will.' He replaced the phone with a sigh. 'They're so busy they might not be here until tomorrow. The officer said Dawn's details have been circulated and we should go to bed.'

'Just as well you phoned,' I said. 'We could have been sitting up all night waiting.'

We went straight upstairs and I was in bed first. When John came in from the bathroom he automatically turned the key in our bedroom door before realising his mistake. And although we were both obviously very worried about Dawn we were also shattered, and were asleep as soon as our heads hit the pillows. It was, however, short-lived.

I came to with a start and immediately looked at the bedside clock. It was 1.00 a.m. John was wide awake too, and for a few seconds we didn't know what had woken us. Then the silence was broken by two long rings on the door bell and we both sat bolt upright.

'Who the hell's that?' John said.

'Dawn?'

We were out of bed, grabbing our dressing gowns as we went. John flicked on the landing light as we passed, and then the one in the hall. I stood just behind him, my heart racing, and my expectations and relief mounting as he slid the bolt and opened the front door. My hopes were immediately dashed. It wasn't Dawn.

On the doorstep stood two uniformed officers; their patrol car parked on the kerb outside and lit up like a beacon.

'You reported a missing person?' one of the officers said.

'Yes, that's right. Dawn,' John said. 'Come in. We were told not to expect you until tomorrow.'

'Sorry. It's been a busy night.'

They came into the hall and took off their hats, and I saw them cast a scrutinising gaze around. I was reminded of the television dramas where the police enter a suspect's home and make a mental note of everything that might be suspicious, and I felt almost guilty.

John went ahead and showed them through to the lounge, where we sat on the sofas. I was conscious that John and I were in our dressing gowns, ruffled and disorientated from suddenly waking, while the two officers were meticulous in their uniforms and professionally alert. The officer who was doing the talking, and seemed to be the more senior, took a printed sheet from his jacket pocket, and began going through Dawn's details. The details were those I had given to the officer when I had reported Dawn missing. As he read them out we confirmed they were correct. The other officer watched and listened, occasionally glancing at John and me; he was only in his mid-twenties and I assumed he was a relatively new recruit. When the senior officer finished checking Dawn's details, he asked us for a recent photograph of Dawn.

'I'm sorry,' I said. 'We don't have one. I explained to the officer I spoke to earlier. He said you might have one on record, as Dawn has gone missing before.'

'No,' he said. 'We returned Dawn's photograph to her mother when Dawn was found. It's usual to do so. I take it Dawn hasn't been in touch?'

'No,' John and I said together.

'Her details have been circulated,' the officer confirmed, 'so it's only a matter of time before she resurfaces and we pick her up.' There was an air of routine in his manner, which I assumed was a result of Dawn having gone missing before. But our worry was that this time the outcome could be different and Dawn might not simply reappear.

'We're very worried,' I stressed. 'I know Dawn went missing when she was at her mother's, but she's never done it before while she's been here. And she's hurt from having cut herself. There was a lot of blood on her pillow.'

The senior office nodded. 'We're aware of that. And we'll have a look at the pillow when we search the house.'

John and I stared at each other aghast. 'Is it necessary to search our house?' John asked. 'Our baby son is asleep upstairs.'

'We search the home of any missing person,' the officer replied. 'You'd be surprised at the number of kids we find hiding in a closet or shed.'

'Dawn's certainly not here,' I said, dismayed. 'I saw her off at the door this morning, and I've been in all day.'

'I'm afraid we still have to make a search to eliminate the possibility,' the senior officer said, 'though we need your permission to do so.' The other officer nodded.

John and I agreed to the search; if it was missing persons procedure, we couldn't do anything else, although I felt it was an intrusion on our privacy, and I knew John felt so too. Both officers stood.

'Let's make a start with the kitchen,' the senior officer said. 'I'm sure you folks want to get back to bed.'

John led the way, and the four of us went into the kitchen. By the back door was the blood-soaked pillow and pillowcase, and the officers' gaze immediately went to it. I felt even more guilty, as if I had committed some unspeakable crime and was about to dispose of the evidence.

'I've changed the pillow,' I clarified. 'I didn't want Dawn to see it when she came home.'

The senior officer went over to it. 'If you don't mind, we'll take the pillowcase with us,' he said. 'Do you have something I can put it in?'

I opened the kitchen drawer where I kept old carrier bags, and taking one out, passed it to him. John and I watched as the officer pinched one edge of the pillowcase between his thumb and forefinger and, carefully lifting it up, dropped it into the carrier bag as if he was removing a piece of evidence from a crime scene. 'I don't suppose you want it back?' he said dryly.

I shook my head.

'Do you have a shed or any outbuildings?' he then asked John.

'No,' John said. 'There's only the garage at the side of the house, and you access that from the front.'

The officer nodded. 'We'll check the garage last, on our way out.' He didn't ask to check the garden, which I thought was a bit of an oversight if they were doing a thorough search.

The officers moved down the hall to the front room, and John and I followed them. John put on the light, and both officers took a couple of steps into the room, gave it a cursory glance and came out again.

'Can we go upstairs now, please?' the senior office asked.

John led the way up, followed by the officers and then me. 'This is Dawn's bedroom,' John said, opening the door and flicking on the light switch. The officers went right in, while John and I waited just inside. I wouldn't say they made a particularly thorough search of Dawn's room; they opened the wardrobe, drawers and bedside cabinet, but didn't really move anything to search beneath the items as I had done. Apparently satisfied, they came out, and John showed them what was to be Adrian's room, and then the bathroom, while I hovered on the landing.

'This is our room,' John said at last, pausing outside our bedroom door. 'Our son is asleep in his cot.'

'We'll try not to disturb him,' the younger officer said, speaking for the first time.

John pushed open our bedroom door.

'Could you put the light on please, sir,' the senior officer asked.

I thought John's patience was being stretched to the limit, as indeed was mine. Did they really think we would have reported Dawn missing if we had concealed her in our bedroom? But I supposed if they search a house, it had to be every room. John switched on the light and we went in, followed by the officers. I immediately crossed to Adrian's cot while the officers surveyed the room. Adrian's eyes flickered open but then obligingly closed again. 'That's fine,' the senior officer said, and he and his colleague went out, followed by John and me.

'We'll take a look in the garage now, please,' the senior officer said as we went downstairs. 'Is it locked?'

'I'll open it for you,' John said picking up the garage key from where we kept it on the hall table.

'I'll say goodnight, then,' the senior officer said to me. 'We'll let you know as soon as we have some news.'

'Thank you,' I said, and I waited in the hall while John went outside with the officers.

John returned two minutes later, dropped the key on the table and closed and bolted the front door without saying anything. I knew from his silence that he was taking the intrusion very badly, and I appreciated why. For while I understood the reasons for the search being necessary, it

Cut   147

was not only a violation of our privacy but had left us with a nasty feeling of being in some way implicated in Dawn's disappearance. I knew from John's look that the search, together with another night's lost sleep, and his ominous silence, was another nail in the coffin for Dawn staying with us.

By the time we returned to bed, it was nearly 3.00 a.m., which meant there were only three hours left before Adrian woke and our morning routine began. I was wide awake now, and lay in bed trying to force myself to sleep while my thoughts chased. Where on earth could Dawn be? Where could she be spending the night? Had she met up with her old crowd, the 'bad lot' her mother had spoken of and getting into trouble with them? Was she sleeping at one of their homes, or was she alone and on the streets, trying to find shelter in a doorway? Although it was the end of April, the nights were still chilly and she didn't have her coat with her. I couldn't think of any other place Dawn could be other than at a friend's house or on the streets. Despite all the worry she had caused us, my main concern, as I was sure it was John's, was for Dawn's safety.

Please God, I prayed, send her back to us, or at least get her to phone to say she is safe. I stared into the darkness and shivered.

Chapter Fourteen

Easier to Cut

Dawn didn't return the next day, nor the day after, although I willed and prayed for her to do so. The next day was Thursday, and the police and duty social worker phoned in the late afternoon to ask if we'd heard anything from her, which we hadn't. The police said they had checked the local hospitals and no one matching Dawn's description had been admitted or visited casualty. I wasn't sure if this made it better or worse. Dawn had been missing for three whole days now and I was thinking that something dreadful must have happened to her, for I was sure she would have returned by now or at least phoned if it hadn't. She had little money and no clothes, and I began to imagine her lifeless body lying undiscovered in a wood or lake. During those days I continued something of a routine for Adrian, but Dawn was constantly in my thoughts and overshadowed everything I did. No matter what I turned to to occupy me, I was always listening out, hoping against hope that the door bell or phone would ring and bring news of Dawn. But it didn't.

When I opened the mail on Friday morning it included a statement from the accounts department at the social services saying that the fostering allowance was now being paid into our bank account, which I thought was cruelly ironic. It had taken over three months for the payments to start and they had finally begun the week Dawn went missing. It was like rubbing salt into an open wound, although it was just the system being slow. I made a mental note to phone the accounts department and tell them Dawn wasn't here, for clearly we had no right to the allowance if we weren't looking after her. I then began morbidly speculating about what I would do with all Dawn's belongings if she didn't come home, visualising having to pack up all her things and then give them to her social worker or mother. It was a truly dreadful week, and John and I felt that we had been left to cope with it alone. Apart from the one phone call from the duty social worker on Thursday there had been nothing from the social services – no offer of support or even a reassuring word.

The school secretary at St James's phoned on Friday morning and asked if Dawn was still missing, and I had to swallow hard before I replied, 'Yes.' The secretary said that the police had visited the school the day before and had spoken to the Head of Year, and also to Dawn's class. The police officer had asked the class if anyone had any idea where Dawn could be, which no one did. He said he'd leave a telephone number with the class teacher, where he could be contacted if anyone remembered anything that might help.

During that weekend John and I decorated the bathroom, more as a displacement for our anxieties than out of any real desire to see it finished. We worked in silence and took little pleasure from the result. The following day and Dawn would have been missing for a whole week.

* * *

On Monday evening, as John and I sat at the table, with Adrian in his high chair, finishing our evening meal, the front door bell rang.

'I'll get it,' I said with no enthusiasm, believing it was a salesperson seeking new business. 'You finish your dinner. I've had mine.'

I went down the hall to the door, wondering why canvassers always managed to call at dinner-time. Double glazing, wall cavity insulation, offers to re-tarmac the drive – we'd had them all at dinner-time. But as I opened the door my heart missed a beat and I struggled for my next breath.

'Dawn!' I cried. 'My God! You're home! Where have you been? Thank goodness you're safe!' I grabbed her hand and, drawing her into the hall, threw my arms around her and hugged her tight.

I felt Dawn's arms tightly around me and I thought she was as pleased to see me as I was to see her.

'Dawn,' I said after a moment, releasing her and standing back. 'Where have you been, love? Are you all right? We've been worried sick.'

She smiled, her pleasant open features unmarred by anything she had experienced or suffered. 'I'm sorry, Cathy. I hope you haven't been too worried.'

I hesitated, taken aback. 'Well, yes, love, we have. John and I have been very worried, and Adrian's missed you.' Which was true. Although Adrian wasn't old enough to be talking yet, he'd continually looked around the rooms as though expecting to see another person besides John and myself.

'Did he really miss me?' Dawn asked, smiling again.

'Yes, love. We all have. Now come through. John's just finishing his dinner with Adrian.'

Dawn dropped her school bag in the hall and then retrieved her slippers from where she'd left them under the coat stand nearly a week before. It was then I noticed she wasn't wearing her school uniform, as she had been when she'd left. She was now dressed in slim-fitting jeans and a black jumper, neither of which I had bought for her.

'You've got some new clothes,' I said lightly, as we went down the hall.

'Don't worry,' she said. 'I haven't lost my school uniform. It's in my bag.' And I was immediately struck by the inappropriateness of what she said – Dawn had cut her arm and had gone missing for a week, and she thought I would be worried about a lost uniform! It was a gross misconception, but I didn't comment.

'Come in and say hi to Adrian and John,' I said as Dawn hesitated outside the breakfast room door. I was aware we had some serious talking to do, but for now I was just pleased to have Dawn safely back and hoped that John would save the lecture for later too.

Following me in, she said a subdued hello to John, and then went straight to Adrian. Adrian grinned, clearly recognising her, and Dawn began chucking him under the chin and coochi-cooing. 'How are you?' she asked. 'Have you missed me? Have you been a good boy?'

'He's crawling now,' I said, returning to my seat at the table and taking a sip of my water. 'Do you want something to eat?'

'No thanks.'

I looked at John opposite, and motioned for him not to say too much, for I could see he was taken aback, as I was, by the ease with which Dawn had strolled in, apparently without a care in the world, and was virtually continuing where she had left off.

'How have you been, Dawn?' John asked stiffly, finishing the last of his dinner.

Dawn looked up from Adrian and smiled politely. 'I'm good, thanks.'

I met John's gaze and shook my head, again saying we must leave talking until later.

'I'm going to shower and change,' John said, pushing back his chair.

'Can I have a bath later?' Dawn asked.

'Of course, love, after John has finished. Are you sure you don't want anything to eat? We've had our dinner but I can do you some pasta or a fry-up.' John threw me a glance as he left the table, suggesting that perhaps I was being too accommodating after all the worry Dawn had caused us, but clearly the poor girl couldn't go hungry.

'No thanks, Cathy,' she said. 'I've had something. I think I'll go to my room for a bit, if that's OK?'

I nodded. 'As you like. We'll have a chat later when I've seen to Adrian.'

She smiled, and went out after John. I heard them both go upstairs without speaking; then John went into the bathroom and Dawn went to her room, and I heard both doors close.

I sat back in my chair and sighed, relief and concern flooding through me. I was so happy to see Dawn again, safe and well, that part of me just wanted to leave what had happened and move on. But there were questions that had to be asked, and reassurances and explanations that had to be given. Dawn needed to appreciate just how much trouble and worry she had caused John and me, for so far nothing Dawn had said had suggested she had the slightest idea what we had been through. I still didn't know what had caused her to cut and then run away, and I needed to hear her promise she wouldn't do it again.

I stood, and went to Adrian, and lifting him from his high chair gave him a big squeeze. 'You won't ever cause us this much worry, will you, little man?'

Adrian babbled his baby talk – 'Da, da, da, mmmmm' – and then I could have sworn he said, 'No.'

At eight o'clock, when John had showered and changed and was in the lounge, and I had settled Adrian for the night, I knocked on Dawn's bedroom door.

'Come in,' she called brightly.

I opened the door and stuck my head round. She was on the bed listening to her Walkman. She took out one earphone so that she could hear me. 'I'd like you to come down now, please, Dawn, so we can have a chat. After that you can have your bath.'

She obligingly took out the other earphone and switched off the Walkman. 'I'll be down in a minute,' she said. 'I need to go to the toilet first.'

'OK, love.'

John and I sat in the lounge, and a couple of minutes later Dawn appeared. 'Is Adrian in bed?' she asked, sitting cross-legged on the floor, as she did sometimes.

'Yes,' I said. 'He tires himself out now he's crawling.'

'I haven't seen him crawl yet.'

I smiled. 'You will do tomorrow. There's no stopping him.'

Dawn was apparently relaxed and chatty, although I could feel the tension rising in me. I glanced at John and wondered which of us would begin what we needed to say. John cleared his throat and, folding the newspaper, laid it to one side.

'Dawn,' he said evenly. 'I don't think you realise the extent of the worry you have caused us. You left the house to go to school on Tuesday morning and we haven't seen or heard from you since. Cathy found blood on your pillow and was beside herself with worry. She had to report you missing to the police.' I let out a small gasp and my hand instinctively shot to my mouth.

'Oh,' I said. 'I haven't phoned the police to tell them Dawn's back.' In all the fervour of Dawn's return I'd completely forgotten, and, apparently so too had John.

Dawn looked at us. 'There's no rush,' she said. 'I can't imagine they're trying to find me – they didn't before.' The leisurely manner in which she said it, coupled with her lack of concern for what had been happening in her absence, didn't go unnoticed.

'Dawn,' John said firmly, his voice rising slightly. 'Quite apart from our worry, do you have any idea of the amount of police time that has been wasted by you going off? The police went to your school, and searched our home. I think you owe us an explanation, and apology.'

'Sorry,' Dawn immediately said. 'I didn't think you would be worried.'

John looked at me, absolutely astounded.

'Of course we were worried,' I said. 'We didn't know where you were or how you were coping. We've been out of our minds with worry and have thought about nothing else all week.'

Dawn looked at us, genuinely surprised. 'I'm sorry,' she said again. 'I didn't realise. Mum and Dad never used to worry – they knew I'd come back.' And I thought that that was probably the truth of the matter and also the explanation for Dawn's apparent indifference to our feelings – she really hadn't thought we would be worried when she disappeared because her parents hadn't worried.

'Dawn,' I said. 'John and I care for you a great deal, and when you vanished without saying anything, and then I found blood on your pillow, we were worried sick.' I paused, hesitating to ask the next question because I didn't want to make her feel cornered. 'Where have you been, Dawn? Can you tell me?'

She shrugged despondently. 'Just hanging out with me mates.'

'What? All week?' John asked. 'Which mates? Where?'

Dawn gave the same shrug. 'My old crowd. Over on Mum's estate. There's always someone there to hang out with – they don't go to school.'

'What, none of them?' John asked. 'Do they work?'

'They're not old enough. They just hang out until the police pick them up.'

'And what do the police do?' I asked, shocked.

'Search them for drugs and booze, and knives, then take them to the station, and phone their parents.' Dawn's casual appraisal left John and me astonished; we were catching a glimpse of a different world, which clearly had also been her world. I noticed that Dawn talked of 'them' and didn't include herself, although clearly she had been part of the group, and apparently still was.

'But where did you eat and sleep, Dawn?' I asked.

'At me mates' houses. We crept in when their parents were out or had gone to bed. I spent all day and night on

Wednesday at one mate's house and her dad was in the whole time and didn't know. He was downstairs with his cans of Special Brew and didn't hear a thing.' And I now understood why the police had searched all of our house, including our bedroom. Dawn flashed a small smile, almost pleased with her accomplishment.

'It's not funny, Dawn,' John said. 'It's not a game. You've wasted a lot of people's time and caused untold worry.' But to Dawn that's exactly what it appeared to be – a game, no doubt goaded on by her mates, and apparently with precious little consequence for any of them.

'Your new clothes, Dawn?' I asked. 'How did you get those?' But I thought I already knew the answer.

'My clothing allowance,' she said, looking slightly concerned. 'I hope you don't mind, Cathy, but I've spent the lot. I couldn't stay in my school uniform and the same knickers all week.' And I acknowledged the police officer's caution about 'runaways' not having too much money, but of course the decision to give Dawn a clothing allowance hadn't been ours but Dawn's social worker's.

'Dawn,' I said gently, after a moment. 'Whatever made you do it, love? When I said goodbye to you on Tuesday morning you seemed fine. Then the school phoned to say you hadn't arrived and I went up to your room and found blood all over your pillow. Is your arm all right?' I'd been wondering about Dawn's cut arm since she had returned. The black jumper she was now wearing was long-sleeved. I was approaching the subject with care, aware that the last time I had talked to her appeared to have made her do it again.

'My arm?' Dawn asked, looking at me questioningly.

'Yes. Didn't you cut your arm?'

She shook her head. 'No, not my arm this time. I cut my leg. But it's OK. It's healed up. I put the pillow under my leg so that it wouldn't make too much mess on the bed. Was that right?'

Our silence said it all: John and I were shocked and horrified. Dawn had admitted to cutting herself so easily, as if it was a normal occurrence and all she needed to be concerned about was limiting the extent of the mess on the bed.

'You need to see a doctor,' John said.

Dawn didn't say anything but sat quietly, cross-legged and apparently unfazed.

'Dawn,' I tried again, aware that I still had to make phone calls to the police and duty social worker. 'Why did you do it? What made you so distressed that you needed to hurt yourself? What was it that you couldn't tell me? Do you know?'

She looked away, and for the first time since she had arrived home, her face dropped, and she actually looked sad. 'Yes,' she said quietly.

'Can you tell me, Dawn? I would really like it if you could.'

She drew a deep breath and concentrated on the carpet, rubbing her fingertips over the weave. 'Natasha, that girl at school. I was her friend, and then she made new friends, and she didn't want to be with me any more. I was angry and upset. So I cut my leg. Cutting takes away the pain and anger.'

I looked at her; John looked too. 'But why didn't you try to talk to me?' I asked. 'I would have understood how upset you were and maybe I could have helped.'

'I know, Cathy. I'm sorry. You have both been so kind to me. But I'm no good at talking about my feelings. The hurt builds up inside me until I can't stand it any more. I have to cut to let it out. Cutting helps. It makes me feel better and puts me in control. It's easier to cut than talk.'

The three of us went quiet. Dawn had taken the first step in talking about her feelings, and had admitted to something she felt deeply; she had obviously found it very difficult to speak of it, and possibly hadn't spoken of it before. John and I were reeling from what she had said – a sane, rational appraisal of what outwardly appeared to be the irrational act of a disturbed mind.

'Next time will you try talking to me rather than hurting yourself?' I asked.

'I'll try,' Dawn said amicably.

'What about a counsellor?' John asked. 'Would that help?'

Dawn shook her head. 'Wouldn't think so.'

'All right, love,' I said slowly. 'At least you have told us now. But I don't want you running off again like that.'

'No, I won't,' she agreed, too readily. 'Can I have my bath now?'

'Yes, if there's nothing else you want to talk about.'

'Not really. I'll go straight to bed after my bath. We didn't get much sleep at me mate's.'

'Does your mate have a name?' John asked.

'I'd rather not say,' she said sheepishly. 'I don't want them getting into trouble.'

She uncrossed her legs and, getting up from the floor, came over and kissed us both goodnight. As soon as she had gone upstairs I picked up the phone to call the duty social worker and the police, while John went into the kitchen to pour us both a strong drink. The duty social worker said he would make a note on Dawn's file, and the police officer said he would take Dawn off the missing persons register, 'until the next time,' he added.

'Hopefully there won't be a next time,' I said.

'Hopefully,' he repeated, but I knew from his tone he believed otherwise.

I had more faith in Dawn.

Chapter Fifteen

Family

The following morning I woke Dawn at 7.15 a.m., and told her it was time to get up for school. She opened her eyes and looked at me, surprised, perhaps thinking that after what she had told about her friendship problems she wouldn't be going to school today. But I thought there was nothing to be gained by putting it off – we needed to deal with the problem, and of course I intended to help.

'I'll take you to school in the car,' I said. 'And I'll speak to your Head of Year.'

'No, it's OK,' Dawn said, hauling herself upright. 'I'll go by myself. I'll be fine, really.'

'I think it's better if I come with you on your first day back. It's bound to be a bit strange seeing everyone again, particularly as the police have been in.' Indeed I would have thought it would have been cripplingly embarrassing to face her class for the first time, but apparently it was not so to Dawn.

'Couldn't you phone instead?' she asked. 'I will go to school, I promise.'

I looked at her carefully. 'Why don't you want me to come in with you, Dawn?'

'I don't want a fuss.'

I couldn't see how my having a quiet word with Jane Matthews could be construed as 'a fuss', but aware that Dawn needed to know that I trusted her, I agreed to phone instead of taking her, and left her to get dressed.

When she came down to breakfast I asked her how her leg was and if she wanted me to check that it was healing properly. I was concerned that it must have been quite a large cut to produce the amount of blood that had been on her pillow and, although the previous evening Dawn had said that it was healing, I would have felt happier having a look to make sure.

'It's fine,' Dawn said, and began eating her toast. Clearly she wasn't going to show me, and I thought that the scar on her leg, like the ones on her arm, were private to her. She wore black tights under her skirt, and her school blouse and jumper were long-sleeved. I wondered if, when the summer came and it was hot, she would still keep her arms and legs covered. The book we had read said that self-harmers often kept themselves covered up even in hot weather.

'Dawn?' I asked hesitantly as she ate and coochi-cooed at Adrian in his high chair. 'What did you use to cut yourself?' I was anxious that whatever it was could still be with her or somewhere in the house. I had checked her school bag the night before when I had taken out her crumpled school uniform and put it in the laundry basket, but there was nothing else in there apart from her books, pencil case and sweet wrappers.

Dawn looked at me guiltily. 'A razor blade,' she said. 'I took one of John's from the bathroom cabinet. I'm sorry. I'll buy him a new one.'

I felt the same shock and confusion that I had the night before when Dawn's concern had been about losing her school uniform and the mess on the bed, rather than the actual cutting. Now Dawn saw her problem as one of taking something that didn't belong to her. And I of course felt guilty that I hadn't thought to remove John's razors from the bathroom cabinet.

'There's no need to replace it,' I said quietly. 'John's got plenty.' As soon as we'd finished breakfast I would remove the razor and blades, and after Dawn had gone to school I would scour the house for any other sharp objects we might have overlooked, although there was a limit – I could hardly lock away all the cutlery in the kitchen drawer. And taking little comfort, I thought that at least the razor blade had been clean, unlike the cans and bottles her mother had said Dawn had used to cut herself in the past.

I gave Dawn her bus fare and lunch money, and saw her off at the door at 8.15 a.m. At 8.30, with Adrian exploring the corners of the lounge for anything he hadn't yet discovered since he'd started crawling, I phoned St James's School. Jane Matthews, Dawn's Head of Year, was in the staff room and I was put through. I said immediately that Dawn had returned home the night before and was now on the bus going to school. I explained that the reason for Dawn's truanting appeared to be a friendship problem: that being responsible for, and being friends with, Natasha had been Dawn's lifeline, and that when Natasha had made new friends Dawn had felt excluded from the group.

Jane Matthews was sympathetic but said exactly what I had anticipated: 'I'll do what I can, but I can't force Natasha, or anyone to be friends with Dawn. I thought

Dawn had been included in that group and they were all friends together. Dawn might have over-reacted or used it as an excuse for not coming to school.'

'I don't know,' I said. 'But Dawn was upset enough to run away for nearly a week.' I hadn't told Jane about Dawn cutting herself; I didn't think she needed to know, and it wouldn't have helped Dawn to have this added to her school notes. The school knew that Dawn had previously cut herself: her mother had mentioned at the meeting that Dawn's father had phoned the school and told them.

'I'll speak to Dawn,' Jane finished by saying, 'and also to that group of girls.'

'Thank you so much. I'd very much appreciate that.'

When Dawn returned home at the end of school she said she'd had a good day. Natasha was her friend again, and so too were the other girls in the group. I praised Dawn, and also silently praised Jane Matthews, for clearly whatever she'd said to the girls had worked. But at the same time I recognised how fragile Dawn was and how little ability she had to cope with life's downers. To have slashed her leg and gone missing for a week after a friendship falling-out obviously wasn't normal or healthy, and not for the first time I wondered what could have possibly gone so badly wrong in Dawn's past to have made her so vulnerable and defenceless.

The week progressed without major incident. Dawn went to school each day, returned home on time, did her homework before and after dinner, and then in the evening sat with John and me in the lounge or went to her room to listen to her Walkman. John's razor and razor blades were now in a drawer in our bedroom; John took the razor into the bathroom each morning and returned it to the drawer straight afterwards, and disposed of the old blades in the dustbin outside. I had also removed the nail scissors from the bathroom cabinet.

In the middle of Wednesday night we were woken by the sound of Dawn's bedroom door slamming shut, having been caught by the wind from her open bedroom window. We immediately got out of bed and went out to the landing, where we found Dawn about to go downstairs. We turned her round and steered her back to bed, where she slept until morning. As usual she didn't remember sleepwalking, and when I asked her if she had slept well she said politely, 'Yes thanks, Cathy, did you?'

I phoned Dawn's social worker on Thursday morning; two weeks had passed and she was due back from holiday. I had a lot to tell her, and John and I had agreed that in the light of recent events we would ask for more information about Dawn. But a colleague of Ruth's answered and said that due to 'family reasons' Ruth had extended her holiday by another week and wouldn't be back in the office until the following Monday. I left another message asking her to call me as soon as possible.

On Friday evening Dawn spent an hour getting ready to go out and then asked for her pocket money and clothing allowance. Mindful that she had used her clothing money to fund her running away, I gave her the pocket money but said, 'I'll give you your clothing allowance tomorrow. The clothes shops are all closed now, so you don't need it tonight.'

Dawn hesitated and looked as though she was about to argue the point but then thought better of it.

'Have a nice time,' I said. 'See you at nine thirty.'

While Dawn was out, John and I spent a relaxing evening catching up on the week, mainly talking about Adrian's progress and various issues John had had to deal with at work. Dawn appeared at exactly 9.30 p.m., and when I asked her if she'd had a good time, she said politely, 'Yes thanks, Cathy,' but as usual she didn't offer any details. In some respects I felt it was like having a house guest or lodger staying with us rather than caring for a child of thirteen – we knew so little about Dawn or her life outside the house. John and I provided shelter, regular meals and money, but precious little else.

I hoped that with time Dawn would start to integrate more into our family life, and allow us to have some part in hers. Although Dawn visited my parents with us, if we suggested other family outings she always found some excuse: something she had to do, like homework, washing her hair or tidying her room. I would have expected this distance from an older teenager, but not someone of thirteen. We couldn't force Dawn into family outings, but her not going limited our outings. John and I didn't feel comfortable about leaving Dawn alone in the house as she wanted; indeed we weren't even certain if it was legal to do so at her age, even for short periods. 'You go,' Dawn said when we'd suggested a visit to a local water mill. 'I'll be fine here, I've plenty to do.' We couldn't persuade her, so none of us went.

On one occasion when it was a fine day John suggested we all went for lunch in a lovely pub garden we knew that held barbecues. 'Why don't you two go and I'll look after Adrian here,' Dawn said helpfully. Clearly this was out of the question, and once again we were forced to change our plans, careful not to hurt Dawn's feelings after her offer to look after Adrian. A couple of times Dawn agreed to come with us to the park with Adrian, but more often she didn't want to, and either John or I stayed at home with Dawn while the other one took Adrian out. It was a pity, because not only was Dawn missing out on these aspects of family life, but John and I were not going out with Adrian as a family as much as we would have liked at weekends.

On Saturday I gave Dawn her clothing allowance, but she didn't go shopping during the day; nor did she want to come shopping with me, which I had suggested. At 6.30 p.m., after dinner, she began getting ready to go out for the evening. She didn't wear a lot of make-up, which I was pleased about, but she always spent a long time washing and blow-drying her hair, and then choosing what to wear. More often than not she ended up in a pair of jeans and long-sleeved sweatshirt, but that was what most girls her age wore. She said, 'Have a nice evening,' before she left, and John and I wished her the same.

At 9.30 p.m. there was no sign of Dawn, and nor was there any sign of her at ten o'clock, or at 10.30.

'I don't believe it!' John said angry and worried. 'She's never run away again!'

I watched the carriage clock on the mantelpiece, aware that before long one of us was going to have to phone the duty social worker and the police to report Dawn missing, with all that that entailed! At 10.50 the door bell rang and didn't stop – one long ring as someone pressed it and didn't let go. John and I shot down the hall, aware it would wake Adrian.

'I'll open the door,' John said, and I waited just behind him.

Dawn was on the doorstep with her shoulder leaning against the bell button. She straightened and the ringing stopped. 'Hi,' she said, grinning inanely and waving one hand. 'Hi! It's me! I'm home!'

'You're drunk,' John said.

'Am I?' she grinned again, then leant forward and tried to navigate the step. 'Oops! I'm h-a-p-p-y,' she slurred. 'I'm happy!' she shouted. She lifted one leg and tried the step again, nearly falling flat on her face.

John and I caught her, and taking an arm each, manoeuvred her up the step and into the hall. 'Ooooh, thanks.' She hiccupped, then tried to kiss John's cheek. John stepped back just in time as Dawn threw up all over the new carpet.

There was no point in trying to talk to Dawn or lecture her while she was in this state, so John and I helped her upstairs to bed. She giggled and talked loudly the whole way – saying nothing of any sense, just the incoherent ramblings of someone who was very drunk. We kept telling her to 'ssshhh' and 'be quiet', as Adrian was asleep and she would wake him.

'Issss he?' she slurred. 'Bless-hisss-little-cotton-socks.'

We steered her into her bedroom, and eased her onto the bed. John took off her shoes, but we left her in her clothes. We turned her onto her side and propped the pillows down her back to keep her in place, so that if she was sick again she wouldn't choke on her vomit.

'I'll get a bucket,' John said, and went downstairs to the kitchen. He returned with the plastic bucket we used for washing the car and put it by the bed.

'Whzz-dat-for?' Dawn slurred.

'To be sick in,' I said.

Her eyes were already starting to close. 'Roooom keeps moving,' she sighed, and then she fell asleep.

John and I waited for a moment but Dawn was in deep sleep. We came out and left her bedroom door wide open so that we would hear if she was sick again or started to choke.

Downstairs I set about clearing up Dawn's vomit. John offered to do it, but I said he could do the next one, if she was sick again and missed the bucket.

'Thanks,' he said dryly. 'I'll look forward to that.'

Ten minutes later, I was warm from the labour of scrubbing, and all that remained on the carpet was a large wet patch, which I hoped would dry without leaving a water mark. The overpowering smell of pine disinfectant pervaded the house.

There wasn't a 'next one' – not that night, at least – so John escaped another clean-up. We checked on Dawn when we went to bed, and she was still on her side, fast asleep, and lightly snoring. We left her bedroom door open, and also left our door unlocked and open, for we were more concerned about the possibility of her choking than sleepwalking.

Amazingly we all slept through, and when Adrian woke at 6.30 a.m., I picked him up and the three of us went in to check on Dawn. The bucket was empty and she hadn't been sick again. She was on her side, exactly as we had left her – her mouth open, breathing slowly, and still sleeping peacefully. 'We'll have to give her a drink more often,' John quipped with a smile.

I now closed her door, for I thought it was highly unlikely she would be sick again or choke, and left her to sleep it off. I looked in on her at eleven o'clock and then again at one. Dawn didn't surface until 3.00 p.m. that Sunday, when she finally staggered downstairs, still in the same clothes, and looking absolutely dreadful – deservedly so I thought. Her face was white, her eyes were red and puffy, and her hair, which she had spent so long styling the evening before, was matted and stuck out all over her head.

'Do you have any paracetamol?' she asked quietly, coming into the kitchen where I was preparing Sunday dinner. 'I've got a dreadful headache.'

'I'm not surprised,' I said. 'And you've only got yourself to blame. I'm afraid that type of headache doesn't get my sympathy.'

'I know,' she said, and her hand went to her forehead as she grimaced.

'Sit down at the table,' I said, 'and I'll get you a para-cetamol, and also a cup of tea and some toast.'

She groaned. 'I can't eat toast. Can I have a biscuit?'

I guessed she was craving sugar after all the alcohol. I made her a large mug of strong tea, took a paracetamol tablet from a bottle in the medicine cabinet and, tucking the biscuit barrel under my arm, carried them over to the table. Setting them in front of her I returned to the kitchen and continued preparing the vegetables, occasion-ally glancing in her direction. I saw her swallow the tablet, drink some tea, then dunk a biscuit and begin to chew. It was time to begin my lecture, I thought.

'Dawn, you know a person can die from too much alco-hol. Apart from trying to cross roads in the state you were in, you could have passed out anywhere. Then what would have happened? Fortunately you got home before you crashed out, but next time you might not be so lucky. It's very silly and very dangerous to get drunk. It's also illegal to drink or to be sold alcohol at your age. Where did you get the drink?'

'Me mate bought it,' she said slowly and grimacing again, clearly finding talking, and probably the sound of my voice, aggravated her headache.

'Which mate?' I asked, none too quietly.

She shrugged.

'She doesn't sound like much of mate to let you get in that state. How old is she?'

'He,' she corrected, rubbing her fingers over her fore-head. 'He's older than me.'

'Where did you go to drink? They wouldn't have served you in a pub – you don't look anywhere near eighteen.'

'The park.'

I chopped another carrot, the knife snapping sharply on the wooden chopping board, while Dawn drank the rest of her tea and then asked for another. I refilled the kettle, and she slowly stood and gingerly carried her mug to me.

'Where did you get the money to buy the drink?' I asked, aware of the answer, but wanting confirmation, and ammunition with which to approach her social worker.

Dawn looked at me sheepishly. 'I'm sorry, Cathy. I used my clothing allowance.'

I nodded, and dropping a teabag into her mug poured on boiling water. When I next spoke to her social worker (hopefully on Monday if she was back) I would tell her how the clothing allowance was being spent, and ask if I could stop giving Dawn the money and take her shopping for clothes as I had done when she'd first arrived.

I poured milk into the tea and passed her the mug. 'Sorry,' she said again, and returned to sit at the table.

Dawn was always so polite and pleasant when she was at home, but something seemed to take over when she left the house. I thought that 'something' was probably her mates, the 'bad lot' her mother had spoken of who had got her into trouble before.

'Dawn,' I said more gently, as she dunked another biscuit into her tea. 'These mates of yours: it seems to me that being with them leads to trouble. Can't you spend some time with girls from your school, who are the same age as you? Natasha sounds nice, and from what your Head of Year said so do the rest of your group. You could invite them here for the evening, or arrange to go to the cinema or ice-skating on Saturday afternoon. I'm sure their parents wouldn't let them hang around the park on your mum's estate. In fact I doubt they'd be allowed out after dark at all.'

'How did you know I was in that park?' she asked, surprised.

'I guessed. It's where all your old friends go, isn't it?'

She shrugged. 'I like going there. We have fun.'

'But what sort of fun, Dawn? There are other ways to have a good time without drinking yourself into oblivion and then throwing up.'

I saw her face set and I knew I had said enough. It was difficult; had she been my own child I would have dealt with it differently, more firmly, and grounded her indefinitely. Indeed, the situation would never have arisen if Dawn had been my child, for there was no way either John or I would have let a girl of her age out alone in the evening unless they were just walking up the road to a friend's house. But the social worker had said that Dawn could go out Friday and Saturday evenings, so unless we could change Ruth's mind there was precious little we could do.

'Why don't you have a bath and change your clothes?' I suggested after a moment. 'Dinner will be ready about four o'clock, and then you're seeing your mum this evening.'

Dawn nodded. She finished the second mug of tea and pushed back her chair to stand. 'Where's Adrian?' she asked, finally realising that she couldn't hear him, or see him scampering around the floor.

'John's taken him out for a breath of fresh air. They'll be back soon.'

She hesitated, then looked at me; some of the colour was returning to her cheeks and she didn't look quite so pale and heavy-eyed. 'I love Adrian,' she said quietly. 'He's very lucky having you and John. I wish I could start my life over again, and be a baby here. I'd like you and John as my parents.'

'Oh, love,' I said, putting down what I was doing and going over to her. 'It's not too late. You're only thirteen – you can start afresh. John and I will give you all the help you need. You're a good girl. You've just got a bit off track – I don't know why.'

'Neither do I,' she said, and she paused. I knew she was about to say something heartfelt, and that she was finding it very difficult. She looked at me, her blue eyes sad and imploring. 'You and John are the only family I've ever had,' she said in a small voice. 'I really like being here with you, and I want to try and change and do what's right. I've made a real mess of it so far. Will you help me, so I can be good? I want to be like Adrian will be when he's my age. I don't want to do bad things – they just happen. I want you to be proud of me.'

I put my arms around her and hugged her hard. I had to swallow before I spoke because of the lump in my throat. 'Dawn, love, you've no idea how happy it makes me to hear you say that. Of course I'll help you all I can. You're a lovely girl, and I know if we all work together we can make big changes.' And I knew at that moment that whatever Dawn threw at us we would deal with it and support her, for if we failed her, her future would mean more of the past, or worse.

'Love you,' she said quietly into my shoulder.

'And you, love.'

Chapter Sixteen

Faking It

'If she's on the other line, I'll wait,' I said. 'I've already left four messages and she hasn't called back.'

I heard Ruth's colleague sigh. 'She might be a while yet. She's very busy.'

'No problem. I'll hold. I do need to speak to her urgently.' The line hummed as I was put on hold.

It was Wednesday morning and, despite Ruth having returned to the office on Monday, and my leaving two more messages for her to phone me, she hadn't. I now intended waiting for as long as it took for Ruth to finish her other call, so that she could speak to me.

Ten minutes later Ruth's voice came on, measured and precise. 'What can I do for you, Mrs Glass?'

I knew in my head what I wanted to say, and there was plenty of it. I began with the most serious – Dawn cutting her leg and going missing for a week, and then her sleep-walking. I told Ruth how Dawn had used her clothing allowance to buy drink, and continued with Dawn's truanting and the friendship fall-out that had caused it, and the hope that it had now been sorted. 'I know,' Ruth put in. 'The school left a message.'

'Good,' I said. I returned to Dawn's habitual sleep-walking, emphasising the seriousness and that it was a regular and disturbing occurrence. I described in detail the incident when Dawn had sleepwalked into the kitchen and re-enacted striking a match, calling herself a 'wicked girl' and 'evil child'. I thought for a moment Ruth was going to say something, for I heard her take a breath, but she didn't; so I continued with my visit to the doctor. I told Ruth that although the doctor hadn't yet received Dawn's medical notes, he had suggested coun-selling, but that we would need Ruth's permission before going ahead.

'You've got it,' Ruth said, 'if that's what Dawn wants.'

I paused. 'Dawn says she doesn't want it at present. But she needs it. John and I can only do so much.'

'You can't force Dawn to go for counselling,' Ruth said, unnecessarily. 'It has to be her decision.'

'I know, but John and I were thinking that perhaps you could talk to her and try to persuade her it would help. There's so much in Dawn's past we don't know about. Something has caused her to behave as she does and want to hurt herself.' I stopped again, hoping that Ruth would pick up this invitation to talk to Dawn and also fill in some details of Dawn's past, but there was nothing. 'I appreciate there are confidentiality issues,' I continued, 'but can you tell us anything about Dawn that might explain her behaviour and help us deal with it, so that we are better equipped to look after Dawn?'

'You can't stop her from going out,' Ruth said, missing the point – purposely? – and returning to what I had said at the beginning. 'She's used to going out and leading her own life. She's had a lot of freedom in the past and if you stop it all now she'll buck against it. Her behaviour could get even worse.'

'I'm not suggesting we stop her going out completely,' I said. 'But I don't think it's a good idea for her to be hanging around the streets two nights a week. If we're going to help Dawn we need to try to get her away from her old crowd. Seeing them just leads to trouble. She shouldn't be arriving home drunk at thirteen!'

There was a moment's silence at the other end of the phone, before Ruth said, 'Look, if I say you can stop giving Dawn her clothing allowance so that she doesn't have so much money on her, will that help?'

I had the feeling that Ruth just wanted to appease me, throw me a small scrap, and finish the phone call. 'Yes, that would be something. The police said it wasn't good for runaways to have a lot of money on them. And from the way the officer spoke it seemed they had dealt with Dawn before. Is that so? I know she ran away when she was with her parents, but has she been in trouble with the police before?'

There was another – poignant – silence before Ruth answered tersely, 'I'm not sure you need to know that, Mrs Glass. It doesn't affect how you look after Dawn.' So I assumed the answer was yes. 'Is Dawn in school today?' Ruth then asked, changing the subject.

'Yes.'

'And she went on Monday and Tuesday?'

'Yes.'

'Well, that's good, isn't it? I think you and John need to be more positive. Praise Dawn when she gets home and try to focus on all the progress she has made. I'm sure in time she'll respond to positive encouragement.'

Ruth's tone was patronising and what she said was demeaning. Give me some credit, I thought! Of course John and I were positive, and praised and encouraged Dawn. 'We do already,' I said bluntly.

'Good. Well, fingers crossed, then. I'm sure Dawn will improve given time. But she's had a really rough ride so far and she won't change overnight.'

And that was it. Ruth finished by telling me to say hi to Dawn, and that she now had to go because there was another call waiting.

I said a curt goodbye and replaced the receiver. I was annoyed. I felt impotent and ineffective, and I thought of all the things I should have said to Ruth or demanded of her; I even wondered if I should have threatened not to look after Dawn if we weren't given more information or given more support. But that would have been a hollow threat because despite our concerns John was now as committed as I was and we would stick by Dawn, with or without Ruth's input and support.

That evening while Dawn was in her in bedroom I told John of the conversation I'd had with Ruth, and he too was affronted, to put it mildly. 'She's got a nerve!' he said. 'I'd like to see her look after Dawn! She wouldn't give any more information – nothing at all?'

'Not a thing. She said knowing wouldn't help us care for Dawn.'

'It might,' he said. 'Knowing what has caused Dawn to behave as she does could help us deal with it.'

'Perhaps Ruth doesn't know,' I offered. 'She's already told us there was a four-year gap when no one knew where Dawn was.'

'But there would be records from when the social services got involved when Dawn was nine. That's nearly five
years ago!'

'I know,' I said with a sigh. 'But whatever is in those
records clearly isn't for our eyes. At least we've got her
clothing allowance changed.' I added.

John nodded absently, deep in thought.

When Dawn joined us in the lounge that evening after
she had done her homework, I told her I had spoken to
Ruth and that she'd said to say hi. I also said that it had
been decided that in future I wouldn't be giving her her
clothing allowance and we would be going shopping
together, as we had done when she had first arrived. I
added that I enjoyed shopping with her. Dawn didn't say
anything, but I could tell from her expression that she
wasn't the happiest bunny in the world, and would rather
have had the money in her hand. I ignored her scowl and
suggested a game of Scrabble.

'I'm no good at Scrabble,' she moaned. 'I can't spell.'

'Well, Scrabble will help your spelling,' I said brightly. I
fetched the game, set out the board and passed around the
alphabet tiles.

An hour and a half later, although Dawn hadn't won (I
had), she had clearly enjoyed playing and joining in what
was for her a rare family activity. She had entered into the
spirit of the game wholeheartedly and it had been lovely to
see her so engrossed and competitive. And while I would-
n't have expected Dawn to sit in every night playing
Scrabble, it had at least shown her that there was more to
family life than meals on the table and pocket money.

* * *

Dawn didn't go to school on Friday. When I woke her she said she was ill, but couldn't be more specific. I felt her forehead and it didn't feel hot, and when I asked her if she felt sick or if anything hurt, she said no. But I gave her the benefit of the doubt and told her to stay in bed. I phoned St James's School and said that Dawn wouldn't be coming in, as she wasn't well, and the secretary kindly wished her a speedy recovery.

It was very speedy!

By ten o'clock Dawn was up, dressed in jeans and sweatshirt, and hungry. I made her a cooked breakfast and then she said she was going out.

'Out?' I said. 'Out where?'

She shrugged. 'Just out. For a breath of fresh air,' she added, using the expression I used.

'Er, no, Dawn,' I said. 'You are off school, ill. If you are well enough to go out, then you are well enough to go to school.'

'No one will see me,' she said, quick as a flash.

'I know they won't, love, because you're not going out.'

She shrugged, and seemed to accept this, so I continued with the housework, even suggesting that she might like to help me, but she didn't find this idea very appealing. A short while later I was carrying Adrian upstairs to change his nappy when I heard the front door open behind me. I looked down, just in time to see Dawn disappear out, and the door close behind her.

I stood for a moment stunned, unable to believe what had happened. Dawn had deliberately defied me. Then with Adrian in my arms, I instinctively turned and shot down the stairs, and out of the front door. I flung open the garden gate and went out on to the pavement.

'Dawn!' I yelled at her retreating back. 'Dawn! Come back now!'

She turned briefly, and then continued at a faster pace up the street. I ran back into the house, grabbed my keys from the hall table and opened the car, which was parked on the driveway. I bundled Adrian into his seat in the rear and, jumping into the driver's seat, I started the engine and pulled from the drive. A few seconds later I was level with Dawn, who was about halfway up our road and heading towards the High Street. She saw me and looked very surprised.

I wound down my window and shouted across the road, 'Dawn! I told you not to go out. Get in the car now! You're coming home.'

She continued walking, and I continued slowly in first gear, kerb-crawling directly opposite her.

'Did you hear me, Dawn?' I shouted again. 'You're not going out! You're coming home with me!' Adrian giggled from the rear, believing it was some sort of game. I continued along the road, with my window down, moving at the same pace as Dawn. 'Dawn! Get in the car. I'm not going home without you!'

She was starting to look embarrassed, and looked even more embarrassed as a couple of lads in their late teens came sauntering down the road towards her. 'Dawn!' I yelled again. 'I've told you to get in the car! You've missed school and you are not going out!' She put her head down and hurried past the lads. The boys glanced at me, said something to each other and grinned. If Dawn thought this was embarrassing, it was nothing compared to what awaited her if she continued into the High Street, where there would be lots of people. I was quite determined that

Dawn would get in the car and return home with me, no matter how much of a scene I had to cause or how far I had to follow her.

Suddenly she crossed the road in front of the car and I guessed she was heading for the bus stop. She was now on the same side of the road as me, and I leant over and wound down the passenger window.

'I'm not going home without you!' I shouted again. Adrian was in fits of giggles now, having never heard me shout before, nor enjoyed such a stop-start ride in the car.

Dawn got to the top of the road and approached the bus stop where three people were already waiting. She glanced at the car and then hovered, clearly uncertain what to do.

I seized the opportunity for my grand finale, and stopping in the kerb, flung open the passenger door. 'Get in now!' I demanded. 'You are not going out. You are supposed to be off school, ill!'

The people waiting stared at Dawn, and then at me, but it was Dawn who felt the most embarrassed. And whether it was from acute embarrassment or the realisation that I really wasn't going to return home without her, I don't know, but she hesitated again, glanced up the High Street – presumably looking for the bus – then jumped in and slammed the car door. Adrian whooped with delight.

'Fasten your seat belt,' I said, as I checked in the mirrors and pulled out. Adrian babbled away excitedly in the rear. And although my heart was racing and I was wound up, I too could see the funny side of the scene.

I turned left and left again, which took us in a loop back to our road, and I pulled on to our drive. I didn't say anything until we were in the hall and Dawn was sullenly taking off her shoes. 'Don't you ever do that again,' I said.

'If I tell you you're not going out, then you are not going out. Do you understand me?'

She nodded, her face like thunder, and then stamped up the stairs and to her room, slamming the door shut behind her. Having no teenage children of my own and therefore no experience of dealing with them, I didn't know if I had handled the situation correctly. I had acted instinctively, feeling it was crucial that Dawn did as I said – it was as if she was testing me. But I recognised that had she not done as I had asked and got into the car I would have had even less authority in the future. I knew enough about looking after children from my friends who had older children and teenagers to be aware that children of all ages need boundaries – not only for their safety but to socialise them into society and make them responsible human beings. Enforcing the boundaries can be hard work but it is a sign of caring, and for someone like Dawn, who had just been left to do as she liked in the past, it was essential proof of my level of concern. I hoped that Dawn now knew that when I said something I meant it, and also that I cared enough for her to put myself out and chase her up the street to get her back home safely.

When Dawn reappeared from her room an hour later, she had stopped sulking and was her usual pleasant self.

'Hi, Cathy,' she said, coming into the lounge, where I was playing with Adrian. 'Do you want a game of Scrabble?'

And while I should have been doing other things, I recognised she was offering an 'olive branch' of reconciliation. 'Yes, that sounds good. Let's take the board into the garden; it's such a nice day.'

She helped me carry the coffee table out on to the lawn and then she fetched two garden chairs from the shed, while I spread a mat for Adrian under the shade of the tree and littered it with some of his toys. We then spent a very enjoyable couple of hours in competitive play, and taking it in turns to retrieve Adrian from the dubious delights of clods of earth, empty snail shells and stray leaves, all of which were heading for his mouth.

That evening as I prepared dinner Dawn sidled into the kitchen, and I half-guessed what was coming next.

'It's Friday,' she said looking at me carefully.

'That's right, love. It is.'

'I usually go out on a Friday evening.'

'Yes, you do.'

'Am I allowed out tonight, Cathy?'

'No, love. You were off school today, ill.'

'But I'm better now.'

'I know, and I'm very pleased you made such a quick recovery. But I don't think it's appropriate for you to be out when you've had a day off school. If one of your teachers were to see you, they might think you had been faking it.'

She looked at me and without further comment went over to amuse Adrian, maybe thinking that perhaps I wasn't so daft after all.

When John came home I told him of my chasing Dawn up the street and he thought it was quite amusing too. After we had eaten Dawn joined us in the lounge and we watched a video together, sharing a large bowl of home-made popcorn. Had we turned a corner? I didn't know, but having set out some ground rules, and showed Dawn that I expected her to do as I asked, at least I felt that the next challenge she threw at me might be that little bit easier.

How wrong could I be!

Chapter Seventeen

Why?

A week passed. Dawn managed to go to school each day and return without any major mishap, although she was late for registration on two mornings, claiming she had lost her bus fare and had had to walk. I wondered if the bus fare was being spent on other things – supplementing her pocket money and replacing the clothing allowance she no longer had. I didn't make an issue of it, but simply told her to try to be more careful in future, and that if she kept losing her bus fare then it might be prudent if I took her to school in the car.

Dawn only sleepwalked once during that week. John and I found her downstairs, on her way to the kitchen. As usual, we turned her round and steered her back to bed. We were taking Dawn's sleepwalking in our stride now and hoping as with all her other behaviour, that it would improve as time went on and she felt more secure and settled with us.

Dawn went out on Friday and Saturday evenings and returned home just after 10.00 p.m. on both nights. I reminded her that her coming-home time was 9.30, but again I didn't make much of it, for on the whole it had been a pretty reasonable week. On Sunday evening she left to go to her mother's at 5.45, but she arrived home again at 7.15. She never stayed the full two hours – there was always something her mother had to do that necessitated Dawn's visit being curtailed. But this was even earlier than usual; I'd just come down from putting Adrian to bed, and Dawn could only have been at her mother's for half an hour.

As soon as I answered the door I knew there was something wrong with Dawn, but I didn't know what. Her eyes appeared glazed and distant, and her pupils were dilated and staring. She was steady on her feet, and when she spoke her speech was slow but not slurred. I couldn't smell alcohol and she didn't seem drunk. I asked her, as I always did when she returned from seeing her mother, if she'd had a nice time and if her mum was OK.

'Don't know,' Dawn said, enunciating each word carefully and separately. 'She went out as soon as I got there.'

'Oh,' I said, disappointed for Dawn. 'Well, I'm pleased you came straight home.' For I realised that Dawn could have used the time to hang out with her old mates on the estate and I would have been none the wiser. I looked at her carefully. 'Dawn, are you all right, love? You don't seem with it.'

She nodded, bent forward and began retching, and then threw up all over the hall carpet. John shot out of the lounge. 'Not again!' he said.

'Can you get the bucket?' I called.

Dawn was still bent forward and now retching violently, gasping for breath as she gagged. John reappeared with the bucket, and running down the hall, placed it on the floor in front of her, just in time. She threw up into it.

'Christ!' he said. 'Whatever have you been drinking?'

'I haven't,' she gasped between breaths and gagging, and then she threw up again into the bucket.

I put my hand on her shoulder to comfort her, for I could see she was frightened. I moved her hair away from her face and tucked it behind her ears. 'It's all right, Dawn,' I reassured her, wondering what on earth could have made her so ill. Unlike before, when she had vomited once from drink, this was continuous and very violent. Then as I looked in the bucket a thick white chalky substance started to appear which certainly wasn't alcohol, and neither was it the dinner I'd given her before she'd left. 'Dawn,' I said, as she paused between retching. 'Have you eaten something since dinner?'

She didn't reply. She retched again, and as she vomited I saw a half a dozen small white partly digested pills appear in the bucket.

'Dawn!' I cried, as fear gripped me. 'Have you taken tablets? Tell me quickly!'

She half nodded, and then vomited again. This time ten or more similar white pills appeared, completely undigested.

'Oh no!' I cried. John saw them too.

'I'll call an ambulance,' he said, going to the phone on the hall table.

I now had my hands on Dawn's shoulders, steadying her, as her body shook and she continued to retch, then vomit, and more pills appeared. She was bent double, with her hands clutching her stomach as she threw up, over and over again. Each time she vomited, a few more white pills appeared. I couldn't believe what I was seeing. I could feel her growing weak from the exertion of retching and vomiting. 'Sit down,' I said, trying to stay calm and hide my fear for Dawn's sake. I guided her the couple of steps to the bottom stair and pulled the bucket after us. She sat, leant forward, gagged repeatedly and was sick again. Another six or more pills appeared. She was gasping for breath now and panicking. 'Take slow deep breaths,' I said, and my voice trembled. I heard John on the phone giving our address, telling them to hurry and confirming she had taken pills.

Dawn collapsed against me, exhausted, then leant forward and began retching again. More whole pills appeared, again completely undigested. I put my arm around her shoulders and held her as she was sick again. There was nothing I could do but comfort Dawn and wait for the ambulance. I felt hot and cold at once.

'It's on its way,' John confirmed, putting down the phone and coming over. 'They said ten minutes.'

I nodded and held Dawn. 'I'll go with her to hospital, if you stay with Adrian.'

John stared in horror at the contents of the slowly filling bucket. 'How many tablets have you taken, Dawn?'

Dawn was too weak to answer; she had her head on my shoulder, only raising it to vomit. There were fifty or more tablets in the bucket, and the ones that were now appearing were still whole and undigested, but they appeared slightly bigger than some of the others, so I thought she must have taken a mixture of tablets. Dear God, why?

The periods between her being sick slowly began to lengthen, and I willed the ambulance to hurry.

'What were the tablets?' I asked her, as her eyes closed and her head lolled on to my shoulder again. She didn't answer. I wondered if we should keep her awake by trying to get her to stand and walk, but she was a dead weight and it would be impossible to keep her upright.

Five minutes later, when Dawn had been sick twice more, we heard the ambulance siren in the distance. Dawn was still collapsed against me. She hadn't moved since the last time she had been sick and I wondered if she was lapsing into unconsciousness. I shook her. She groaned, but didn't open her eyes. Terror gripped me as I pictured her in a coma from which she never recovered. I shook her again and her eyes briefly flickered open. 'Hurry up!' I willed the ambulance again as John hovered by the door.

The siren grew louder as it entered the top of our road, then louder still as it approached the house. We saw the blue light flashing through the glass in the front door, and the siren stopped. John immediately opened the door as I held Dawn. She raised her head at the sound of the door opening, but her eyes were still closed. She groaned, and was sick again. Two paramedics appeared in the doorway, stepped round the vomit on the carpet and came over to where Dawn and I sat at the foot of the stairs.

'What's her name?' One of the paramedics asked, kneeling, and opening his bag.

'Dawn,' I said.

'Hello, Dawn. Can you hear me?' He spoke to her loudly, and took a pen torch from his bag. 'How old are you, Dawn?'

She groaned but didn't open her eyes or say anything. 'She's thirteen,' I said, 'and she's taken tablets, lots of them.'

The paramedic glanced in the bucket. 'Do you know what she's taken?' he asked, lifting Dawn's eyelids and shining the torch into her eyes.

'No. She's just come home from seeing her mother. She started being sick as soon as she came in.'

'You're not her parents?'

'No, foster parents,' John said, coming to stand beside us.

'And you've no idea what she could have taken?'

'No,' I said. 'The tablets couldn't have come from here. We've only got a small bottle of paracetamol, and that's in a locked medicine cabinet.'

'Dawn?' the paramedic who was examining her said, now taking her pulse. 'What have you taken, love? Can you remember?'

Dawn groaned, raised her head and retched, but wasn't actually sick.

'She's taken a lot,' I said again. 'And it must have been since six o'clock – that's when she left to go to her mother's.'

'OK, let's get her into the ambulance. You can come in with her. We'll take the bucket in case we need to identify what's she's taken.' Please God, I said silently, make everything all right.

The paramedic who had examined Dawn took my place on the bottom stair next to Dawn, while the other paramedic went to the ambulance and came back with a wheelchair. John and I stood to one side as they manoeuvred Dawn into the chair, talking to her and reassuring her the whole time. Dawn groaned and her eyes flickered open. She looked at me, afraid. 'It's all right, love,' I soothed. I took a step forward and patted her hand. 'I'm coming with you. We're going to hospital.'

'Phone me as soon as you know anything,' John said. 'And take your bag: you'll need money for the phone.'

He passed me my handbag, and I picked up the bucket; then I waited while the paramedics lifted the wheelchair over the step and on to the front path. 'Phone as soon as you can,' John called again before the doors closed.

'I'm Dave,' the paramedic who was with us said in the ambulance as he worked on Dawn.

'Cathy.' I looked at Dawn's colourless face. 'She is going to be all right, isn't she? She must have brought up most of the tablets – there are loads in the bucket.'

'There are certainly a lot,' he said, fitting electrode pads to Dawn's chest. The wires ran to a portable heart monitor, which he placed on the bed beside her.

I sat in silence, looking at Dawn, as the monitor bleeped and the ambulance siren whirred as we pulled away. Dawn's eyes were closed, but when we went over a bump in the road she groaned and her eyes flickered.

'Has she done anything like this before?' Dave asked.

'No, not as far as I know. God knows why she did it. She didn't seem unhappy, and she'd had a good week at school. I don't know why she can't talk to me. I keep asking her to and she says she will, but it seems she can't. It must all build up inside her and then ...' I stopped, feeling tears welling in my eyes. Dave nodded and concentrated on Dawn and the heart monitor.

Ten minutes later we pulled into the hospital grounds and the flashing light and siren stopped. As soon as the ambulance came to a halt, the rear doors opened from the outside, and a nurse was waiting with a gurney.

Dave roused Dawn again. 'Come on love, let's get you out.' He eased her into a sitting position and the nurse came forward and helped him manoeuvre Dawn out of the ambulance and on to the gurney. Dawn's eyes immediately closed again as she lay down. 'This is Dawn,' the paramedic said to the nurse. 'She's thirteen and has taken an overdose. Tablets not identified, but we've brought the bucket she's been sick in. This is her foster carer, Cathy.'

I took the bucket with me as I left the ambulance; then I followed Dave and the nurse as they wheeled the gurney through the double doors of the Accident and Emergency entrance. Dave then disappeared as another nurse took over, and we went into a curtained cubicle where a doctor was waiting.

'Could you come and give me a few details?' the nurse who had just joined us asked me. I glanced anxiously at Dawn, who was now being transferred from the gurney to the bed. The doctor was placing his stethoscope in his ears. 'It won't take long,' the nurse reassured me. 'She's being well looked after.'

I went with the nurse, back along the corridor, where she stopped outside a door. 'I'll take the bucket,' she said. 'We'll send a sample for analysis if necessary.' I passed her the bucket and she disappeared through the door, reappearing a moment later. I then went with her into the main waiting area, where she went behind the reception desk and logged on to a computer. My head spun and I felt pretty nauseous. I leant on the edge of the desk as I answered her questions. She asked for Dawn's full name, and then her date of birth, which I now knew off by heart. I gave her our address and telephone number. She wanted details of Dawn's parents and I could only give her what I knew, which was her mother's name.

'We'll contact her social worker,' the nurse said, tapping the keyboard as she spoke. I gave her Ruth's name.

'Reasons for admittance,' she said, reading the next question off the screen. 'Overdose,' she said and typed. My eyes started to moisten and I felt peculiarly distant – I simply couldn't take in what was happening. The nurse then asked the name and contact details of our GP, and if Dawn was on any medication, and I said she wasn't.

'Thank you,' she said. 'You can go back to Dawn now.'

I turned and retraced my steps; my head was light and my breath was coming fast and shallow. As I approached the cubicle, a nurse came out and held the curtain aside for me. I went in. The doctor was on one side of the bed and another nurse was on the other; they glanced up as I entered. Dawn was wired to a monitor and I assumed the lines I could see on the screen were readings of her heart rate and blood pressure. Her eyes were flickering open and closed as she tried to answer the doctor's questions.

'You're Dawn's carer?' the doctor asked me.

'Yes. She is going to be all right, isn't she?'

'Dawn told me she's taken a lot of tablets. We're going to irrigate her stomach to make sure there aren't any left. Stomach pump,' he qualified. 'The fact that she has taken so many may have saved her life. Her stomach couldn't cope, and she has vomited most of them up. Had she taken a smaller number, or had you left it longer before seeking help, more of the tablets would have been absorbed. Without doubt they would have killed her.' His face was stern as he said this and he looked at Dawn. It was a dire warning and, although it was intended for Dawn, I felt responsible.

He nodded to the nurse and she left, presumably to get what was needed to pump Dawn's stomach.

'Has Dawn told you what the tablets were?' I asked, praying that she hadn't found the key to the medicine cabinet and taken the paracetamol, although the bottle only contained half a dozen tablets – far less than Dawn had swallowed.

'Her mother's Valium,' the doctor said, 'and a bottle of artificial sweetener tablets, which are just as dangerous in the quantity Dawn has taken them.'

I looked at him. 'But she will be all right, won't she?'

'Let's hope so,' he said nodding stiffly, and looked from Dawn to the monitor.

The nurse returned, carrying a number of sealed sterilised packages and a small plastic bucket. Dawn's eyes opened as the nurse approached the bed, then closed again.

'I need to phone my husband and tell him what's happening,' I said. 'Can I come back in a minute? I want to be with her.'

The doctor nodded.

'I'll be back soon,' I said to Dawn. I didn't know if she had heard me or not.

I returned to reception, where I found a pay phone. Delving into my bag for coins, I dialled our number and when John answered I told him what the doctor had said.

'So she is going to be all right?' he asked.

'From what they're saying I think so.'

'Will they keep her in?' he asked.

'I don't know. I'll find out and call you again later. If it gets too late you go to bed you've got work tomorrow. I'll get a taxi home.'

John said he would, although he added he wouldn't sleep until we had both returned safely. We said goodbye and I returned to the cubicle. There were two nurses present now, one on either side of the bed, but the doctor had left. Dawn was on her left side with her head slightly lowered. One nurse stood behind her, with her hands on Dawn's shoulder, steadying her into position, while the other nurse sat on a chair with Dawn facing her. A thin tube ran from Dawn's nose into the bucket and I could hear a gurgling and suction noise coming from it. Both nurses glanced at me as I entered, and then returned their attention to Dawn.

I stood out of the way, at the end of the bed, and looked at Dawn. The stomach pumping didn't appear to be causing her too much discomfort – less, I thought, than when she had been continuously retching and vomiting. Her eyes flickered open and she moaned slightly, but I thought the worst part was probably when the tube had been inserted up her nose and down the back of her throat. From what I could see, the fluid in the bucket wasn't so chalky and I hoped this was a good sign. After a few minutes the nurse attached what looked like a large syringe to the end of the tube and slowly depressed it, injecting a clear solution down the tube and into Dawn's stomach. She removed the syringe and the suction began again, with fluid appearing in the bucket. The nurse repeated the procedure a second time and then glanced at me.

'It's all clear now,' she said.

'Does that mean all the pills have gone?'

She nodded. 'Apart from those she has already digested. Her blood pressure is down and her heart is racing slightly. We'll monitor her overnight.'

'Thank you,' I said. 'Thank you so much.'

The nurse slid the tube from Dawn's nose and Dawn coughed and retched. 'Don't worry,' the nurse said. 'It's a reflex action as the tube comes out.'

I remained at the end of the bed as the nurse wiped Dawn's mouth, and then both nurses gathered up the tube, empty packages and bucket, and left the cubicle. I went over and sat on the chair the nurse had vacated and gazed down at Dawn. She was still on her side and appeared to be sleeping. She looked so young and vulnerable. Thirteen years, I thought; thirteen short years. Whatever had happened to make her do this? And what life experience had made her hate herself so much that she slashed her flesh, and had now actually tried to take her life? The books had said that self-harming was a coping mechanism and rarely a suicide attempt, but this was certainly a suicide attempt. And the number of tablets Dawn had swallowed suggested it was a serious attempt, in which Dawn had thought she'd guaranteed the outcome. She had only been saved by taking so many tablets that her body had rejected them, and by coming home in time for us to call an ambulance. Dear God, I thought, if she had taken less tablets, or not come home in time, I would have been identifying her body in the mortuary.

Chapter Eighteen

Rejected

I waited with Dawn until she was found a bed on the children's ward. She slept the whole time, while I listened to the comings and goings the other side of the curtained cubicle. A porter helped Dawn into a wheelchair and then pushed her to the ward, while the nurse and I walked behind. Once I had seen that she was comfortable, and the nurse had reassured me that she would most likely remain asleep until morning, I kissed Dawn goodnight and went down to reception, where I phoned for a taxi.

It was after midnight by the time I arrived home, and I was utterly exhausted. John looked gaunt and strained too. I told him what had happened at the hospital while I drank the mug of tea he had made for me. Then we both went upstairs, and I stood for a moment looking at Adrian's little sleeping face before I climbed into bed. John said he would take the following day off work so that I could return to the hospital without having to take Adrian with me.

It was 7.30 a.m. when I woke, and John had taken Adrian downstairs and was giving him breakfast. I quickly washed and dressed, then packed Dawn's nightdress, some clean clothes and her wash bag in a small overnight case. I gulped down a mug of coffee, and giving Adrian and John a big hug, I drove to the hospital.

It was just before nine o'clock as I pressed the security buzzer on the wall beside the locked doors of the children's ward. 'It's Cathy Glass, Dawn Jennings' foster carer,' I said as a female voice came through the security intercom. There was a short pause before the door clicked open, and I went in, making my way to where I had left Dawn the night before.

To my surprise and absolute delight Dawn was sitting up in bed in a hospital gown and eating breakfast. Her face lit up when she saw me.

'Hi, Cathy,' she called across the ward.

'Hello, love,' I said, going over and giving her a big kiss. 'How are you? You look so much better.'

'I am, but my throat is sore.'

I smiled and pulled up a chair. 'I expect your throat is sore from being sick yesterday. Didn't they have anything softer you could have had?'

'Only porridge and I didn't like it.' She carried on eating the toast, so I thought the discomfort couldn't be too bad.

'Did you sleep well?' I asked, glancing at the other occupants in the four-bedded ward.

'I must have. I don't remember anything until they woke me to take my blood pressure.'

A television mounted on a tall stand was on at one end of the room and Dawn, like the other children, was looking at it. In the bed next to her was a young boy of about nine or ten with his father sprawled beside him, also watching the television. Opposite was a girl of a similar age to Dawn who was by herself, and in the bed next to her was a much younger girl of about five or six, who had her mother with her. I smiled at the woman as she looked over and she smiled back.

'The doctor's going to do his rounds soon,' Dawn said very knowledgeably. 'And then I can go home.'

'Great!' I said. 'You won't be needing this, then. I put your nightdress in just in case.'

Dawn nodded absently and returned her attention to the television; I looked at it too. Clearly I wasn't going to start talking to Dawn about what had happened the day before. That would come later; for now it was enough that she had recovered.

Fifteen minutes or so later a nurse came on to the ward and, removing Dawn's breakfast things, said that the doctor was doing his rounds now. I felt somewhat apprehensive and nervous as we waited for the doctor to arrive; so too apparently did the nurse, judging from the way she was tidying the ward and straightening all the bed covers. When the doctor appeared half an hour later, with an entourage of two nurses and three young student doctors, it was a different doctor to the one we had seen the night before. Coming straight to the end of Dawn's bed, he unhooked the clipboard and, without saying hello, began studying the chart. The students grouped around him. I sat upright and waited in respectful silence, while Dawn, apparently less impressed by our visitors, gave them a cursory glance and then returned her attention to the television.

'How are you today?' the doctor eventually said, glancing up from the clipboard and finally acknowledging Dawn. The students looked at Dawn too.

'Good,' Dawn said, not taking her eyes from the screen.

He looked at me. 'Are you mum?'

'No, I'm Dawn's foster carer.'

One of the nurses said something quietly to the doctor, which I couldn't hear, and he in turn said something quietly to the students, which I also couldn't hear. Replacing the clipboard at the end of the bed he took a couple of steps closer to Dawn. 'You've had a very lucky escape, young lady,' he said brusquely. 'Next time you might not be so lucky.' Dawn took her eyes off the television and looked at him, while I wondered at the wisdom of even suggesting the vaguest possibility of their being a 'next time'.

'I'm discharging you with a letter for your GP,' he said, no less tersely. 'You'll be sent an appointment to see a psychiatrist.' Then addressing me, 'We always refer to a psychiatrist after a suicide attempt. And she needs to talk about why she's cutting herself too.'

I assumed the nurses had noticed the scars on Dawn's arms and leg when they had changed her into her hospital gown. I opened my mouth to speak, but the doctor was already turning and moving away from the bed. With a brief glance around the ward he left, followed by his entourage. I had hoped for a chance to discuss what Dawn had done, and maybe to have even received a few words of advice, but clearly that would now have to wait until we saw a psychiatrist. The doctor's manner had been so terse that I wondered if he resented having to deal with a patient who had tried to take her own life when his work centred on trying to save lives. However, I thought, if one good thing had come from all this, it was that Dawn was now being referred to a psychiatrist and would get the help she so badly needed.

* * *

An hour later, Dawn having had a wash and in her clean clothes, I thanked the nurses and we left the hospital. Once we were in the car I didn't immediately start the engine.

'Dawn,' I said, looking straight ahead through the windscreen. 'Did any of the nurses or doctors ask you why you did what you did?' I found it too difficult to say the words 'taken an overdose' or 'attempted suicide'.

'No,' she said, fastening her seatbelt. 'I was asleep until breakfast.'

I hesitated. 'Can I ask you, Dawn? Can you tell me why?'

I turned sideways to look at her. She gave a small shrug. 'It was Mum, I guess. I wanted to teach her a lesson.'

'Why?' I asked slowly. 'Did she do something?' It was a pretty dire lesson, I thought, and the outcome could have been far, far worse.

Dawn shrugged again. 'It seems a bit silly now, but at the time I was angry and upset with her. When I went to see her yesterday she went out as soon as I got there, to see that Mike.'

'And was she planning on returning home again to spend time with you?'

'No. That's what made me upset and angry. She can see Mike any time, but we only have one hour a week. I went all that way on the bus and she just said hi and left me. They were going to the cinema. She's done it before – gone out as soon as I got there.' Dawn paused and looked at her hands, clasped tightly in her lap. 'I don't suppose you understand, but one hour a week isn't going to hurt her, is it? I mean it's not much of her time.'

'No, Dawn, it isn't,' I said quietly. 'And I *do* understand.'

She paused again, still gazing down at her hands. 'I know I shouldn't have done it, Cathy, but I thought if I swallowed all her tablets, when she came home and found me it would make her feel really bad. Then she would be sorry she hadn't spent more time with me. I just wanted to punish her.'

I nodded slowly. 'I see. Thank you for telling me.' I could see the logic only too clearly, but Christ, what a way to go about teaching your mother a lesson! We were still sitting side by side in the car park with the engine off. 'Dawn,' I said after a moment. 'Did you actually intend to kill yourself or was it more to shock your mother so that she would spend time with you in future?'

She wrung her hands together. 'To begin with I wanted to kill myself, as I was so upset she didn't want to see me. But once I'd finished taking all the tablets and began feeling ill, I wasn't so sure. That's why I came home to you. I hoped you'd make me better.'

'Thank God you did,' I said, placing my hand on her arm. 'And it was just in time. Dawn, you won't ever do anything like that again, will you? There are ways of working out problems even when they seem huge, without doing something like that.'

'I won't,' she said. 'I didn't like being sick. It frightened me. Has anyone told my mum yet?'

'I would think so,' I said, wondering if Dawn was still hoping her mother would learn from the 'lesson' and be sorry. 'The hospital was going to notify your social worker, so I think Ruth will have phoned your mum. I'm going to phone Ruth later. I think we need to do something about the time you spend with your mum. There's no point in you going over there if she's not going to be in.'

'No,' Dawn agreed quietly. 'I'm not sure I want to go again.'

Cut

I started the engine and drove slowly out of the car park, winding my window down as I went. Dawn lowered her window too. At just after eleven o'clock the heat was already building up, heralding another very hot June day. As I drove, my thoughts centred on Dawn and all her problems, as they were increasingly doing now; indeed I was always thinking or worrying about Dawn, and what was going on in her head. I was desperate to try to find a key: something that would unlock her past and better explain her disturbed behaviour, thereby hopefully giving us a way forward. I realised she had been rejected by her parents, but while that in itself was bad enough, I couldn't help feeling that it didn't fully explain her extreme behaviour – even more so after last night – and I kept returning to one point in particular.

'Dawn,' I said as the engine idled at a set of traffic lights that had just turned red. 'Your social worker said that there was a gap in your life when no one knew where you were. Between the ages of five and nine,' Dawn nodded and again looked down into her lap. 'Do you have any memories of that time? Do you know where you were or who you were living with? I expect Ruth has asked you the same question.'

'She did,' Dawn said flatly. 'And she asked Mum and Dad if they knew where I was.'

'And?' I prompted after a moment when she hadn't said any more.

'Mum says I was living with my dad, and Dad says I was with Mum.' Which was what Ruth had told me after the meeting. And I remembered the essay Dawn had written for school about being five, which she had made up, claiming she couldn't remember that time. It seemed ludicrous: either she or her parents must have some recollection of where she was and who she was living with.

'And what about you, Dawn?' I asked. 'Do you know where you were? It wasn't so long ago. Do you remember?' The lights changed to green and I pulled away.

I glanced between the road ahead and Dawn, and as I did I saw her face crumple. Tears began streaming down her cheeks and her chest heaved with silent sobs. 'Oh, Dawn, love, I'm sorry. I didn't mean to upset you.' I immediately pulled over and switched off the engine. Releasing my seatbelt, I leant over and put my arms around her. 'It's all right, love. Please don't upset yourself.'

'Cathy, I don't know, I really don't know,' she stammered between breaths. 'I can't remember anything. Anything at all.' I reached down and pulled some tissues from my bag and passed them to her. 'I remember being with Mum and Dad when I was very little. And I remember Dad leaving. Then there's nothing. The next thing I remember is living with Mum again. It's like I suddenly woke up and I was there. I was nine and at a different school. Then I spent time living at Dad's place and then at Mum's, going backwards and forwards because I was so naughty – neither of them wanted me for long. And I know I was bad – I felt bad, and I did bad things – but I don't know why. The time before that is like a big black hole. Sometimes I get weird dreams and think I remember things, but the dreams are awful and I get really frightened and confused.'

I hugged her. 'I understand, love. I'm sorry. Please don't cry.' I waited as she blew her nose and dried her eyes.

'Dawn, when you see the psychiatrist I want you to tell him all this. It might help. All right?'

She nodded and blew her nose again. Then looked at me, her cheeks flushed and her eyes red from crying. 'It's really scary, not knowing. It's like part of me is missing. But the more I try to remember, the worse it gets. I see me at Mum's when I was five and I know those memories are real; then I disappear, and suddenly come back again all those years later. I was already being naughty then; I don't know why – I just was. I think something might have happened to change me, something dreadful that I can't remember.'

I hugged her again and thought that she might be right. What she had described sounded like a type of amnesia. I remembered reading an article in a newspaper about people who had lost their memories after a really bad experience, a trauma. I thought the condition was called dissociative amnesia, when the brain blots out what it can't cope with, but I didn't know any more. 'It must be dreadfully worrying for you, love, but I'm sure the psychiatrist will be able to help you.'

'Will he?' she asked, looking at me with a spark of hope.

'Yes, that's his job – to help unravel the past and make sense of it. So let's leave it to him, shall we? Don't force yourself to remember. Let's concentrate on the present.' I smiled, and Dawn smiled back.

'Thanks, Cathy. Can we go home now? I'm starving. Can I have a fry-up?'

'Of course, love, anything you like.'

It was just before midday when we arrived home and John greeted us at the door.

'Welcome home,' he said to Dawn and kissed us both on the cheek.

Dawn smiled, and then went to Adrian, who was scuttling on all fours down the hall.

John said that his work had phoned with a problem, and as we were now home he would go in for the afternoon. He went upstairs to change into his suit while I cooked Dawn a fry-up. John said goodbye and left half an hour later. While Dawn was eating Ruth phoned and said that in view of what had happened she would come and visit Dawn that afternoon. I told Dawn and she shrugged.

'I can't tell her any more than I told you,' she said.

'No. I think she's just coming to make sure you're all right now.'

That afternoon Dawn, Adrian and I spent a pleasant couple of hours in the garden under the shade of the tree. Dawn and I chatted for a while about things in general; then she fetched her Walkman from her bedroom and listened to music, while I flicked through the paper, and we both kept an eye on Adrian and his forages into the flower beds. Ruth arrived shortly after three o'clock and said she wanted to talk to Dawn alone. I showed her through to the garden, and scooping up Adrian, I went inside, pulling the French doors to behind me.

From where I sat with Adrian in the lounge I could see them. Ruth was sitting where I had been and looked the more serious of the two. She leant forward as she spoke to Dawn, and Dawn just looked glum. Ruth did most of the talking, with Dawn giving the occasional small nod, or shrugging. After about twenty minutes Ruth stood and headed back towards the lounge. I opened the French doors to let her in.

'Everything all right?' I asked as she came in, hoping for some feedback that might help.

Ruth sighed. 'As right as it's going to be.' She crossed the lounge towards the hall.

Leaving Adrian in the lounge with the door open so I could keep an eye on him, I followed her to the door to see her out. She arrived at the front door without saying anything further and clearly with no intention of doing so.

'She's been referred to a psychiatrist,' I said. 'That should help, shouldn't it?'

'If she goes,' Ruth said dryly, with one hand on the doorknob. 'I'll speak to Barbara and see if I can persuade her to stay in on Sunday evenings when Dawn visits.'

'And if you can't persuade her?' I asked, feeling that Ruth should be taking a firmer line with Barbara, given what had happened. 'Is it worth Dawn going? Dawn says she's not sure she wants to go any more if her mum's not going to be in.'

'Dawn says that now but she'll probably change her mind come Sunday.' Ruth sighed again. 'I'll speak to Barbara, but obviously I can't force the woman to stay in and see her daughter.' With that she turned the doorknob and let herself out. 'Phone me when the psychiatrist's appointment arrives. I want to speak to him before Dawn does,' she added.

'Yes, I will.' Ruth was already halfway down the front path. 'Ruth?' I called after her.

She paused and turned. 'Yes?'

I went up to her. 'Is there anything you can tell me that might help us? John and I are very worried about Dawn, and I know it's confidential, but we're struggling to look after her. Dawn is so polite and pleasant when she is with us, but obviously her behaviour is very disturbed. I've been reading up on —'.

'She's had a rough ride,' Ruth said, cutting in. 'Let me know when her appointment arrives and we'll take it from there.' She turned and continued down the path.

I went inside, not a little put out by Ruth's dismissive attitude, and closed the front door. Collecting Adrian from the lounge, where he was exploring the soil in a potted plant, I returned to the garden. Dawn was still sitting under the tree with her Walkman in her lap and the earpieces out.

'All right?' I said with a smile. 'Did your chat with Ruth help?'

'Not really,' she shrugged. 'She's always on Mum's side, and just lectures me.'

'What? About the tablets?'

'And other things.' She stood, and leaving her Walkman on her chair went over to play with Adrian on the lawn.

Dawn clearly didn't want to talk to me about her conversation with her social worker any more than Ruth had wanted to, and it wasn't appropriate for me to press Dawn. I thought it was sad, and not at all good for Dawn, that she felt Ruth was on her mother's side, as though there was a battle going on, when we should all have been working together to help Dawn. I also felt that Ruth should have given Barbara an ultimatum: make sure you're in when Dawn visits or she won't come in future. But clearly that wasn't going to happen, and it seemed that if Dawn went on Sunday it would be on the off chance that her mother was in, as apparently had been the case in the past. It was hardly likely to help Dawn's feelings of inadequacy and self-loathing to know that her mother would only stay in and see her if she didn't have a better offer or there was nothing good on at the cinema. And if their relationship was so bad anyway, I wondered what the point was in them seeing each other at all? But then again Barbara was Dawn's mother, so I supposed there was a bond of some sort.

Chapter Nineteen

A Weapon?

I would like to say that Dawn received her appointment to see the psychiatrist, began therapy and
slowly started to improve. But it didn't happen. Far from
improving the situation grew a lot, lot worse.

The following morning Dawn insisted she felt well
enough to go to school, and refused my offer of a lift. The
school secretary had phoned on Monday, the day before,
when Dawn hadn't arrived at school, and John had said only
that Dawn was ill. He didn't say that Dawn had taken an
overdose or that she was in hospital, assuming that if the
school needed to know Ruth would inform them. I saw Dawn
off at the door on that Tuesday morning and had no reason
to believe she hadn't arrived at school – the secretary didn't
phone. Likewise on Wednesday and Thursday I said goodbye
to Dawn at 7.45 a.m., and she left with her school bag to
catch the bus, and I then welcomed her home at 3.45 p.m.

On Friday lunchtime the phone rang. It was from a call
box and a girl asked if she could speak to Dawn.

'She's at school,' I said. 'Can I give her a message?' I
was pleasantly surprised that Dawn had given our phone
number to a friend. It was the first time she had been
called at home and I felt it was a positive sign that she was
starting to include us in her life.

There was a pause on the other end of the line before the girl said, 'No, she's not.'

'Sorry?' I asked.

'Dawn's not in school. This is Natasha from her class and I was wondering how Dawn was. She hasn't been in all week and our teacher said she was ill.'

'Are you sure?' I asked, my heart starting to pound.

'Positive. We sit next to each other in most lessons.'

'But I don't understand. The school secretary phones me if Dawn doesn't arrive. Dawn was ill on Monday but she's been all right since. She's been leaving every morning to go to school. And you're sure she's not there?'

'Yes, and I have to go for my lunch now,' Natasha said quickly, clearly feeling uncomfortable that she had been the one to tell me. And she hung up.

I replaced the receiver and stood for a moment in the hall, my thoughts racing, and wondering why the school secretary hadn't phoned to say Dawn wasn't in school. It didn't make sense. I picked up the phone again and dialled St James's School.

When the secretary answered I asked if Dawn was there.

'No,' she said, surprised by my question. 'Your husband said she was ill.'

'She was ill on Monday, but she should have been in school the rest of the week.'

'Oh, I'm sorry. I assumed she was still ill. That's why I didn't phone to check.'

'I see,' I said, understanding what had happened. My spirits fell. 'It's not your fault. I should have phoned on Tuesday to tell you she was returning.'

She apologised again and we said goodbye.

My heart was heavy. School hadn't checked with me, assuming Dawn was still ill, and I hadn't seen the need to check with the school, assuming Dawn had arrived and that I would be told if she hadn't. Dawn had cunningly seized the opportunity in the breakdown of communication between the school and me and used it to her advantage. Apart from feeling badly let down I was now worried as to where Dawn could be and what she was doing. She had been leaving the house each morning with her school bag and returning home as normal, answering my question as to whether she'd had a good day with a pleasant smile and, 'Yes thanks, Cathy,' without the slightest indication to the contrary. After all the chats we'd had, and the promises she'd made to confide her worries in me so that I could help her, it had all come to nothing. I felt hurt, worried and betrayed. What on earth did I have to do to change her behaviour and get her back on track? I had no idea.

Dawn came home at 3.45 p.m. that Friday afternoon, as though she had just returned from school. She dropped her bag in its usual place in the hall and slipped out of her shoes.

'Good day?' I asked as normal.

'Yes thanks, Cathy.' She smiled.

I felt sly – I hate deception in any form – but now I had the upper hand. 'What did you do today, Dawn?' I asked. 'Anything exciting?'

'Only the usual lessons.' She smiled again and bent down to Adrian, who was trying to pull himself into a standing position using the hem of her skirt.

'Which were?' I asked. 'What subjects did you have?'

She hesitated – this was more than my usual greeting – and I couldn't keep the deception going any longer.

'Natasha phoned,' I said bluntly. 'She wondered how you were.'

I watched as Dawn let go of Adrian and slowly straightened. 'I'm sorry, Cathy,' she said too easily. 'But I couldn't face going into school after everything.'

'So why didn't you tell me instead of running off? I thought we'd agreed that you would tell me if something was bothering you so that I could help. Now you've done what you always do and just disappeared!'

She continued to look at me, her expression neutral. 'I know I've let you down again,' she said matter-of-factly. 'And I'm sorry, but I can't help it. I did tell you I was bad; now perhaps you'll believe me.'

I was furious at Dawn's easy acceptance of what she saw as her badness. 'You're not bad. But you take the easy option sometimes. I don't understand why you couldn't have said something on Tuesday. I wouldn't have forced you to go to school, having come out of hospital the day before. But oh no, you decided it was easier just to slip off. It's not good, Dawn, and I'm very disappointed. I also felt a right fool when I told Natasha you were in school.'

'Sorry,' she said again but with no great conviction.

'Right, Dawn,' I said. 'I accept your apology but you're grounded for the weekend. You are not going out tonight or on Saturday. You can spend the time catching up on the school work you've missed.'

She looked at me, quite surprised. 'I don't have my books,' she grumbled; then, turning, she stomped up to her room.

I left her there for half an hour and then went up to check on her, for I was now worried that if she was upset she could self-harm or, heaven forbid, even make another suicide attempt. But when I knocked on her door and poked my head round she was lying on her bed listening to her music. I returned downstairs without saying anything and only called her when John came home and dinner was ready.

I told John of Dawn's truancy before she arrived at the table. After a particularly demanding week at work, which hadn't been without its problems, he needed it like a hole in the head. 'I'll speak to her after dinner,' he said.

Dinner passed in unnatural silence; even Adrian in his high chair seemed to sense the atmosphere and kept his chuntering to a minimum. When we had finished, I cleared away while John told Dawn he wanted to speak to her in the lounge. She followed him in and I heard him tell her to sit down and listen. I could hear him through the open lounge door as he gave her a good talking to – father to daughter. Dawn was very quiet as John lectured her about her behaviour and how she had let down not only herself but us as well. When he asked her where she had been all week, she predictably said, 'Just hanging out with my mates.'

'Well, don't in future!' he stormed. 'On a school day, you are in school, not with your friends. Do you understand me, Dawn?'

I heard her small voice answer yes, and then she said she was sorry for all the trouble she'd caused and promised she wouldn't do it again; it sounded heartfelt. John said he was pleased to hear that and he'd say no more of the matter, as he didn't want an atmosphere all weekend. He reiterated that she wouldn't be going out, and then sent her through to apologise to me. I accepted her apology, and said, as John had done, that we would put it behind us and move on, for what else could we do?

On Saturday we had a barbecue in the garden, as the weather was so good, and I hoped the family activity might help cement Dawn's loyalty and feelings of belonging. On Sunday evening Dawn said she would go to see her mother, but agreed that if her mum wasn't there, or went out while she was there, she would come straight home.

When Dawn returned, dead on time, she said her mother had been in and had stayed in for the hour of Dawn's visit. I wondered if Barbara had spoken to Dawn about her overdose the previous Sunday, but when I asked Dawn she said no, and that they had watched television. I found it incredible that Dawn had attempted suicide, using her mother's tablets, and Barbara hadn't seen fit to mention it, let alone discuss it with her daughter.

That night Dawn was up at 2.00 a.m., sleepwalking out of her bedroom. I don't know how we knew she was out of bed: perhaps it was a sixth sense, or we had subconsciously heard her, for suddenly John and I were wide awake and knew instantly why. We found her in the hall on her way to the kitchen, and as usual we turned her round and steered her back to bed, where she slept until I woke her for school in the morning.

The occasions on which Dawn sleepwalked varied but it was still happening at least twice a week. Sometimes John and I could spot something that had happened during the day that might have triggered her disturbance, as on Sunday, when she had seen her mother. But at other times there appeared to be no root cause, or none that we could see at least. We consoled ourselves that, as with all Dawn's other disturbing behaviour, it would be addressed when she started therapy.

The promised appointment to see the psychiatrist arrived at the end of the following week, in a letter addressed to Mrs Cathy Jennings (Dawn's and her mother's surname), which suggested the hospital had made a complete mess of inputting our names and contact details on their computer. When I opened the letter, I found the appointment was for 3 August, two months away. It seemed a ridiculous wait for a teenage girl who had tried to commit suicide, but I guessed she was on an NHS waiting list. I made a note of the date in my diary and, when Dawn returned home from school, I told her of the appointment.

'Good,' she said, and I wasn't sure she was referring to the fact that the appointment had at last arrived or that it was so far ahead.

Dawn completed a full week at school, so she was allowed out on Friday and Saturday evenings. As usual we didn't know where she was going, but we guessed her evening's activities centred around hanging out with her mates. She returned at 9.30 p.m. on Friday and I praised her. On Saturday she went out again, but this time she didn't return. John and I waited in the lounge, anxiously watching the clock. We were not only worried for Dawn's safety but also frustrated and angry at her apparent total disregard for everything we had said, and by her hollow promises.

At 10.30 p.m. I phoned the duty social worker. 'Wait until eleven o'clock,' he said, 'and if Dawn still hasn't returned, report her missing to the police.' Which I did – spending ten minutes in a call waiting system and then half an hour giving details of Dawn and the circumstances in which she had gone missing. Apparently each time a person went missing it was treated as a new case and the details weren't retrieved from any previous instances. However, I now had a photograph of Dawn, which I took out of the album, ready for when the police arrived. And after the last time John and I knew better than to go to bed, for the police could arrive at any time during the night to search the house.

At nearly 12.30 a.m., as we were dozing in the lounge with the television on low, the door bell rang.

'At last!' John said, and heaving himself out of the chair, he went down the hall to answer it. I heard the front door open and then John's surprised voice – 'Dawn!'

I immediately went into the hall, to find Dawn and two uniformed officers stepping in from the porch. Quite clearly Dawn was drunk. She was giggling and trying to hang on to one of the officer's arms. The officers didn't look impressed by Dawn antics.

'Hi-John-n-Cathy,' she slurred. 'Hows-ya-been? I'm-sorry-I'zz-late, suppose-I should-ave-phoned-ya.' We had told Dawn that if she was delayed for any reason she should phone us so that we wouldn't worry.

'It's a bit late for that now,' I snapped.

Dawn snuggled her head against the officer's arm, looked up at him and grinned. 'Szz-nice-of-ya-to-'elp-me,' she slurred; then she hiccupped and took a deep breath.

'Dawn, you're not going to be sick, are you?' I said. Stepping forward, I drew her away from the officer.

'Sss-no, I'm-good,' she said, and she hiccupped again.

'Can we have a quick chat?' asked the officer whom I had just rescued from Dawn.

John showed the officers through to the lounge, while I steered Dawn in the same direction, with her grinning inanely and apologising. 'Sooo-sorry. I'zz sorry I'zz late,' she giggled. As we entered the lounge she burst into song: 'What-shall-we-do-wid-da-drunken-sailor …'

'Sit down, Dawn,' John said sharply. I eased her on to the sofa and then went into the kitchen for the plastic bucket, which I positioned at her feet just in case.

'Izz-not-sick,' she slurred. 'Izzz-happy – h-a-p-p-y.'

'Enough!' John barked.

Any humour in the situation now vanished as one of the officers began to speak. 'We picked Dawn up half an hour ago after a 999 call. She was outside the Queen's Head.' The Queen's Head was a pub on the edge of town with a notorious reputation for fights and affrays. It featured regularly in our local press as the residents had been campaigning for years to get it shut down. 'Two lads are now in hospital,' the officer continued, 'having their faces stitched up after being bottled outside the pub. We found Dawn in the crowd of onlookers. She wasn't involved in the fight, but she was cheering them on. It's not the best place to go for entertainment,' he added dryly.

I was shocked and immediately felt responsible for Dawn being there. 'She was supposed to be home by nine thirty,' I said. 'And she's no business being anywhere near a pub at her age, let alone the Queen's Head.'

The officer looked at me with a mixture of sympathy and warning. 'We're clamping down on under-age drinking and the last time we picked Dawn up from the pub we told her to stay away.'

'Last time?' John said, horrified.

'It's a regular haunt of hers, isn't it, Dawn?' Dawn nodded and hiccupped.

I shook my head in dismay. 'So is that where you've been going on Friday and Saturday evenings?'

'Sometimes,' she slurred.

'Well, don't!' John said, then addressing the officers, 'I'm sorry. I'm sure you've got better things to do than bring home drunken teenagers.'

The officer who was doing the talking nodded stoically. 'Will Dawn be going back to live with Barbara?' From his familiar use of Barbara's first name I assumed the police knew Dawn's mother quite well, presumably from having regularly returned Dawn to her.

'We don't know yet,' I said.

The other officer's phone crackled loudly and a message came through. 'Unit five to Dusmore Close. We've received a report of a disturbance in the street.'

'That's us,' he said. Both officers stood, and so did John and I. 'We've told Dawn that if we pick her up again she'll be cautioned,' the office said. 'And she doesn't need any more of those. Do you, Dawn?'

Dawn smiled and hiccupped, and then shook her head playfully. John raised his eyebrows in warning. We followed the officers out of the lounge, leaving Dawn on the sofa trying to control her hiccups and giggling in between.

'Make sure you use the bucket if you're sick,' I said as I left the room.

John paused before he opened the front door. 'How many formal cautions has Dawn had?'

'Too many,' the officer said, clearly unwilling or not at liberty to give details. 'And there won't be many more before they start charging her.'

With what? I wondered. What exactly had Dawn been cautioned for? But the officers were out of the door and on their way to answer the next call. John and I returned to the lounge, where Dawn was still hiccupping and giggling. She hadn't been sick but we took the bucket with us anyway as we manoeuvred her upstairs and into her bedroom. John placed the bucket beside her bed then left the room. I cajoled and helped Dawn out of her clothes and into her nightdress. It was like trying to undress a very large baby, although I usually had more cooperation from Adrian; she giggled and hiccupped the whole time. As I pulled off her jeans, I saw scars on her – not one as I had anticipated but four bright pink parallel lines, about two inches long and equally spaced. The last looked very recent.

'Dawn! You've been cutting yourself again,' I said, horrified. 'You told me you had stopped.'

'Sorry,' she slurred in much the same tone as she had been apologising for everything that night. 'I couldn't kick the habit.'

'Habit! But when did you do it? You haven't said anything to me, and there's been no blood on your clothes.' I continued to stare in horror at her leg.

She was sitting on the edge of the bed with her legs dangling down. Leaning forward, she began pointing to the scars one at a time, telling me when she had made each cut as though they were achievement badges she had collected. 'That one was when Mum was horrible to me,' she said pointing to the top scar, which was halfway down her left thigh. 'That one was when Mike called me an interfering bitch,' she said moving her finger to the one beneath. 'That one you know about already. It was when Natasha wouldn't be my friend and I got blood on the pillow. And this one,' she said arriving at the fourth, 'was the other week when you and John grounded me and I wasn't allowed out.'

I started with shock, and could have wept. 'Because you were angry with us? But Dawn, couldn't you have just accepted the punishment? It was reasonable. Other teenagers are grounded for not doing as they're told.' Yet while I felt we had been justified in punishing Dawn's truanting, it didn't help the guilt that was now welling inside me.

Dawn had been accepting and almost nonchalant about her cutting when we had first talked about it. Now drunk, she was flippant and dismissive. 'It's no problem,' she said with a smile. 'Don't worry. It's my leg and I like to cut it. It helps.'

'But it's dreadful, Dawn, upsetting. I just don't understand.'

'It's not your fault. Don't worry,' she said again; then, drawing up her feet, lay down, and curled up into bed. Within seconds her eyes had closed and she was asleep. I looked at her for a moment, then switched off the light and came out.

Downstairs I told John what I had discovered and he was as shocked and horrified as I was. 'What are we supposed to do?' he said, equally frustrated. 'Never tell her off? Or stop her from doing what she wants because she might harm herself? It's emotional blackmail.' Except of course it wasn't, because Dawn hadn't used her cutting as a weapon against us – she hadn't said, 'If you ground me I'm going to cut' – any more than presumably she had used it against her mother, Mike or Natasha. She had appeared to accept the sanction and then gone away and slashed her leg. How we should deal with it I'd no idea, and once again I clung to the belief that when she started seeing the psychiatrist in August he would be able to help. I dearly hoped so, for I didn't know what else I could do.

Chapter Twenty

Added Violation

Dawn managed to get to school three days the following week and two days the week after that. The school secretary phoned each time Dawn failed to arrive, and when Dawn came home at 3.45 p.m. I told her off and lectured her. But my telling off and lecturing were starting to sound as hollow as Dawn's apologies and promises not to do it again, for we had both said it all so many times before.

'I do try, Cathy,' she said, 'but something just takes over when I leave the house.'

'I know, love,' I said exasperated. 'But how can we stop it?'

'I don't know,' she shrugged.

Neither did I!

It was now nearly the end of June, and John and I had booked a holiday – a week in south Cornwall – for the beginning of July before the schools broke up. We had made the booking in December, when we hadn't had Dawn staying with us. But it was a self-catering cottage which could sleep five, so with only John, Adrian (who would be in the cot) and me there would be plenty of room for Dawn. I thought a holiday was exactly what Dawn could do with – a relaxing week away from the area where all her problems seemed to stem from. John thought so too. But it would mean Dawn missing school for a week, and on top of all the days she'd already missed I wondered if her social worker would agree to Dawn going. Without mentioning the prospect of a holiday to Dawn, I phoned Ruth and asked if Dawn could come with us.

Ruth readily agreed. 'Yes, if she wants to. It might do her good.'

There was no doubt in my mind that Dawn would jump at the chance, if for no other reason than it meant a week off school. But when John and I asked her that evening, both of us excited and looking forward to a family holiday, Dawn shook her head.

'It's nice of you, but I don't want to miss any more school.'

John and I looked at each other, flabbergasted; then we looked at Dawn. 'But you hardly ever go to school,' John said. 'You spend more time playing truant than you are there.'

'I know. I've got a lot of catching up to do. And we've got end-of-year exams in two weeks, so I need to revise.'

'You can take your books with us,' I said. 'There will be time to revise in the evenings or even on the beach.'

'I wouldn't be able to concentrate. You go and I'll stay here.'

'Absolutely not,' John said.

'You're too young,' I added. 'Ruth would never agree.' And neither would we, I thought, but didn't say.

John and I spent the entire evening trying to persuade Dawn to change her mind, pointing out all the attractions that the south coast of Cornwall had to offer, but Dawn remained adamant that her studying had to come first and she couldn't afford to miss more time from school. Call me a Doubting Thomas, but I had the sneaking suspicion that Dawn's sudden conscientious enthusiasm towards her school work had more to do with not wanting to be out of the area and away from her mates – going out on Friday and Saturday evenings was the highlight of her week.

Clearly Dawn refusing to go was not only disappointing for John and me but also going to cause a problem: where was Dawn going to stay while we were away? Certainly not alone in the house, as she had suggested. I phoned Ruth the following day and told her that Dawn didn't want to come with us and we couldn't persuade her otherwise.

Ruth sighed. 'I'll have to try to find her other carers to stay with, which won't be easy. Or perhaps she could stay with her mother for the week.'

I didn't think the second option was a good idea, given the lack of concern or parental control Barbara seemed to have for or be able to exert over her daughter, not to mention the rejection Dawn would feel if her mother didn't stay in. 'Do you think Barbara will want Dawn to stay?' I asked. 'And I'm not sure Dawn will want to go, even if her mother agrees.'

'Ask her,' Ruth said. 'And if Dawn says yes, I'll approach Barbara.'

So I did. And Dawn's eyes lit up. 'Yes, I can stay at Mum's! What a good idea.'

I didn't think that Dawn's excitement was because she had suddenly repaired her relationship with her mother; it was more that freedom loomed.

'But your mum is hardly ever at home and she works until late each day,' I said. 'And what happens when Mike comes in the evening?'

'I'll go out with my mates,' she said, barely able to contain her excitement.

With little or no parental supervision or control, an empty house, and Dawn coming and going as she pleased and hanging out with her mates, it was, I thought, a recipe for disaster. This was pretty much the situation that had led to her coming into care in the first place and, as far as I could see, nothing had changed. I asked Dawn again if she would like to come on holiday with us, pointing out that a week wasn't very long and she could phone her friends.

'I'll be fine,' she said. 'I promise I won't drink, and I'll try to get back in at nine thirty like I do here.' Clearly all thoughts of studying had now gone.

I phoned Ruth the following day and told her that Dawn wanted to stay at her mother's, although I had concerns about what Dawn might get up to. 'No more than she does when she's with you,' Ruth put in tartly; then she said she would now phone Barbara and run it past her. 'It's easier than trying to find another foster carer,' she added, which I could have guessed.

Two days later Ruth phoned and asked to speak to Dawn. When Dawn came off the phone, she was delighted that her mother had agreed to her going to stay. And while, at one level, I was pleased that Barbara hadn't rejected her daughter outright by refusing to have her, I could see only too clearly the problems looming.

The following week I helped Dawn pack her case and school bag, and John helped me pack for our holiday. I had told the school of the arrangements, and that if Dawn didn't arrive they were to phone Barbara, as clearly we couldn't deal with any problems, being 250 miles away. On

Friday evening I gave Dawn her pocket money for the week and, kissing her goodbye, saw her into the car. John was taking Dawn to Barbara's flat while I finished the packing. When John returned he said that her mother hadn't been there, and Dawn had used the spare front door key hidden under the mat to get in. He said he felt concerned about leaving her alone in the empty flat, but Dawn had said she would be fine and that she was going out soon, which no lessened our concern. But we had to remind ourselves that Dawn wasn't our responsibility now, and we couldn't spend the entire week worrying about what she was getting up to. We had to put some trust in her and Barbara and hope for the best.

Nevertheless, although there was an element of relief in not having to worry about Dawn, and particularly her sleepwalking, which might have been an even bigger problem in a strange house, we were sad that we were leaving her behind. Despite everything that had happened, and the continual worry of Dawn's behaviour and what she would do next, she was still part of our family and, if we were honest, we had grown very fond of her. 'Hopefully she'll come on our next holiday,' I said, as I switched off the bedside lamp.

John agreed. 'She'll be in therapy by then and feeling much better.'

The cottage overlooked the small sandy bay of Gorran Haven, and because the schools hadn't broken up there were only a few families on the beach with pre-school children. Adrian was in his element exploring the fine golden sand, which he prodded, rubbed between the palms of his hands, rubbed into his hair and then tried to eat. He had perfected crawling to an art form and was very fast scampering over the sand, and we had to keep a watchful eye on him the whole time. He was mesmerised by the sea, and John and I stood on the shoreline with him and, taking an arm each, jumped him over the small waves much to his delight and shouts of glee. It wasn't only the moving sea which fascinated Adrian but everything it brought in, including the seaweed and shells which he tried to eat, and the little bubbles that the receding waves left behind which he poked and popped with his finger.

The weather was excellent, and in the late afternoon and early evening we explored the coastal paths and the walks through the National Trust land which flanked the bay, as well as taking in some local sights. By the end of the week we were suntanned, relaxed, and somewhat reluctant to pack for the journey home. For while we had spoken of Dawn, and wondered how she had been getting on, the responsibility, with its continual anxiety, had been kept well away by the distance, and the knowledge that there was nothing we could do about any problems that might have arisen.

On Saturday morning we were on the road by 9.30 a.m. The traffic was heavier than it had been on the way down and the journey slower. Adrian, confined to his car seat, quickly grew restless. John pulled into a lay-by and I moved to the back seat so that I could amuse and comfort Adrian until eventually he dropped off to sleep. While it was lovely to have been on holiday, I knew I would be pleased to be home again with the familiar comfort of my own bed – or I would have been, had we not been broken into.

We didn't notice immediately. The bottle of milk I'd ordered was on the doorstep, the front door was locked, and there was no sign of a forced entry or broken window. It was only when we went into the kitchen to make a cup of tea and found the cupboard doors open that I started to feel something was wrong.

'I'm sure I shut those,' I said to John. I looked in the cupboards and saw that the biscuits and crisps were missing, together with an unopened carton of fresh juice. But even then I didn't immediately think they had been stolen. Then I noticed that the dish on the side, which usually contained loose change for emergencies, was empty, and at the same time the cat flap blew open.

'What the hell?' John said. The cat flap had been fitted by the previous owners and was always kept shut by us, as we didn't have a cat. It was now open and flapping in the wind.

My heart began to race as John went to the back door and, turning the handle, found it unlocked. He went out and looked down the sideway. 'The side gate's open too,' he said, returning stony-faced.

Picking up Adrian, I followed John through to the lounge. The television was still there, and when we went into the front room we found that the hi-fi system hadn't been taken either. The burglar had been through our cassettes, though, for instead of being on the shelves they were in a heap on the floor; whether any were missing wasn't immediately obvious. We flew upstairs and found all the bedroom doors open – we had definitely shut them before leaving as a fire precaution. Our bedroom was the only one that contained anything of value – two rings I had inherited from my grandmother, and thankfully they were still in my jewellery box. However, Adrian's money-box, which I kept on the cabinet beside my jewellery box, had been broken into and was now empty. I guessed there must have been over £30 in it, for John and I had started dropping one pound coins into it, with the intention of opening a savings account for Adrian.

Going round to Dawn's room, we found her wardrobe doors open. I didn't know if anything had been taken, for Dawn had packed her own casual clothes while I had seen to her uniform.

'Did she take her Walkman with her?' John asked.

'Yes. Definitely.' Fortunately Dawn was inseparable from her Walkman, so it was with her and not stolen.

The third bedroom, which was to be Adrian's room, was untouched; likewise the bathroom and toilet appeared not to have been entered. But while it could have been a lot worse in terms of things taken or damage done, there was an awful feeling of violation from knowing that a stranger had been in our house and gone through our possessions. I felt it was an added violation that Adrian's moneybox had been forced open and cleared: it was as though it was a personal attack on a toddler. It was the last thing we needed on our return after a six-hour journey, and it immediately blighted the relaxed feeling we'd had after our week away.

John phoned the police, and while we waited for them to arrive we checked for anything else that might have been taken. We thought it was odd that the food and juice had been taken but the 'valuable' items had been left. When we double-checked the kitchen cupboards we found that John's bottle of Scotch was also missing; apart from a bottle of red wine, which had been left, the Scotch was the only alcohol we had in the house. Then we found that three of the six cut-glass tumblers, which we kept for best,

were also missing. It was almost as if the thieves had been
on their way to a party, and had stopped by for nibbles and
drink.

We made a list of everything that was missing and
handed it to the police officer when he arrived. I couldn't
remember ever having the police come to my house before,
even as a child, and now it had happened three times in the
last six months. It was a different officer to the ones who
had visited us before in connection with Dawn, and I
thought that before long the entire local constabulary
would have come through our front door.

'It's kids,' the officer said, looking at the inventory, as
we showed him around the house. 'You're lucky they didn't
graffiti the walls or pee in the bed. Usually they make
more mess.'

We didn't feel very lucky – far from it – but we did
appreciate that the intruders (the officer said it would have
been more than one) could have done more damage.

'Get rid of that cat flap,' he said as we entered the
kitchen. 'That's where they got in.'

John and I looked at the cat flap and then at the officer.
'But it's not big enough for someone to get through,' I
said, aware than not even Adrian could have squeezed
through the nine-inch square gap.

'They didn't come through it,' the officer said. 'They
reached in. Here, I'll show you.'

We watched as he unlocked the back door, and then,
stepping outside, knelt down and closed the door. To my
amazement and eerie disconcertion his disembodied hand
appeared through the cat flap followed by his arm, gradually extending to its full length. His hand reached across
until his fingers alighted on the bolt at the bottom of the

door, and then moved up to the key in the lock. Both the bolt and the key were within easy reach and he turned the key, locking it and unlocking it, to prove the point.

'But how did they know they could enter that way?' John asked, as the officer returned into the kitchen, shutting and locking the door behind him.

'It's a tried-and-tested method,' he said. 'Cat flaps, open windows and letterboxes feature in most house burglaries. Fix a padlock on your side gate, and my advice would be to do away with the cat flap completely. I'm sure moggy can be let out to do its business.'

Neither John nor I admitted we hadn't got a moggy, as doubtless it would have only compounded our apparent stupidity in maintaining this lapse in security.

'Does anyone else live here besides you and the baby?' the officer asked.

'Only our foster daughter, Dawn,' John said.

'How old is she?'

'Thirteen,' I said, and I saw the officer's expression. 'No, she wouldn't. Absolutely not. She's no angel but she certainly wouldn't do this.'

'Good, but you won't mind if I have a chat with her?'

'She's not here,' John said. 'She's been staying with her mother while we've been away. She's not due back until tomorrow.'

He nodded. 'OK. Perhaps I could call back. I'm on duty tomorrow evening. I'll make it as close to the start of my shift as possible – about seven o'clock.'

We reluctantly agreed – we didn't really have much choice – and I bitterly hoped that Dawn wouldn't see his visit as a sign of our distrust in her. The officer said he would bring a form with him, which we would need for claiming on our insurance, and thanking him, John saw him out.

'She wouldn't,' I said again, as John returned to the lounge. 'Dawn wouldn't break into her own home!'

'No,' John said thoughtfully. 'Unless Dawn's told her dubious mates that the house was empty and that there was an easy route in via the cat flap.'

I couldn't disagree that it was a possibility.

John made a cup of tea while I threw together a quick pasta meal. Then I got Adrian ready for bed. I checked the sheets on our bed and Adrian's cot, to see that they hadn't been 'peed in', but they were clean and dry. Once Adrian was settled for the night we opened the week's mail. Then John secured the cat flap by nailing a piece of wood over the opening, while I finished most of the unpacking. It was nearly ten o'clock and we watched television for an hour before going up to bed. Neither of us had mentioned Dawn since the officer had left, but I knew her name hung in the air.

'I'm sure she's not implicated in any way,' I said as we prepared for bed.

'No, but I'm not convinced it wasn't one of her mates. You must admit it's a bit of a coincidence. Not only did someone know we were away, but they also knew about the cat flap. Unless of course it was an opportunist who struck lucky. But then why take biscuits and booze and leave the valuables? It doesn't add up.'

The following day, while I set the washing machine going, John went to collect Dawn from her mother's, as arranged, at twelve noon. When he returned, without Dawn, he said that Barbara had had to get up to answer the door, and had told him that Dawn wasn't there as she had stayed at one of her mate's for the night. Not best pleased by the wasted trip, John had pointed out that we had arranged to collect Dawn at twelve, and then asked when she was expected back. Barbara said she didn't know but guessed it would be late afternoon, which was the time Dawn had been returning during the week. Apparently Dawn had only slept at her mother's one night, and when John asked Barbara about school, she said she didn't know if Dawn had been going or not.

John returned to Barbara's at five o'clock and Dawn was there, in the middle of a big argument with Mike. Mike had helped, or rather bundled, Dawn and her cases into the car and yelled 'Good riddance,' as they pulled away.

'Good week?' John had asked Dawn dryly. Then he told her that we had been broken into.

Dawn said, 'That's dreadful.'

As I welcomed Dawn home, she seemed very pleased to be back and gave me a big kiss and a hug. I set about her suitcase full of dirty washing – an entire week's worth.

'Didn't you wash anything?' I asked in dismay. 'Not even your underwear?'

'No. Mum wouldn't let me use the washing machine.'

I would have thought her mother could have done her washing for her daughter, but I didn't comment. I had other, more pressing, matters on my mind – the police officer's return visit in an hour's time – and I was very worried. I hoped Dawn wouldn't take it personally, as it could seriously damage our relationship.

Chapter Twenty-One

Broken—Down Bus

'Hello, Dawn,' the officer said, when he returned as promised at seven o'clock and I showed him into the lounge. 'Remember me? I thought your name rang a bell. How are you doing, Dawn?'

I exchanged a pointed glance with John, wondering how the officer knew Dawn.

Dawn was sitting on the sofa and I had told her the officer would be coming – to speak to *all* of us about the robbery. 'I'm good,' she said, smiling sheepishly.

'I expect your foster parents have told you why I'm here?' the officer said, taking a seat opposite Dawn.

Dawn nodded and smiled again, this time I thought a little apprehensively.

'You know this house was broken into and burgled last week?' he continued.

'Yes, John told me. But it wasn't me,' Dawn said far too quickly. My heart sank.

'I'm not suggesting it was you,' the officer said. 'But I'm wondering if you could help me find who did do it. It's not very nice to go away on holiday and come back to find you have been burgled, and this is your home too. I'm sure you'd like to help catch who was responsible.'

Very diplomatically put, I thought. Dawn didn't say anything but was eyeing the officer carefully, while John and I looked at her.

'Have you got a house key, Dawn?' the officer asked after a moment.

Dawn shook her head.

'We didn't think she was old enough,' I said, feeling the need to justify our decision. 'I'm always in when Dawn comes home.'

'Did you need anything from the house while your foster parents were away?' he asked.

'No!' Dawn said adamantly. 'I haven't been anywhere near this place. I've been at me mum's.'

'Not very often,' the officer said. 'I've spoken to your mum and she hardly saw you last week.'

There was silence as Dawn looked away, and John and I exchanged another pointed glance, before the officer said, 'Your mates, Dawn. Are you still in with the same crowd?'

'Some of them,' Dawn said, almost under her breath.

'The Bates lad, and the Melson twins?' the officer said, raising his eyebrows.

'Sometimes.' Clearly the officer was more aware of who Dawn saw than we were, and it sounded as though these friendships weren't for the best.

The officer shifted position, leant slightly forward, and looked seriously at Dawn. 'They're not good company, Dawn. In fact they're bad news. They've landed you in trouble before, haven't they?'

Dawn didn't say anything.

'What sort of trouble?' John asked.

'I'll leave Dawn to tell you about that.' The officer's eyes met Dawn's in almost conspiratorial silence and I guessed he was bound by confidentiality as much as Ruth was. 'I'd really like to find out who broke in here,' he continued, addressing Dawn. 'Do you think your mates might be able to throw any light on that?'

Dawn remained quiet, and then shrugged.

'OK,' the officer said. 'I think it might be best if we continue this chat at the station. We can call in for Bates and the Melson twins on the way.'

'No!' Dawn suddenly cried, clearly as shocked by this as I was. 'I didn't have anything to do with it!'

'So who did? Did you mention the house was empty to your mates?'

'No,' she said; then, after a pause, 'I don't think so.'

'Dawn,' the officer said forcefully. 'You were hanging out with your mates every night last week. They must have wondered why you were suddenly on the streets again until all hours, as your foster parents don't let you. I'm sure one of the gang asked you how come.'

There was another, longer, pause before Dawn shrugged. 'I guess I might have said they were away.'

'And did you give them this address?'

Dawn shook her head. 'No way.'

'Do they know where you live, Dawn?' the officer persisted. 'Might you have told them before?'

Another pause; then, 'I guess I might. I don't know.'

The officer transferred his gaze from Dawn to John and me. 'I'll be out that way tonight and I'll stop by and have a chat with that group. I know where they hang out.'

'Don't say I told you anything,' Dawn put in quickly.

'They're not good mates if you're frightened of them,' the officer said with a frown.

'I'm not,' Dawn retaliated. 'I just don't want them to think I've grassed.'

Standing, the officer took a folded sheet of paper from his jacket pocket and passed it to John. 'That's the statement you'll need when you claim on your insurance.'

John thanked him, although we wouldn't be claiming on our insurance: we had an excess of £100 on the policy, and the broken cat flap, £30 from Adrian's moneybox, drink and biscuits didn't amount to that much.

'Goodbye then, Dawn,' the officer said before he left. 'Behave yourself. You've got a nice home here and good foster parents. Try to keep out of trouble.'

Dawn nodded and smiled pleasantly. I stayed in the lounge with Dawn as John saw the officer out.

'I wouldn't,' Dawn said in earnest as soon as they had gone. 'I wouldn't break in my own home. Why should I?'

I shook my head. 'I don't know.' But I could have guessed. If Dawn had been involved it would have been for kicks: an empty house, an easy way in, goaded by a group of lads into helping themselves to alcohol, crisps and biscuits. It would have been out of bravado – sitting in the park, probably after dark, sharing out the Scotch, crisps and biscuits, and generally having a laugh. I doubted Dawn would have been the instigator, but neither would she have had the gumption to stand up to them.

'What happened to the glasses?' I said, unintentionally voicing my thoughts.

'We ...' Dawn began; then, 'What glasses?' Which rather confirmed my suspicion.

'Three of our best glasses were taken,' I said.

Dawn shrugged but didn't say anything further.

John returned to the lounge and sat on the sofa with a sigh. 'Are all your mates boys?' he asked.

'No, the Melson twins are girls – Sandy and Patsy.'

He nodded, and then picked up the remote control for the television and flicked it on low. 'Remember, Dawn, if you do think of something that might help, I'd be grateful if you could tell us or the police. OK?'

'Of course I will,' Dawn said. And we left it at that. The matter was in the hands of the police and we didn't want to sour our relationship with her by questioning Dawn further.

We watched television for an hour and then Dawn went up for her bath. Once she was in bed I said goodnight and reminded her that we would be back in the routine of school the following morning, and I expected her to go everyday, which she promised she would.

Any residue of the relaxing week's holiday had vanished by the following morning. We were up most of the night with Dawn. She didn't actually sleepwalk but she kept shouting out in her sleep. We took it in turns to go in and settle her and each time we found her sitting up in bed, eyes open and staring straight ahead, as though in the grip of a repeating nightmare. 'It wasn't me!' she cried out. 'You must believe me! I wouldn't do that. I like babies. I was there, but I didn't do it!' All the time she was oblivious to our presence and remained asleep.

We assumed her conscience had got the better of her and the reference to babies was to do with Adrian's moneybox. And her hysterical assertion 'I was there but I didn't do it' suggested she had been an accomplice – perhaps an unwilling one – but now regretted her actions.

Her sleeptalking admission left John and me in the unenviable position of knowing Dawn's guilt without her having told us. Apart from feeling badly let down, we didn't know what we could or should do with this information. We decided to do nothing. Such a confession was hardly admissible evidence, and we wouldn't have felt comfortable by adding to Dawn's troubles by telling the police.

John left for work the following morning absolutely exhausted after the broken night. I felt pretty rough too, and it took me ages to wake Dawn for school. The only person who hadn't been up most of the night was Adrian, and he was his usual chirpy self. Dawn hugged and petted him during breakfast, although she'd seen him the evening before.

'I missed him while you were away,' she said, chucking his chin.

'You could have come with us, Dawn,' I reminded her.

'I know. Maybe I should have done. It would have kept me out of trouble.' So I was all the more convinced she had been party to the break-in but now regretted what had happened.

And as if to prove her regret, she had a very good week. She went to school each day, arrived home on time, and then set about revising for the end-of-year exams. On Friday evening she went out and was home on time. On Saturday she was half an hour late, and although she wasn't drunk, she had clearly been drinking and smoking, for we could smell alcohol and smoke on her breath. John and I lectured her about the effects of both on her health, adding that it was illegal for someone of her age to drink or smoke.

Nevertheless when Ruth phoned on Monday to ask if Dawn had settled in again with us, I was able to say a positive yes. I told her about the burglary and that Dawn had been interviewed by the police with us present, for I thought that as her social worker she should know. Ruth didn't comment but said that she was pleased we were back and Dawn had resettled and was going to school. Apparently Dawn had only been to school one day the week we had been away, and the school secretary, unable to reach Barbara, had phoned Ruth each morning when Dawn hadn't appeared.

'I don't know what she expected me to do about it,' Ruth said dryly.

Very little, I thought, but didn't say.

There were three weeks until the end of term and school broke up for the long summer holidays. Out of the fifteen school days Dawn managed to go to school on ten of them, which included some, but not all, of her exams. Having had to lower my expectations in respect of Dawn's progress, I accepted that on the scale of things this wasn't too bad. She had come home drunk twice during that period, and I'd had to report her missing one Saturday evening, although she'd reappeared before the police arrived, so I cancelled the missing persons. Dawn went to her mother's on all three Sunday evenings, although Barbara was only in for two of them, and then only for an hour each time.

Dawn remained pleasant and co-operative while she was in the house, although I'd no idea what she was getting up to while out. This had become the pattern of our life with Dawn, and together with her sleepwalking it made for a very rocky ride. But John and I were determined to stand by Dawn, believing that at some point we must turn a corner and things would start to improve. We didn't hear any more from the police about the break-in, and John bought and fitted a new back door, rather than just removing and boarding up the cat flap.

The six weeks of summer holidays were upon us and Dawn wanted to go out and meet up with her friends during the day, which seemed reasonable at one level – that's what young people did in the summer holidays – but it clearly increased her potential for getting into trouble.

'Which friends?' I asked. I was only aware of Natasha.

'My friends from school,' she said non-commitally.

'Not the Bates lad and the Melson twins?' I thought I was starting to sound like the police officer.

'No,' Dawn said. 'They only come out at night.'

'What, like vampires?'

She laughed.

'All right, but not every day,' I said. 'I want us to go out together some days. Also I want to know who you are meeting and where.'

Dawn agreed to this, but then Dawn had a habit of agreeing to everything I said and then going off and doing something completely different.

On 1 August I reminded Dawn that her appointment to see the psychiatrist was in two days' time. I told her that I had asked my neighbour to look after Adrian so that I could go with her to the hospital. I knew it was asking too much of Adrian to sit still through an hour-long appointment.

'Don't worry,' Dawn said. 'I can go alone.'

'It's no bother,' I said. 'I'd like to come.' Then I wondered if she didn't want me in the consulting room and party to anything she might confide in the psychiatrist. 'I'll wait outside while you go in and see the doctor,' I said. 'But it's nice to have some support and company.'

'No, really, I'll be fine,' she insisted. 'I'd rather catch the bus. Thanks anyway.'

Clearly I couldn't force my presence on Dawn, so having asked her again on the morning of the third if she wanted me to go with her, and received the same reply, I gave her the appointment card and money for the bus fare, and explained where the outpatients department was.

'Good luck,' I called from the front door step as she left, and she gave me a little wave.

Dawn didn't arrive.

At 11.30 a.m., half an hour after the consultation should have started, the psychiatrist's secretary phoned and asked to speak to Mrs Jennings.

'It's Mrs Glass,' I said. 'Dawn's foster carer.'

'Oh, I see. Well, we were expecting Dawn for an eleven o'clock appointment. She's very late.'

'She left over an hour ago,' I said, 'in plenty of time. I'm sorry – perhaps she'll arrive soon.'

The secretary explained that Mr Gibbons, the psychiatrist, had another appointment booked for 12.00 p.m, but she added that he could give Dawn whatever time was left of her hour's appointment when she arrived. I thanked her, apologised again and asked if she would call me when Dawn arrived.

She didn't call back and at twelve ten I phoned the secretary to be told that Dawn hadn't appeared. I apologised again, and said that I didn't know what had happened, for Dawn knew how important the appointment was. The secretary was quite understanding, considering Dawn had wasted an hour of the psychiatrist's time when he could have seen another patient. She asked me if I wanted to book another appointment, which wouldn't be for another three months. I said I'd speak to Dawn first, as clearly there was no point if she wasn't going to attend.

I was worried as to where Dawn could have got to, although not as worried as I would have been with another child who didn't have a reputation for going missing. I was also frustrated and disappointed, for we had all viewed Dawn going into therapy as a turning point, when she would be able to share her problems and hopefully alter course towards a better future. I was also somewhat annoyed with Dawn – she had gone off with the bus fare and, without saying a word to me, simply decided not to attend the appointment, unless of course there was a very good reason for her not arriving.

'The bus broke down,' she said, when she finally appeared two hours later. 'By the time they sent another bus to pick us up it was too late to go to the hospital, so I walked home.'

It was plausible; the buses did have a reputation for breaking down in the country lanes, particularly the one that led to the hospital, which had a steep gradient. And Dawn had offered the excuse with enough sincerity that I could believe her, just.

'Next time I'll take you in the car,' I said. 'And I'll drop you off. I won't come into the hospital if you don't want me to, but at least I'll know you have arrived safely.'

'Oh,' Dawn said, her thoughts clearly racing ten to the dozen. 'Oh, OK. When is it?'

'Not for another three months.' I looked at her carefully. We had walked through to the lounge where Adrian was, and we were now standing facing each other. 'Dawn, love, it is important you see the psychiatrist. You're not talking to me about your problems, and as far as I'm aware you've not talking to anyone else either. What you tell the psychiatrist is confidential. Dr Gibbons won't tell anyone – not me, your mother, or your social worker. But it's important you share your burden with someone.'

'What about the police?' Dawn asked, squatting on the floor beside Adrian. 'If the police went to see the psychiatrist and asked him to tell them what I'd said, would he?'

'No.'

'Are you sure?'

'Yes. The psychiatrist is bound by confidentiality like a doctor. What you tell him is just between the two of you.' I hesitated. 'Dawn, is there something badly worrying you that you need to share? Something that caused you to harm yourself, and attempt suicide? If so, rather than wait another three months, couldn't you tell me? I'm a good listener and it wouldn't go any further. I promise.'

I watched her as she concentrated on Adrian. Then she said quietly without looking at me, 'If only I could tell you, Cathy. But I'll have to wait until I see Dr Gibbons.'

And I knew at that moment that the bus hadn't broken down, and that Dawn had missed her appointment because she had been worried that what she told the psychiatrist could be accessed by the police. What her burden was I didn't know, but I bitterly regretted not telling her the consultation was confidential before she went, and also that I hadn't taken her to the hospital in the car. But at least she'd had enough trust in me to confide that there was something badly worrying her; I viewed this as a huge step forward, and hoped we could build on it in the future.

That afternoon I telephoned Dr Gibbons' secretary and, apologising again for Dawn's non-attendance, told her the bus had broken down. Then I booked the next available appointment, which wasn't until 4 November.

Chapter Twenty-Two

The Lifeline Vanishes

I negotiated with Dawn that while she was on holiday from school she could go out with her friends during the day on Tuesdays and Thursdays, in addition to her usual Friday and Saturday evenings. Dawn cannily suggested that if she went out during the day on Friday instead of Thursday it would save me the bus fare, as she could stay out all day and continue into the evening.

'I can afford the bus fare, Dawn,' I said. 'And I wouldn't want you out from ten o'clock in the morning until nine thirty at night. I want to see more of you, not less.' Which was true, in addition to feeling that the less time Dawn spent out of the house the less opportunity there was for trouble to present itself to Dawn and be accepted.

The six-week break from school fell into something of a routine. Dawn met her friends – who she assured me were school friends and not the 'old lot' – between ten o'clock and four o'clock on Tuesdays and Thursdays, and spent Mondays, Wednesdays and Fridays with Adrian and me. I took Dawn on outings. She seemed more comfortable going out when there was just her, Adrian and me, rather than family outings at weekends, which were still being curtailed because of Dawn's refusal to join in. I didn't know why, because she got on very well with John;

perhaps it had something to do with appearing in public as a family group and loyalty to her own father. We went to museums, a theme park, swimming, ice-skating and for walks in the country. Dawn appeared to enjoy herself and most of the experiences were new to her, as she had missed out on such things as a child. I also drove us to the coast for the day – leaving at 8.00 a.m. with a picnic and returning in the late evening. Dawn was as excited as Adrian to see the sea, and to my amazement she told me it was only the second time she had been to the seaside, although we were only forty miles from the coast. Her first visit was a vague memory of a family holiday before her parents had divorced.

Dawn's Friday and Saturday evenings followed the same pattern as they had during term time, with her arriving home at 9.30 p.m. on Friday and late (and often drunk) on Saturday. She wasn't daft, and knew that if she was late on a Friday she wouldn't be allowed out on the Saturday. Clearly we couldn't stop her going to her mother's on Sundays as a sanction, so eventually I said if she wasn't home on time (and sober) on Saturdays she wouldn't be meeting up with her friends the following Tuesday. This had the desired effect for one week before she forgot again the next week. Not wishing to be locked in a continuous battle with Dawn, John and I decided we had to give her some leeway and accept that she pushed the limits. If we had been too strict and grounded her every time she hadn't adhered to the rules, then it could have easily tipped her into rebelling completely. At least, with some flexibility on our part and by overlooking some of her behaviour, we had Dawn's co-operation most of the time.

But during the summer holidays something strange happened. It was in relation to Dawn's attitude to Adrian, and I couldn't understand why. Whereas before she had been all over Adrian and couldn't get enough of him (or babies in general), she became guarded in approaching him and seemed to back off. It suddenly became apparent that not only did she now spend very little time fussing over Adrian, picking him up and playing with him, but she seemed to be actively avoiding him. Adrian was on his feet most of the time now, staggering around, and into everything. I sometimes asked Dawn if she would keep an eye on him, while I popped into another room, or answered the phone or door bell, or went upstairs to the toilet. And whereas before she would have not only have kept watch on him but played with him, she now said, 'Can't he go with you?'

'I'll only be a minute,' I would say.

But as I left the room Adrian invariably followed with Dawn steering him towards me. 'He wants you,' she would say.

If I asked her to hold him for a moment, or take his hand, she now refused. 'I might hurt him,' she said. 'He's very little.' Which didn't add up. Adrian would be a year old in seven weeks' time and was now a strong robust little chap. He had been far smaller and more vulnerable when Dawn had first arrived and then she'd been only too keen to hold him.

I reassured Dawn that she wouldn't hurt him, and I wondered if her sudden distrust of her competence had anything to do with Adrian's moneybox. Was she feeling guilty that she had been party to taking his savings, as John and I now believed she had? Perhaps, with a heavy conscience, she felt she didn't have the right to pet and cuddle him. While the whole incident of the break-in was unfortunate, to say the least, I didn't want Dawn bearing a heavy burden of guilt. She had enough to contend with without adding to her problems, and I wanted her to know that I had forgiven her.

While we were feeding the ducks in the park one sunny afternoon, I casually remarked, 'You know, Dawn, we all make mistakes and errors of judgement. Things that we regret afterwards, and would have done differently, or not done at all, if we had the chance over again. No one is perfect. But we can learn from our mistakes, and then we must forgive ourselves and move on. We can't punish ourselves for ever.'

Dawn went very quiet and, breaking off another piece of bread from the slice I had given her, absently threw it into the pond. I was helping Adrian tear up his slice of bread and feed the ducks rather than himself.

'You can't forgive yourself if you've done something really bad,' she said quietly, not looking at me. 'It stays with you.'

'Well, yes, I know it can play on your conscience, and make you angry that you did it in the first place. But there still comes a point when you have to forgive yourself. Otherwise the guilt eats away and can make you very unhappy, and even depressed.'

There was another pause. 'Even if it's something really wicked?' she asked. 'Something so bad that if you told some-one they would hate you?' She was concentrating on the bread, holding the slice, but not tearing off the next piece.

'Yes,' I said. 'But I don't think for one moment that anything you have done could be that bad. Although it might seem like it at your age.'

'It is,' she said, without looking up. 'You wouldn't know because you and John are nice. You wouldn't do really horrible things.'

Whatever Dawn had done in the past, I didn't think that it deserved the guilt she seemed now to be inflicting on herself. Children and teenagers can easily let worries build up and get out of perspective.

'I've said and done things which seemed dreadful and unforgivable at the time, Dawn.'

'But not evil wicked things,' she persisted.

'No. And I'm sure you haven't either.'

Without saying anything further she tore of another piece of bread and threw it into the pond.

I half expected that now we had broached the subject, she would revisit it at some point and hopefully tell me what was causing her so much anxiety. But she didn't. And her attitude to Adrian continued to be removed and almost cold, as if by putting distance between them she was protecting Adrian from herself.

John, too, had noticed the change in Dawn's attitude, and was convinced, as I was, that it was the result of having plundered Adrian's moneybox. But he was philosophical: 'If her guilty conscience stops her getting herself into more trouble, that's no bad thing,' he said.

But it didn't. During the six-week summer holiday Dawn was brought home, worse the wear for drink, by the police on three occasions, having been found outside the notorious Queen's Head pub cheering on a fight. And her guilty conscience seemed to be fuelling the ramblings in her sleepwalking, which often included Dawn telling herself she was wicked and evil.

* * *

Dawn returned to school for the autumn term on 4 September and continued with her part-time education. She managed to attend the whole first week, but given that school hadn't gone back until the Thursday that wasn't exactly a runaway achievement. The following week she went in four days.

When the secretary phoned me on Tuesday to say that Dawn hadn't arrived, she greeted me like an old friend – 'How are you, Cathy? Did you have a nice summer?' – before telling me that Dawn wasn't in school. Then she asked if I could sign and return Dawn's report slip as soon as possible, as it was supposed to have been handed in on the first day back.

'What report slip?' I asked, guessing the answer.

'The one attached to Dawn's report that was sent home with her at the end of term.'

'It didn't arrive, I'm afraid. I'll speak to Dawn and find out where it's got to.'

'Dustbin, probably,' the secretary said with a small laugh. 'She's not the only one. I'll send a copy in the post addressed to you.'

I thanked her and we said goodbye.

When Dawn wandered in at 3.45 p.m., I asked her where her school report for last year was.

'I left it on the bus,' she said. 'It wasn't very good anyway.'

'But I would have liked to have seen it, Dawn, and there was a tear-off slip for me to sign.'

'Sorry, it won't happen again.'

'No worries. The secretary is going to send me a copy.'

'Oh,' said Dawn.

'Yes, "oh". Although I doubt it will hold any surprises.' I paused and looked at her. 'Dawn, you are a bright girl, but you are throwing away your education. Where have you been today?'

She gave me one of her usual shrugs, followed by the usual answer: 'Just hanging around. I couldn't face school today.' I thought that if I avoided every situation I didn't feel like facing then we wouldn't have any clean or ironed clothes and there would be no food in the fridge. But then I wasn't thirteen with all Dawn's problems.

No longer having the sanction of stopping her going out on Tuesday, I said she would be grounded on Friday if she didn't go to school, which got her in the rest of that week at least.

Two weeks into the term, Dawn's sleepwalking escalated for no obvious reason and we were up four nights out of seven. One night we found her in the kitchen with the cutlery drawn open and a knife pressed into the soft flesh of her arm. John grabbed the knife and we quickly examined her arm. It wasn't bleeding. Fortunately she'd used a fish knife, which wasn't sharp, and had done no real harm other than leaving an indentation in her skin, which soon faded.

The following day John stopped off on the way home from work and bought another lock, which he fitted to the kitchen door after Dawn had gone up for her bath. Before we went to bed John locked the kitchen door and we took the key up with us.

That night we were woken in the early hours by the sound of Dawn rattling the kitchen door and trying to get in.

Hurrying downstairs, I thought I would try to talk to her – try to talk her through whatever it was she wanted to do while sleepwalking, as the books had suggested and I'd tried before. But when Dawn said in her slow, heavy, sleep-induced voice, 'I want to cut,' meaning she wanted to self-harm, I realised it was impossible. I couldn't say, 'OK, Dawn you've cut yourself, it's dripping with blood, now let's go back to bed.' I just couldn't say it, so instead I said, 'It's all right, love. There's nothing for you to worry about. Time to go to bed.' I turned her round and steered her upstairs and into her room, where she slept until I woke her for school.

Adrian had his first birthday on 12 October and I invited my parents, brother, some friends with similar aged children and my neighbour, Sue, to a little party. It was a Sunday afternoon and Dawn was with us until she left at six o'clock to see her mother. She was very helpful, passing round the plates of sandwiches I had made for the buffet and refilling glasses, but again I noticed she stayed well clear of Adrian. Even when she gave him his birthday present she dropped it into his lap and then went to a far corner of the room while we all watched him open it. And when John took group photographs Dawn didn't want to be in them to begin with and, once persuaded, positioned herself as far away from Adrian as possible.

My mother noticed the difference in Dawn too, and asked me quietly in the kitchen, 'What's the matter with Dawn? She used to be all over Adrian like a rash. Now she runs away, as if she's scared of him.'

I agreed, and said I didn't know what was the matter. Although we had told my parents of the burglary, we hadn't said anything of our suspicions of Dawn being involved, as it could have worried them. Yet I now began to wonder if stealing Adrian's money was really the reason for Dawn's rejection of him. Four months had passed since the break-in, and it seemed a bit drastic if she was still punishing herself for a relatively minor crime. But what else could be causing it? I'd no idea, and Dawn certainly wasn't going to tell me, although I tried repeatedly to get her talking about her thoughts and feelings.

By the end of October John and I had our hopes once more pinned on Dawn seeing the psychiatrist on 4 November.

When the day came, I kept Dawn off school for the whole day – she didn't resist – and I drove her to the hospital for her 1.30 p.m. appointment. I had asked her again that morning if she would like me to come into the hospital with her and wait outside the consultation room, but she didn't. So having dropped her off at the main entrance and watched her go in, I returned home for half an hour before setting out to collect her. I had Adrian with me in the car, and I hovered with the engine running at the 'drop off and collection' parking space until Dawn appeared. She gave me a little wave and smiled when she saw us, which I took as a positive sign.

'Was it useful?' I asked hopefully, as we pulled away.

'No,' she said bluntly. 'And I've told him I don't want to go again.' My spirits fell as our lifeline disappeared. 'He said if I changed my mind, I could call and book another appointment. He told me to think about it and I said I would.' Which I had to accept.

Although Dawn was only thirteen and had been referred to the psychiatrist after a suicide attempt, it was ultimately her decision whether she entered therapy or not. I had done all the persuading I would, for I sensed that any more pressure was likely to do more harm than good, and possibly strengthen her resolve not to go.

The following day was 5 November, a Friday, and Bonfire Night. John and I had decided that Adrian was too young to go to a firework display, as he would be frightened by the loud bangs and flashing crackling lights. Dawn said she wanted to go to a firework display which was to be held in a park fifteen minutes' walk away. The entrance fee was £4 and I gave her this, plus extra to buy a burger and a hot drink. Seeing her off at the door, I wished her a good time and told her to be back by 9.30 p.m. at the latest, for I knew the display finished at 9.00.

Dawn returned early, at 8.45 – in a police car. We recognised one of the two officers from the last time Dawn had been brought home by the police. The officer said they had picked her up, together with two lads, for causing a nuisance in a street near the park. Apparently they had been throwing lighted fireworks in people's dustbins and watching the lids fly off. While this was no more than high jinks to them, as the officer pointed out it had damaged the dustbins and was also very dangerous. John and I apologised to the officers, and once they had gone, told Dawn off and lectured her about the dangers of the misuse of fireworks. She admitted that she had spent the money I had given her for the entrance fee on buying fireworks, then immediately apologised and said she had let us down, again. We agreed she had, and we stopped her from going out on Saturday, which she accepted without complaint.

It was exhausting and frustrating dealing with Dawn's behaviour, and we no longer had the comfort of the

forthcoming psychiatrist's appointment. But John and I
still believed that at some point, when Dawn realised that
we would always be there for her no matter what she did,
she would stop rebelling, begin to come to terms with her
past and settle on a more even track.

Christmas was approaching and I was looking forward to
it for a number of reasons. It would be Adrian's first
proper Christmas, as he had only been ten weeks old the
previous one and clearly wouldn't remember it. I also
hoped it would give Dawn a boost to be part of a family
Christmas. Judging from what she had told me of her past
Christmases, it would be her first real one for many years,
for like our visit to the seaside her last recollection of
having a good Christmas was before her parents had
divorced when she had been five.

However, at the beginning of December, as the fervour
towards the twenty-fifth increased with earnest, a phone
call from Ruth put paid to my hopes. 'Barbara wants Dawn
home with her,' Ruth said. 'From Christmas Eve to the
first of January.'

Chapter Twenty-Three

Christmas Comes Early

'Why?' I asked, shocked. 'Whatever for?'

'Mike's away, and Barbara doesn't want to be alone over Christmas and the New Year,' Ruth said.

While I could appreciate Barbara's need for company over the festive season, I was bitterly disappointed. Christmas is such a family time and, if I was honest, I viewed Dawn more as a member of our family than she was of Barbara's, although I respected that Dawn was her daughter and therefore Barbara had a right to lay claim to her.

'Ask Dawn what she wants to do,' Ruth said. 'If she wants to stay with you, I'll tell Barbara she'll visit her for Christmas Day only.'

This would still limit my plans for giving Dawn a really special Christmas, but it was better than nothing.

'And what about her father?' I asked. 'Is Dawn going to see him too?'

'No,' Ruth said. 'He will be spending it with his partner and baby.'

'OK,' I said dejectedly. 'I'll ask Dawn what she wants to do.'

Later, when I told Dawn about her mother wanting her for Christmas, I could tell she was struggling with the decision, clearly having divided loyalties.

'Look, Dawn,' I said after a while. 'She is your mother, and if that is where you feel you should be over Christmas then I'll give you a little Christmas here before you go.'

'Oh, will you?' she cried, clearly relieved. 'And you won't mind if I go?'

'I'll mind because I'll miss you, but I do understand, love.'

'Thanks, Cathy. You're terrific!' Throwing her arms around me she planted a big kiss on my cheek.

So that's what we did. We had a mini Christmas on the weekend before Christmas. School had broken up, the decorations and tree were in place, and on the Saturday evening (21 December), instead of going out and getting up to mischief, Dawn stayed in and hung her pillowcase on the end of her bed. Once she was asleep I crept into her room and took the pillowcase into my room where, careful not to wake Adrian, I filled it with the wrapped presents I had hidden in my wardrobe. I carried the bulging pillowcase back to her room and propped it beside her bed, making sure she wouldn't trip over it if she sleepwalked.

Dawn slept well that night and in the morning I didn't have to wake her. We heard her cries of glee at 6.45 a.m. as Adrian began to stir. 'Cathy! John! Come quickly. Look! Father Christmas has been.'

John and I smiled as we put on our dressing gowns and, collecting Adrian from his cot, went to Dawn's room. I don't think she actually believed Father Christmas had been, but she was like a young child, accepting of and embracing all the magic Christmas had to offer. Her face was a picture of awe and delight as she sat up in bed and delved into the pillowcase, bringing out the gifts one at a time. She studied each present first, turning it in her hand, savouring the anticipation, before slowly removing the paper. For her, as with children (and many adults), the unwrapping of the present was as exciting as receiving the actual gift.

I perched on the edge of the bed while John stood to one side holding Adrian, and we watched as she unwrapped and admired the gifts. They weren't all expensive presents – many were 'stocking fillers' – but I had bought Dawn the wristwatch, denim shirt and shoulder bag she wanted; together with cassettes for her Walkman, a chocolate selection box, bubble bath, a photograph album and a bracelet, which she wasn't expecting. I could have wept as she looked, eyes big with wonder, at each unwrapped gift for some moments before placing it carefully on the bed beside her, as though unable to believe what she saw. She thanked us over and over again, and said how lucky she was, and how did Father Christmas know what she wanted? Dear, sweet, innocent Dawn, I could, and did, forgive her everything, and I thought if only I could have had her five years earlier how different things might have been.

Once all her presents were open and the pillowcase was empty, she sat in bed overawed, and gazing at the presents which surrounded her. I asked if I could take a photograph of her for the albums – hers and mine – and she agreed. I fetched my camera and then stood at the end of her bed and looked through the lens. She sat in a nest of wrapping paper and gifts and smiled up at me with pure joy, and I knew it was an image that would stay in my mind's eye for ever.

'Merry Christmas, love,' I said, after I had taken the photograph.

'Merry Christmas,' Dawn said, and we laughed in conspiracy, for the outside world had to wait another three days before they started their Christmases.

We dressed, and I made a cooked breakfast. Then we went through to the lounge, where more presents awaited Dawn under the tree. And while I had been in the kitchen three presents had appeared of which I had no knowledge.

'It looks like Father Christmas has been in here too,' I said.

Dawn smiled. 'Merry Christmas and thanks for everything. It's not much but I hope you all like them.'

'That's very sweet of you, Dawn,' I said. 'I'm sure we will. Thanks, love.'

John took the present that Dawn had put under the tree for Adrian and passed it to him. I took a photograph as he opened it, and while Dawn didn't sit next to him, or even help him, as she would have done in the past, she didn't put a huge distance between them as she had been doing. Pulling off the last of the paper, Adrian revealed a soft toy.

'It's a panda,' Dawn said. 'Do you like it, Adrian?'

Adrian grinned and nodded. 'Dank u,' he said before rubbing his face in the soft fur of the toy.

'He does, very much,' I said, and Dawn smiled, pleased.

She watched as John and I opened our presents from her – perfume for me and aftershave for John.

'That's lovely, Dawn,' I said, and going over I kissed her. 'Thanks, love. We'll smell delightful now.' John thanked her too.

'I hope you don't mind,' Dawn said sheepishly. 'But I used my clothing money to buy the presents.'

'No,' I said. 'That's very generous, and much better than spending it on beer.'

She looked sideways at me for a moment, unsure if I was joking, and then realising I was, laughed.

There were presents under the tree for Dawn from my parents, brother, my neighbour Sue, and my good friend Pat, who had met Dawn a few times when she had come to the house. Adrian couldn't understand why he wasn't allowed to open any more presents – at fourteen months the concept of a pre-Christmas Christmas for Dawn's sake was a bit beyond him. We kept him amused with the discarded wrapping paper while Dawn opened her presents: makeup in a presentation box, a set of teenage novels, a music voucher, and a denim skirt from my parents which I had chosen to match the shirt and bag Dawn had had from Father Christmas. Dawn said she would thank everyone the next time she saw them, which would be in the New Year.

With the other presents (for John, Adrian, me and our Christmas guests) remaining unopened under the tree until the twenty-fifth, we played games, as we would be doing again on Christmas Day. I popped into the kitchen every so often to see how the chicken was doing, and later as I set the vegetables to boil, John and Dawn laid the table.

At two o'clock we sat around the table with its festive cloth, pulled the crackers, put on our paper hats and tucked into the Christmas dinner with all the trimmings – roast chicken with stuffing, roast potatoes and parsnips, carrots, peas and sweetcorn, with lashings of thick gravy. Christmas music played on the hi-fi in the background as we ate, and John told us of his Christmases as a child in Norway where has father had worked. Adrian's paper hat, which was far too big, slipped further and further down

until if finally covered his face and stopped him from
eating, and I took it off. He was in his high chair and made
a good attempt at feeding himself with a combination of
small fork and fingers. John and I didn't open a bottle of
wine as we would be doing on Christmas day for we felt it
was putting temptation in Dawn's way and she was really
too young to be drinking alcohol.

We had a rest from eating after the main course, and
returned to the lounge for a couple of hours. Adrian
dropped off to sleep on the sofa, and we played card games,
and then Cluedo, which Dawn won. Adrian woke just as I
was giving Dawn a chocolate off the tree for a prize and
protested so loudly that I gave him a chocolate too.

It was Sunday and Dawn had told her mother she
wouldn't be making her usual evening visit as she would
be with her for all the following week. Dawn had therefore
been with us continuously since coming home at 9.30 p.m.
on Friday, and while I knew it wasn't an ordinary weekend, with our mini Christmas, she had been so relaxed and
happy that I wished I could have curtailed her going out
more often, for I was sure the gang she hung around with
was largely responsible for the trouble she got into.

We had cold chicken sandwiches for tea, and then once
Adrian was in bed John, Dawn and I set about the washing
up. We were amazed at how much there was considering
there was just the four of us, yet there was a cosy, homey
feel in the warm kitchen as John washed, Dawn wiped and
I put away the pots, pans, cutlery and crockery – a
comfortable family feeling that encompassed Dawn and
which I hoped would be repeated more often in the future.

Once the kitchen was clear, we returned to the lounge
with a cup of tea and slice of Christmas cake each – I had

bought a small cake, as I had the Christmas pudding, with a larger one in the cupboard for Christmas Day, when there would be eleven of us.

Before Dawn went up to bed, carrying her presents, she thanked us again. 'It's been great,' she said giving us both another kiss. 'My best Christmas ever!' While I was pleased, I also thought this was a little sad, for Adrian, like many children, would grow up anticipating and enjoying these Christmases every year, almost as a right.

When I went to say goodnight to Dawn she had put her presents in two neat piles on the floor so that she could see them from her bed.

''Night, love,' I said. 'Merry Christmas.'

'Merry Christmas, and thanks for giving me a good time. Now I won't be so disappointed on Christmas morning.'

'Have you been disappointed by Christmas in the past, then, Dawn?' I asked gently, sitting on the edge of her bed.

She nodded, and her face clouded. 'But I won't think of that now. I don't want to be sad again. I'm happy now and I want to stay happy for as long as possible.' Throwing both arms around me she hugged me for all she was worth.

On the morning of Christmas Eve John took Dawn with her suitcase to her mother's for the week. Barbara was in and awaiting Dawn's arrival and – perhaps because Mike was away – Barbara seemed really pleased to see her daughter, John said. She welcomed her in and wished John a Merry Christmas, and said he could collect Dawn any time on 1 January, although not too early, as they would be celebrating the New Year together.

As I began the last of the preparations for our second Christmas – collecting the pre-ordered turkey and shopping for fresh vegetables – the house was strangely quiet and empty without Dawn, and I closed her bedroom door against the reminder of her vacant bed. Adrian missed her too and kept saying, 'Daw'? Daw'?' as he went from room to room looking for her. For although Dawn hadn't given him any attention in the last five months she was still a member of our family and her sudden vanishing was inexplicable to Adrian at his age.

'Dawn will be back soon,' I reassured him, and myself.

Our Christmas went as planned. On Christmas morning my parents, my brother, John's brother and his family, and an elderly aunt of mine who had never married and would have been alone over Christmas arrived, and we had drinks and mince pies. We chatted, and swapped presents as the turkey browned in the oven, and then ate ourselves to a standstill. After dinner we played silly games – charades, consequences, and sardines – and the noise and excitement grew as the day went on.

I thought about Dawn more than once during the day and hoped she was having a nice time with her mother. It was after midnight by the time everyone left, but all the hard work had been worth it, and we'd gone through two reels of film, photographing Adrian's first real Christmas.

John had taken the week off work between Boxing Day and New Year and we spent most of it socialising, visiting old friends and distant relatives whom we only had the chance to see at this time of year. A last-minute invitation saw us at an impromptu gathering next door at Sue's for New Year's Eve. There were twenty of us, all with babies or young children, whom we carried upstairs as they fell asleep, settling them in the main bedroom. The adults and older children saw in the New Year with party poppers and a rowdy chorus of 'Auld Lang Syne'. A little after one o'clock I lifted Adrian from the travel cot upstairs and, thanking Sue, we said our goodbyes, and left to the shouts of Happy New Year reverberating down the road.

I quickly settled Adrian in his cot and, happily exhausted, John and I climbed into bed, leaving our bedroom door unlocked for the eighth night in a row and looking forward to another night of unbroken sleep.

It didn't happen.

Shortly after 5.00 a.m. we were woken by the door bell. Throwing on our dressing gowns and wondering what on earth was the matter, we stumbled downstairs to find Dawn with her suitcase on the doorstep with a police officer in tow.

'It's New Year's Day!' John said, utterly amazed.

'Tell me about it,' the officer said dryly. 'I believe this young lady is living with you?'

'Yes,' I said. 'Come in, Dawn. Whatever has happened?'

Tired, and clearly worse for drink, Dawn came into the hall, as John lifted in her suitcase. 'What's happened?' I asked again, glancing between the officer and Dawn, who was now halfway up the stairs.

'I need to go to bed,' she said, continuing upstairs.

I looked at the officer.

'Her mother phoned us an hour ago and said she was throwing Dawn out on to the street. They'd been drinking heavily and had argued. Doubtless Dawn will be able to give you more details when she's recovered. I need to be going. It's been a busy night and it's not over yet.'

'And there's nothing more you can tell us?' John asked.

'Sorry, mate, that's all I know.'

We thanked him, and he returned to the police car where another office sat with the engine running. 'Happy New Year,' John said sardonically as he closed the door.

Upstairs I found Dawn, having dropped her coat on the floor, getting into bed with her clothes and shoes on. 'I need to sleep,' she said, lying down and immediately closing her eyes.

Clearly there was nothing to be had by trying to talk to her now, so easing her out of her shoes and leaving her fully clothed, I pulled the duvet over her and came out, leaving the door slightly ajar.

What an end to Christmas, I thought, as I lay on my back in bed staring at the ceiling! What a start to the New Year! And my heart went out to Dawn, who had left us so happy and full of the wonder of Christmas, and had now returned drunk after an argument with her mother.

Chapter Twenty-Four

Why, Dawn?

Dawn slept most of New Year's Day, only getting up for dinner in the evening, before showering and returning to bed. While we ate, I asked her if she wanted to talk about the argument she'd had with her mother, but she didn't. I also asked her if she'd had a nice Christmas and what her mother had bought her, but she shrugged and said, 'It was OK.'

I was disappointed, I had hoped that by giving Dawn a really good time she would have happy memories of Christmas, but it seemed that this one would be no better than the previous one, now blighted by what had happened. I now felt that our pre-Christmas celebrations had completely gone to waste. However, aware it was the start of a new year and we had to be positive, I decided to put it behind us and press on.

I cajoled Dawn into coming to the January sales with me to see if we could pick up some good bargains. Normally Dawn wouldn't have needed any encouragement to shop, but even when we were in her favourite store and I was pointing out clothes she might like to try on, she was withdrawn and quiet. She hardly uttered a word, avoided all eye contact and stood as far away from me as possible during the whole trip. The distance she was putting between us continued when we got home, and throughout the following two days. I was starting to feel that for some reason she was withdrawing from me, as she had done from Adrian, although I couldn't for the life of me understand why. Any question, or stab at conversation on my part, was met with a shrug or a nod. This wasn't like Dawn, for even when she had got into trouble in the past she had quickly bounced back to being her usual chatty and pleasant self. I realised that the week at her mother's had been a disaster, but I could hardly be held responsible for all of that.

'Is everything all right?' I asked her again, over breakfast the next morning. 'You've been very quiet since you came back from your mum's.'

She shrugged. 'I guess.'

'Is there anything you want to talk about?' I asked, as I'd asked many times before.

Dawn shook her head. 'No.'

'It's your birthday on the sixth of January,' I said, seizing upon this to try to cheer her up. 'That's only three days' time. Have you thought what you'd like to do to celebrate? It's your special day, so you must choose.'

She shrugged. 'Don't mind.'

'We could go out for a meal or have a takeaway,' I suggested, not easily put off. 'You like Chinese food. And at the weekend, when there's more time, you could have a few friends round and have a little party.'

'Don't mind,' Dawn said again, no more enthused.

'Well, how about we have a birthday tea with a takeaway here on the sixth and then you can think about what you want to do at the weekend?'

Dawn nodded, just.

I looked at her carefully. 'Are you sure there's nothing you can tell me? I really don't like to see you like this. '

She shook her head again. 'I'm OK. A takeaway sounds good.' But her flat emotionless voice and slumped shoulders suggested it was far from good.

Dawn returned to school for the first day of the spring term on 5 January, and that evening she went up to her room, where she remained, uncommunicative, only coming down for dinner, which she ate in silence. When I went up to say goodnight I asked her again what was worrying her and she said, 'Nothing. It doesn't matter.'

'Dawn, love, it's your birthday tomorrow. I want you to be happy and have a good time.'

'I will,' she said. 'Tomorrow everything will be fine. I promise you, Cathy.'

I smiled. 'Good. Now, would you like your presents in the morning before you go to school? Or when you come home, when there's more time?'

'When I come home,' she said, rallying a little.

I paused and looked at her; then, saying goodnight, I kissed her forehead and came out.

The following morning when I woke her for school I said, 'Happy Birthday', and Dawn smiled. When she came down for breakfast, John wished her a happy birthday before he left for work, and Adrian added his "appie bir'day, Daw", which got another smile from Dawn.

I saw her off to school at the door, feeling that things were looking up – she seemed a bit brighter and more responsive. As soon as she had gone I got Adrian dressed and we went into town to collect the birthday cake I had ordered for Dawn. It was iced and had pink and white roses, and *Happy Birthday to a special 14-year-old* written on it in fancy icing. On our return I blew up balloons and hung them in groups of three to go with the birthday banners; John had taken down the Christmas decorations the evening before. I arranged Dawn's cake on the coffee table in the lounge, together with her cards and presents, which included ones from my parents and brother, ready for when she came home. With her birthday coming so soon after Christmas, it had been difficult for me to know what to buy her, and I'd settled on a rather ornate jewellery box and a silver necklace, plus gift vouchers which she could spend at her leisure. I didn't know what was in the parcels from my parents and my brother.

By 3.30 p.m. I was ready for Dawn's return at 3.45. I would order the Chinese takeaway when John got home from work. Adrian had sensed the build-up in anticipation and was busy practising his "appie bir'day, Daw", which I had told him we would say as we opened the front door. I thought if he got the same reaction from Dawn that he had that morning, when she had smiled openly at him and not immediately run away, we could be well on the way to bridging the gap between them, which would be great.

At 3.40 p.m. Adrian and I were positioned at the bay windows in the front room, looking up the street for the first sign of Dawn. Usually I was busy in the kitchen when she returned home from school, and I left whatever I was doing to answer the door. Now, on her birthday, we were ready and waiting: ready to fling open the door as she came up the path and shout, 'Happy Birthday, Dawn!' At 3.50 our gaze was intent on the street, as she was expected any minute. A few lads from the local school sauntered past with their blazers flapping open despite the cold. I glanced upwards: the sky was grey and overcast, and the winter's night was already drawing in.

At four o'clock we were still watching and waiting, and by 4.15 I was starting to get a little irritated. Usually Dawn was in dead on 3.45, whether she'd been to school or not. There'd only been a handful of occasions when she'd been over half an hour late, and tonight she knew her presents and cards would be waiting for her.

By 4.30 I was struggling keep Adrian amused in the front room, and I was both worried and annoyed. It was nearly dark now and there was still no sign of Dawn. Where on earth could she be? I switched on the light in the hall so that we could still see out of the front room but not be seen. I couldn't believe she wouldn't come straight home on her birthday – she knew we were waiting to celebrate it with her. I searched through the reasons that could have made her so late, including the bus breaking down, her staying on at school or dropping in at her mother's to collect a present. But Dawn knew if she was going to be late she should have phoned me. Then I wondered if she was just spending some time with her friends after school, as it was her birthday, which was understandable, but again she should have phoned.

By 5.15, when there was still no sign of Dawn, I reluctantly drew the front room curtains and took Adrian into the lounge, where his toys were. I was bitterly disappointed in Dawn and also extremely worried. If she wasn't home by six o'clock, I would have to phone the duty social worker and report her missing. On her birthday! I looked at the coffee table with its cake, cards and presents, all waiting for her return, and wondered again where on earth she could have got to. I now had Barbara's telephone number – Dawn had given it to me a while back, although I hadn't previously had cause to use it. Picking up my address book, I keyed in the numbers and listened to it ringing. No one answered. It was now 5.30.

John had said he would try to leave work early for Dawn's birthday, and I was expecting him shortly after six. Dawn was now over an hour and a half late. Although it was still early evening, I was beside myself with worry, and at the same time annoyed that she was being so thoughtless. I tried her mother's number again ten minutes later – again, no response. Then at six o'clock I heard the front door open as John returned from work.

'Where's the birthday girl?' he called from the hall. Adrian shot out of the lounge to greet him, and I followed. John knew immediately from my expression that something was wrong.

'She hasn't come home,' I said.

'I don't believe it! On her birthday!' He threw up his hands in despair.

'I've tried her mother's number, but there's no answer. Can you look after Adrian while I phone the social services?'

Scooping up Adrian, John went into the kitchen to make a cup of tea while I returned to the lounge to make the call. When the switchboard operator connected me to the duty social worker I gave my name, explained who I was and that Dawn hadn't come home from school, despite it being her birthday. He thought, as I had, that it was possible she had stayed behind with some friends, and I agreed that that might still be an option. He said to leave it another hour, and if she still hadn't returned or been in touch to phone the police and report her missing.

I went through to the kitchen and told John what the duty social worker had said. He had given Adrian a snack to keep him going until we had the takeaway, for we still assumed that Dawn would appear at any moment and we would celebrate as we had planned.

At 6.45 p.m. I made sandwiches for John and me, for we were both hungry now, and I also gave Adrian some scrambled egg. It was past Adrian's usual teatime, and indeed he would be going to bed shortly. We ate at the table in the breakfast room in silence and then went through to the lounge. John took Adrian on his lap while I, with a very heavy heart, picked up the phone and dialled the police station. I was held for five minutes in the usual queuing system; then when the office came on the line, I gave my name and said I was Dawn Jennings' carer and I had to report her missing.

The officer recognised Dawn's name. 'You've reported her missing before,' he said.

'Yes.'

He told me to hold the line and I assumed he was going to retrieve Dawn's details, although this hadn't happened before. Perhaps, I thought, there was a new procedure.

As I waited, listening to the empty line, I was also listening for the front door bell, hoping, willing, that Dawn would return. We would tell her off, yes, but we would accept her excuse and apology, then watch her open her presents and order the takeaway. But instead of the door bell going, the officer's voice came back on the phone, sounding more formal and sombre.

'Mrs Glass?'

'Yes.'

'We were going to send an officer out to you as soon as one became available. Dawn's not missing: she's in hospital. She was admitted an hour ago.'

'What? What for?' I stared at John.

'I don't know all the details, but I understand her mother found her at her flat when she got home from work. She called an ambulance. I believe Dawn tried to commit suicide.'

I froze and a rushing noise filled my ears as the officer continued. 'She's at the general hospital. Her mother is with her.'

I continued to stare at John. 'Thank you,' I managed to say to the officer, and I hung up.

'Dawn's in hospital,' I said, immediately standing. 'She's tried to commit suicide.'

'Jesus!' John said. 'You go to her; I'll look after Adrian.'

I was already down the hall, pushing my feet into my shoes and grabbing my coat and bag.

In the car my thoughts raced and my heart thumped wildly. Dawn had tried to commit suicide and was in hospital! I couldn't believe it. Despite being quiet and withdrawn the previous days, she had left that morning with a smile and a wave, and, I thought, looking forward to the takeaway and opening her presents. She must have been in school, for the secretary hadn't phoned. So what on earth could have happened since she'd left that morning, to send her spiralling down into abject despair and make her do this? Her mother's flat was an hour's bus ride from St James's School – Dawn must have gone there straight after school. The officer had said she had been

admitted to hospital an hour ago, which explained why
there had been no answer when I'd phoned Barbara's flat –
they were in the ambulance on their way to hospital. But
why? Why today, Dawn? Whatever could have happened?

Then an icy shudder ran down my spine as I remembered Dawn's words the night before, when I'd gone up to
say goodnight: 'Tomorrow everything will be fine, I promise you, Cathy.' Had Dawn been planning this? Had she
known last night what she was going to do? Is that why
everything was going to be 'fine' – because she was planning on going to her mother's and committing suicide?
Dear God! I shuddered again and gripped the wheel as her
words rung in my ears and the reality hit me. I had said
goodnight and left her in bed, thinking she seemed
brighter and was looking forward to her birthday, when all
along she had been relieved at the prospect of ending her
life!

As I pulled into the hospital grounds another thought
hit me. If Barbara was with Dawn, would she want me
there? I'd only met Barbara once, at the meeting when
Dawn had first arrived. John had seen her a few times
since, when he'd taken Dawn to her flat, in the summer
and again on Christmas Eve. Barbara had been polite with
him then, but now she might well hold me responsible for
what Dawn had done. And I felt she had every right to
hold me responsible, for I was. I had missed all the signs of
Dawn's depression and what she was planning to do. Yes,
I'd recognised she had been quiet and I'd tried to talk to
her, but a fat lot of good that had done.

I came to a halt in a parking space, switched off the
engine and sat staring through the windscreen into the
dark outside. My immediate reaction had been to come to

Dawn, feeling she needed me, but now I wasn't so sure. Apart from Barbara blaming me, Dawn might not want me there, preferring to be with her mother at a time like this. But then again if I didn't go in, Dawn could think I didn't care.

Fighting back tears, I got out and, with my head down against the cold night air, I quickly crossed the car park to the Accident and Emergency entrance. I hadn't brought any of Dawn's clothes or her wash bag with me; it hadn't occurred to me as I'd dashed from the house. If Barbara and Dawn didn't want me there, I would leave and return to the house for what Dawn needed and bring her things in. What would happen after that I'd no idea, for clearly staying with us wasn't helping Dawn, and perhaps this was Dawn's way of telling us.

Chapter Twenty-Five

A Dreadful Burden

As the hospital doors swished closed behind me, I blinked against the sudden brightness of the fluorescent lights after the dark outside. The seating area was directly in front of me, and a dozen or so people were waiting to be seen. I walked past the seated area, and over to reception on the far right. A woman at the computer looked up as I approached.

'Dawn Jennings was admitted earlier this evening,' I said, my voice shaking. 'I'd like to see her. I'm her foster carer, Cathy Glass.'

She flicked through a pile of cards beside her on the desk and pulled out one, which I assumed related to Dawn. She read the few handwritten notes on the card and then looked up. 'The doctor has seen Dawn. Go through those double doors and turn right. She's in a cubicle on the left.'

I thanked her, and crossing the waiting area to where she had pointed I went through the double doors and turned right. Six cubicles were on my left, all with their curtains drawn around the beds. A nurse came out of one.

'Can you tell me where Dawn Jennings is, please?' I asked.

She pointed to the third cubicle.

I went over, and stopped. The curtains were completely closed and there was no sound coming from the other side. I hesitated, uncertain whether I should go in, but I hadn't come this far not to see Dawn. Slightly parting the curtains, I said, 'Dawn?' I could see her on the bed, with her mother seated beside her. I opened the curtains just enough to go through and, stepping in, closed them behind me.

Dawn was on her back, propped up on three pillows, with a drip coming from the bandages on her left arm. I hid my shock. Both her arms were heavily bandaged from just below her elbows to her wrists, with only her fingers jutting out; I assumed she had cut her wrists. She was very pale and her pupils were dilated, perhaps from the pain relief she had been given. She looked at me and managed a small smile. Barbara looked at me too but didn't smile.

'Hello, Dawn, Barbara,' I said.

'Cathy,' Barbara acknowledged evenly.

Barbara was as pale as Dawn. She was dressed in a light grey suit and white blouse, presumably having arrived home from work and found Dawn and then come straight here. She was leaning slightly forward, towards her daughter, as though she had been talking quietly to her before I had come in. I hovered at the end of the bed, not wanting to intrude on their privacy.

'How is she?' I asked awkwardly, addressing Barbara.

Barbara nodded. 'She'll live, but she's made a right mess of my bathroom. Blood everywhere! I've told her she can clean it up when she's better.' It was said lightly, as a stab at humour. Barbara didn't appear hostile towards me, and seemed very concerned for Dawn. I moved further in and closer to the bed.

'What did the doctor say?' I asked after a moment.

'They've stitched her up,' Barbara said, 'and they're keeping her in for a few days. Hopefully she'll get the help she needs now, after all this.'

Dawn didn't say anything but looked at me with the same wistful smile.

I assumed by 'help' Barbara meant another appointment with a psychiatrist, which would only help if Dawn actually attended. But that wasn't what she meant.

'I've tried,' Barbara said quietly, looking at me. 'You've tried, her father has tried and the teenage unit was no good. They need to find her somewhere else to live before she makes another attempt on her life and succeeds.'

I acknowledged the truth of Barbara's words, and again felt a surge of responsibility for Dawn being here. I had failed her, as had her mother and father; only the results of my failure appeared to be far worse than theirs. I looked at Dawn and her expression remained blank.

'Has anyone told her social worker?' Barbara asked, looking at her daughter.

'I reported Dawn missing to the social services, but I haven't told them Dawn's in hospital. Perhaps the police have.'

Barbara shrugged.

'I'll phone the duty social worker when I go home,' I offered. 'And if Dawn is staying here for few days I'd better get her nightdress and wash things.'

'Thanks, Cathy.' Barbara said evenly with a small sigh. She seemed far less critical of Dawn than when I had first met her, and was also more attentive and caring. I supposed coming home and finding Dawn like that had perhaps given her the shock she needed, yet there was an air of resignation as she spoke, as though this was yet another incident in Dawn's litany of self-abuse.

'All your birthday presents are waiting for you,' I said quietly, glancing at Dawn. 'And your birthday cake.'

Barbara looked at Dawn. 'Some birthday this turned out to be.'

Dawn threw me another small smile, apparently more bemused by what had happened to her than upset or distressed, I still wasn't sure what to say or do for the best. I would have liked to have sat on the edge of the bed and given Dawn a big hug, but that seemed inappropriate and intrusive with her mother there.

'Are you staying with Dawn?' I asked Barbara presently.

'Until they take her up to the ward. Then I'll go. I've got work tomorrow. I've told Dawn I'll come back tomorrow evening.'

'Shall I come in during the day tomorrow, then?' I suggested. 'So she has some company?'

Barbara and Dawn nodded.

I still hesitated, reluctant to go but feeling I should leave them together. 'I'll get your things, then, Dawn,' I said. 'And I could bring your birthday presents in tomorrow, once you're settled on the ward.'

Dawn nodded again. I looked at her. Lost in the pile of starched white pillows, she looked so young and vulnerable. 'Dawn, love,' I blurted out. 'I so wish you could have told me how you were feeling. I'd no idea.' Tears stung the back of my eyes and I swallowed hard.

Dawn gave me the same small smile as Barbara looked at her daughter. I turned and, parting the curtains, left the cubicle. As I did I heard Barbara's voice behind me saying to Dawn, 'I'll be back in a few minutes.' Then, 'Cathy, can I have a word?'

I stopped on the other side of the curtains and waited as Barbara appeared through them. 'I'd like to talk to you – not here, though. Let's go where we can't be overheard.' She nodded behind her, so I assumed she meant so that Dawn couldn't hear.

Barbara fell into step beside me, and we went through the double doors and to the waiting area. Choosing some seats in the far corner, away from where others waited, we sat down. Barbara leant back and sighed, pushing her hair away from her face. 'Look, Cathy, there's stuff you need to know about Dawn. Things you should have been told a long time ago. Ruth told me not to say anything: she said it was confidential and you didn't need to know. But I think you do, especially as you have a young baby. I don't want to be held responsible '

A feeling of deep disquiet settled within me as I looked at Barbara and waited. Her face was tired and drawn, and set in an expression of earnest, anxious sincerity. 'I'm telling you now,' she continued, 'because I want you to help me get Dawn the care she needs, before it's too late.'

I nodded, wondering what on earth she was about to tell me, while Barbara took a breath and collected her thoughts.

'I'm not the best mum,' she began. 'In fact I'm probably the world's worst, and her father's no better. Our marriage was shaky from the start and we only married because I was pregnant with Dawn. We struggled in a one-bedroom flat and things got worse and worse. Although if you asked Dawn she would probably say those were the best years of her life. But I guess that's kids.' She gave a small tight laugh. 'When Dawn was nearly five, my ex and I decided to call it quits. We weren't doing each other any good, and the continual fighting wasn't doing Dawn any good either. We both needed time by ourselves to recover and think what to do for the best. I know what Ruth told you about the next four years – that I claim Dawn was with her father and he says she was with me, but it's not true.' I held Barbara's gaze as she continued. 'I have family in Ireland, and an uncle and aunt offered to have Dawn while we sorted things out. I'd never been close to them, but it seemed a good idea: they'd got grown kids of their own who were doing OK. So my ex took Dawn over to Ireland. It was supposed to be for a couple of months. I stayed on in the flat and my ex moved out. I tried to find a job, but I hadn't any qualifications. It was a difficult time for me and I got very depressed. Dawn's dad quickly met someone else and wasn't interested in me or my problems – or Dawn, come to that. It wasn't the same woman he's with now, but that's another story.

'Anyway, weeks passed, then months. I missed Dawn, though not as much as I should have done – I was too wound up in my own problems. I phoned Dawn when I could afford it, and my aunt and uncle always said she was fine and had settled in well. But I rarely got to actually speak to Dawn. She was always out on the farm, playing, and I didn't like to have her called in if she was having so much fun. She began school out there, and my uncle said she was doing well. Then suddenly I found a year had passed. I had a job by then, cleaning, and was starting to get my life together. I wanted Dawn back, but when I phoned and asked, my uncle said it was selfish of me, as she was so settled. He said she was having a far better life than I could give her, with all the fresh air and a stable family. I didn't have the fare to go and see Dawn, so I believed what he said and she stayed. During the next three years, I still phoned, but not so often; I felt that my uncle and aunt had become her family and I didn't have the right to intrude.'

Barbara paused and glanced up as a man passed near our chairs; she waited until he had gone before continuing. 'The first thing I knew that something was wrong was when Dawn was nine, and I got a phone call from the social services saying they had Dawn in their office. It was late one afternoon and I'd just got in from work. By that time I'd stopped cleaning and was working in the department store where I am now. I was shocked. I thought Dawn was in Ireland. My uncle and aunt hadn't phoned me to say she was coming to England. I found out later that they'd just put her on a plane, and the police had been called to the airport when no one arrived to collect her.'

I looked at Barbara, horrified, and she nodded.

'Anyway, the social worker brought her to me that same night. I was her mother, after all, and I hadn't done anything wrong, so there was no reason why I shouldn't have her back. But as soon as I saw Dawn, I knew something was wrong. She was a different child. I mean obviously she had changed in appearance – four years had passed. But she was so unruly and aggressive that she was like a wild child. She spat and hit me and screamed that she hated me. When I tried to find out what was wrong, she went quiet and said she couldn't remember.

'I couldn't cope with Dawn,' Barbara continued. 'And eventually I got in contact with her father. He had just moved in with his present girlfriend and they offered to

share the care of Dawn. That was before they had their
baby and I think his girlfriend quite liked the idea of playing happy families, but it soon wore off. Dawn started
spending time with them and time with me. But none of us
could really deal with her and she got worse. By the age of
ten she was doing whatever she wanted. She was out on
the streets, rarely went to school and then started getting
in trouble with the police. She was also having horrendous
nightmares and began sleepwalking. It was really scary to
watch and I didn't feel safe in my own house. I wanted her
to go the doctor and talk to him, but she wouldn't. Then
she began harming herself. To begin with she was pulling
her hair out or banging her head against a wall. Later she
began burning herself and jabbing pins into her arms and
legs. Six months before she went into care she started
cutting herself. I couldn't believe it when I first saw what
she had done. But she was relaxed about it and said it
helped her to cope.'

I nodded seriously. 'She told me that too.'

'And in some ways it's true,' Barbara said quietly.
'Dawn's behaviour has improved. It's as if the cutting is
her way of controlling her anger. She no longer hits me or
swears at me, and she can be very polite. But when she
started hanging out with that bad lot off the estate I knew
she would get into even more trouble, and she did. Ruth
thought that if she came to you it might help. But clearly
it hasn't. It's not your fault, Cathy.' Barbara paused and sat
back, taking a deep breath. 'I don't know what happened to
Dawn in Ireland during those four years, but whatever it
was took away my little girl and gave me someone who
hates me, herself, and life, so much that she wants to end
it.'

'And she's never told you or your ex husband what happened?' I asked.

'No, never.' Barbara shook her head. 'When I have asked her, she says she can't remember anything of that time. Maybe she's telling the truth. Ruth says that maybe it was so bad that she's blocked it out. I've tried phoning my aunt and uncle, but as soon as they hear my voice they hang up. Ruth said you didn't need to know all this, but I've realised that unless someone speaks up, Dawn won't get the help she needs, and then it will be too late.'

Barbara fell silent, and I looked at her, shocked by everything I had heard. It had taken Barbara a lot of courage to tell me all this, and I was thankful that she was now putting the needs of her daughter first in order to get her the help she so badly needed.

'If only Ruth had told John and me,' I said at last. 'It might have helped us understand some of Dawn's behaviour. We've been so very worried, not knowing what to do for the best.'

Barbara nodded. 'I'm sorry, Cathy.'

'It's not your fault. Ruth should have been the one to tell us. But what's this got to do with my son? You said I should have been told because I have a baby.'

Barbara met my gaze and looked deathly serious. 'As you know, Dawn spends a lot of time hanging out with her mates – sometimes on the streets, sometimes at their houses when their parents are out. I can't stop here. The week before she was taken into care she was babysitting with one of those mates, a girl called Tina. She's fifteen. Tina's mother has a young baby, and she had gone out with her boyfriend, leaving Tina and Dawn babysitting. I wouldn't have left two young girls in charge of a baby, but

that was her decision. What happened next is unclear.
Dawn was so hysterical at the time she couldn't tell the
police, and hasn't been able to tell them since. But it seems
the two girls were either playing with matches or smoking
and the flat caught fire. They fled in panic and called the
fire brigade. By the time the fire crew arrived at the flat it
was ablaze. The baby was burnt on one arm and suffered
severe smoke inhalation.'

I gasped, and stared in horror at Barbara as she continued.

'It was touch and go for a while, but the baby survived,
although he needs more skin grafts on his arm. The police
have interviewed Dawn and Tina a number of times, and
the file is still open. Arson is a very serious crime. Tina is
blaming Dawn, and Dawn is accepting the blame,
although she's not giving any details. I think she's probably protecting Tina. Tina's mum wants nothing more to
do with her daughter and Tina is living at the teenage
unit. Once, when Dawn stayed with her father, his wife
found Dawn trying to strike a match while sleepwalking.
Dawn was very upset and anxious and kept muttering
about saving a baby, as though she was going to recreate
the scene and try to change the outcome. Well, that's what
they thought at least. They have a young baby, so you can
see why they don't want Dawn in the house any more.
And for the same reason you should have been told – it's
too dangerous.'

Barbara fell silent and I continued to stare at her, only
too aware of the danger we had all been placed in, especially Adrian. With horror, I remembered the night we
had found Dawn in the kitchen sleepwalking and trying to
strike a match, and all the times she had sleepwalked to

Adrian's cot before John had fitted a lock on our bedroom door. In sleep, had she been led by her subconscious to seek out Adrian, and the matches, in order to try to re-create the night of the fire, and then stop what had happened, as Barbara now suggested? Supposing Dawn had found the matches and lit one? Or John hadn't fitted the locks to the bedroom and kitchen doors? What then? I shuddered; it didn't bear thinking about.

Then my thoughts turned to Dawn and the dreadful burden she had been carrying, alone, and suffering for in silence: both of her time in Ireland and whatever had happened there, and the fire that had nearly taken the baby's life and for which she was accepting full and silent responsibility.

'What a dreadful, dreadful mess,' I said at last. 'No wonder Dawn has been behaving is the way she has. If only she could have talked to someone.'

Barbara nodded. 'Dawn badly needs help to come to terms with everything that has happened, before it's too late. I'm useless, and I feel so guilty that I can hardly bear to be in the same room as her.'

I continued to look at Barbara. 'You know, Dawn used to be all over Adrian when she first came to live with us. Then last summer she suddenly withdrew from him. Since then she won't have anything to do with him.'

'Perhaps it's her way of protecting him,' Barbara said sadly. 'Dawn is naturally a loving child, and is very sweet and caring, especially to those younger or more vulnerable.'

'I'm sure what happened to the baby must have been a horrendous accident,' I said.

Barbara nodded. 'Dawn was interviewed again by the police last summer, when you were away and she was staying with me. That's when they told her that Tina was blaming her and the police file would remain open. They said if they found sufficient evidence they would prosecute her. I have to say the police were very heavy handed. I'm not minimising what happened to the baby: it was awful, and the child is still suffering. But it was an accident, and Dawn can't blame herself forever.'

'No,' I agreed. 'She can't. And she's been carrying all this around with her, plus whatever happened in Ireland, and punishing herself by cutting, and trying to end her life. No wonder she's in such a state.'

'Exactly,' Barbara said, and I saw her bottom lip tremble and her eyes fill. 'And of course, I am to blame.'

We were both silent for some minutes. Then I leant forward and, placing my hand on Barbara's, I said, 'Thank you for telling me all this. John and I will obviously do all we can to help get Dawn the care she needs. Since she's been with us we've grown very fond of her – in fact we love her.'

'I know you do,' Barbara said quietly, 'which is why I've told you.'

Chapter Twenty-Six

The Last Smile

I drove home almost on autopilot, absorbed in my thoughts and overwhelmed by what Barbara had told me. I was very sad and felt very sorry for what Dawn had suffered, but I was also angry that Ruth hadn't told us. Our lack of knowledge had placed us all in danger and, while I realised that confidentiality had to be respected, it should never have been at the expense of the safety of my family, which included Dawn. It was only our instinctive feeling that locks should be placed on the kitchen and bedroom doors, and the matches put away, that had saved us. It wasn't Dawn's fault; I certainly didn't blame her. Goodness only knew what had happened to the poor kid in Ireland during her 'missing' years to send her on the downward spiral that had eventually led to the fire at Tina's house. Then I remembered the conversation Dawn and I had had when we had been feeding the ducks. Believing Dawn was feeling guilty about plundering Adrian's moneybox, I had told her we had to learn from our mistakes and forgive ourselves: Dawn had asked 'even if it's something really wicked?' and had not been re-assured when I'd said yes. My words now seemed simplistic and naïve in the light of what I now knew had been crucifying her.

By the time I returned home, John had put Adrian to bed and was in the shower. I poked my head round the bathroom door and reassured him that Dawn was comfortable and that Barbara was with her. I said I was taking Dawn's overnight things, as they were keeping her in for a few days, and that I would come straight home again.

'I've got a lot to tell you,' I said. 'Barbara has told me so much. And could you phone social services please, and tell them Dawn's in hospital?' John said he would.

I went into our bedroom, where Adrian was asleep in his cot, and I gazed down on him. So small and innocent, so vulnerable and precious: I'd never have forgiven myself if he'd been hurt. I leant over and gave him a goodnight kiss; then I went through to Dawn's room. I gathered together her nightdress, wash bag, Walkman and cassettes, and packed them into a holdall. Downstairs I took her birthday cards from the table in the lounge and packed those too. I thought she could open them with Barbara, and then display them on her beside cabinet in the ward – a token of the birthday she had missed. I would take her presents when I visited the following day.

When I returned to the hospital that evening with Dawn's overnight bag, I found she hadn't gone to the ward but was still in the cubicle, fast asleep, with Barbara sitting at her bedside. I gave Barbara Dawn's belongings and she thanked me.

'You've done so much for Dawn,' she said, her eyes misting again. 'I dread to think what would have happened if she hadn't come to you.'

I smiled sadly. 'It's nice of you to say so, Barbara. But I'm not sure we've really done her much good at all.'

I looked at Dawn, propped high on her pillows, eyes closed, face relaxed and with both wrists heavily bandaged. She looked so peaceful in sleep, as though she hadn't a care in the world – until her subconscious kicked in, I thought, and plunged her into the depths of hell.

'We'll all pull together and make sure Dawn gets the help she needs,' I said positively to Barbara. 'The poor kid certainly deserves it.'

Barbara nodded, and thanked me again. I left, confirming I would come back the following afternoon.

When I got home, John was in the lounge, having just poured himself a Scotch. Dawn's unopened presents and unlit birthday cake lay on the coffee table, like a shrine to her absence. I flopped down on the sofa and sighed.

'Do you want a drink?' John offered.

I shook my head. 'No thanks. Perhaps later. Let me tell you what's happened first. It's pretty awful.'

I began by saying that I thought Dawn could have been planning her suicide attempt, and told him what she had said to me the night before about everything being fine tomorrow. I told him how Dawn had gone to her mother's straight from school, and that her mother had come home from work and had found Dawn in the kitchen with her wrists cut. I recounted what Barbara had said about Dawn's past – the 'missing' years in Ireland, which had completely changed Dawn, and the fire at Tina's flat. By the time I got to last summer and Dawn's interview with the police, where they had said Tina was blaming her, and Dawn, by her silence, had appeared to accept responsibility, John's face was ashen.

'Jesus!' he said. 'It all makes sense now: a dreadful sickening sense. Her sleepwalking to Adrian, her re-enactment of the fire with the matches – it was as though she was trying to purge her conscience. Whatever happened to her in Ireland? Has anyone tried to find out?'

I shook my head. 'Not as far as I know, and whenever Barbara phones her uncle, he just hangs up. I don't think the social services are following it up.'

John nodded slowly and thoughtfully. 'So Barbara thinks she'll be able to get Dawn the help she needs now?'

'She's going to speak to Ruth first thing tomorrow, and I've told Barbara we're behind her and will do all we can.'

'Absolutely,' John said. 'Dawn should have had help sooner. And as for Ruth not telling us – that's criminal!'

The following afternoon I packed Dawn's birthday presents in a large carrier bag; then I sliced half the birthday cake, put the slices in a polythene container and packed that too, together with a few paper plates. I drove to the hospital with Adrian, having told him we were going to see Dawn.

Dawn was in the children's ward now, and when we went in I found her sitting up in bed and talking to girl about the same age, who was in dressing gown and slippers. Dawn's birthday cards were strung across her bedhead, and as soon as she saw me she smiled. I thought she looked brighter and more relaxed.

'Hi, Cathy,' she called, as I went over. 'This is Susie, my new friend.'

'Hello, Susie,' I said. 'How are you?'

'Good, thanks.'

'Cathy is my carer,' Dawn explained, so I assumed she had told Susie she was in care. 'And this is Adrian,' she added proudly, spreading her arms wide to receive him.

'Be careful he doesn't hurt your wrists,' I said as I placed him on the bed next to Dawn.

Adrian snuggled up beside her and she kissed his head. Surprised and delighted by her acceptance of him, I thought Dawn probably felt it was safe in hospital to allow him near her. Susie was perched on the bed, and I sat in the chair. 'I've brought your presents,' I said, delving into the carrier bag and setting them on the bed.

'Oh goodie!' Dawn said, smiling, while Susie made a move to go.

'Why don't you stay and watch Dawn open her presents?' I suggested. 'You can have a piece of birthday cake as well.'

'Yes, stay, please,' Dawn said. 'It will be like a little party.'

Susie smiled and perched on the bed again. She and I watched while Adrian helped Dawn unwrap her presents. The other children on the ward also looked over, and so too did their visitors. A nurse passed the end of the bed on her way to another child. 'Happy birthday for yesterday,' she called.

'Thanks,' Dawn said, and she smiled.

A lump rose in my throat as I looked at Dawn, propped up in bed with her bandaged arms and carefully unwrapping her presents. It reminded me of our pre-Christmas Christmas – she was so child-like and innocent in the pleasure, and I held and savoured every moment.

'That's lovely,' she exclaimed after opening each one. 'Thank you so much. And will you thank John, and your brother, and Gran and Grandpa?'

'Of course, love. You're very welcome.'

When all the presents were open I delved into my bag again and pulled out the paper plates and polythene box containing the sliced birthday cake. 'I haven't brought all your cake,' I said. 'I thought it would go stale here. And I didn't bring any candles because I didn't think we would be allowed to light them on the ward. We'll save those for another day.'

'But we can still sing "Happy Birthday",' Susie said.

'Of course. It's a must.'

'Oh no.' Dawn groaned with embarrassment.

Adrian clapped with glee at the prospect of at last being able to sing the song he had been practising so hard the day before.

I set out four paper plates, and then placed a slice of cake on each one.

'Only a small piece for me, please,' Susie said. 'I've just started chemo again and it makes me feel a bit sick.'

'Sure love,' I said, and my heart went out to her. She was about the same age as Dawn and having to battle against cancer for what sounded like the second time. What some kids had to go through, I thought, and I felt very humble beside her courage.

With the cake on our plates Susie and I began to sing 'Happy Birthday', with Adrian adding what he could. Then the girl in the bed opposite and her visitors joined in. Soon everyone on the ward was singing, including the nurse who was taking the blood pressure of the child in the bed next to Dawn's. By the time we got to the final rousing last line I was blinking back the tears. 'Hip hip,' someone shouted, and we all responded – 'Hooray!' Everyone clapped, and I swallowed hard. 'Happy birth-day, love,' I said leaning forward and kissing Dawn's cheek.

"appy bir'day, Daw',' Adrian added.

We ate our cake, and I wished I'd brought the whole cake in and given everyone a slice, but I hadn't envisaged the embracing warmth of the others on the ward. The nurse came over and asked to see Dawn's presents. Dawn proudly showed her the jewellery box, silver necklace and gift vouchers, and a handbag from my mother and a huge box of chocolates from my brother.

'Lucky girl,' the nurse said.

Dawn smiled, but didn't say anything, and I thought she looked a little sad. Once we'd finished our cake, I gathered up the plates and brushed the crumbs off the bed. Susie left us a little while later, as her parents had arrived. Adrian was still curled into Dawn, making the most of her company, and she had her arm round him.

'It's nice to see you two friends again,' I said lightly.

Dawn nodded and kissed his head, but she still looked sad. 'Has Mum told you about me, about what happened to the baby?' she asked, subdued.

I nodded. 'Yes, she has, love.'

'I can't bear to think about it. We didn't mean to, but it was still our fault. Cathy, I've done the most dreadful things, and made a right mess of my life.'

I took her hand and gently rubbed her fingers, which jutted from the end of the bandage. 'You've had a pretty rough ride, love, but I understand a lot more now your mum has told me.'

'She says I probably won't be coming back to live with you – that I need to go somewhere I will be kept safe and given help. I'll be sad to go, but I suppose it's for the best. I can't keep on like this.'

'We'll make sure you get the help you need. Your mum said she was going to speak to Ruth, but nothing has been

cut

decided yet. Don't worry yourself now, love. Just rest and get better.'

'I will, Cathy. I will be all right.'

I visited Dawn in hospital the next afternoon, and she was still quiet and subdued, perhaps reflecting on the things that had happened to her, although she was pleased to see Adrian and me.

The following morning the phone rang and it was Barbara. She said they were going to move Dawn that afternoon and she asked me to pack her belongings. I was taken aback by the suddenness of the move, although I wasn't surprised that Dawn was going. She couldn't have continued as she was, and John and I had recognised for a long while that she needed professional help – more than we could offer.

'Where is she going?' I asked Barbara.

'Ruth's found her a special teenage psychiatric unit where they can keep her safe and give her therapy and counselling. Ruth says it's a big house standing in its own grounds, and all the residents have their own rooms. It sounds very nice.'

'I see,' I said thoughtfully. 'You've done very well to get things moving so quickly. Will we be able to visit her?'

'Not to begin with. Ruth said they like to give them time to settle in and stabilise. Then they take it at the child's pace. Not even I will be able to visit to begin with. Apparently the house is on the outskirts of a village over a hundred miles away. Ruth said there aren't many of these homes and this is one of the best.'

'I see,' I said again. 'Well, Dawn, deserves the best.' I paused. 'What time are you coming?'

'Ruth and I are collecting Dawn from hospital at twelve noon, so we will be with you just after twelve-thirty.'

'I'd better get packing, then,' I said quietly. 'It's already eleven o'clock.'

I replaced the receiver and, taking Adrian upstairs with me, heaved a large suitcase from the top of my wardrobe and carried it through to Dawn's room. I had soon filled the case with Dawn's many clothes, and continued with a number of holdalls, wrapping her ornaments and anything that could break in newspaper before I packed them. To begin with I concentrated on the task, putting aside my own thoughts and feelings – about the fact that very soon Dawn wouldn't be with us any more. It was nearly a year since she had arrived, but in many ways it seemed a lot longer, with the bond that had formed between us and what we had overcome together, as a family.

But as I neared the end of the packing and saw Dawn's empty shelves and cupboards, and the cases and bags lined up by the door, I sat on the bed and cried. Dear Dawn, how badly I would miss her! I had come to see her as my daughter, and while I knew she was leaving us to get the help she needed, it wouldn't make the loss any easier, and we couldn't even visit her. Adrian, seeing my tears, toddled over, and climbing on to my lap, kissed my wet cheeks.

'It's all right, love,' I said, pulling a tissue from my pocket. 'Mummy's sad.'

'Sad,' he repeated. 'Mummy sad.'

I wiped my eyes and looked at him. How could I possibly explain to him that Dawn was leaving, and the reasons why? It was impossible. 'Dawn's going,' I said at last. 'We will have to say goodbye to Dawn.'

'Daw' bye,' he said; then he crumpled his face to look like mine. I couldn't help but smile.

'Dawn's going, and we will be sad,' I said. 'So we need to be brave and say goodbye to Dawn.'

'Bye Daw',' Adrian said, and taking my tissue he wiped away the last of my tears. I kissed him and gave him a big hug.

Rallying myself I heaved the suitcase and all the bags downstairs, one at a time, opening and closing the stair gate each time so that Adrian couldn't follow me downstairs. By the time I had finished and they were all stacked in the hall, it was just after twelve. I brought Adrian down and took him through to the lounge, where I phoned John at work and told him Dawn was going.

'That's quick,' he said, shocked. 'I won't have a chance to say goodbye.'

'I know. I'll have to say goodbye for you.'

'And give her my love and say we'll visit as soon as we are allowed to.'

'I will.'

At exactly 12.30 p.m. the door bell rang and, steeling myself, I took hold of Adrian's hand, and led him down the hall.

Dawn was on the doorstep, with Barbara and Ruth standing just behind.

'Come on in,' I said, welcoming her. 'You're looking so much better, Dawn.' She had some colour to her face, and I thought her expression had lost some of its quiet, reflective sadness, which I had seen so often in the past. It was as if she had decided, at last, to accept help and was relieved to have made that decision.

She smiled, and the three of them came into the hall.

'I've got everything ready,' I said, nodding at the cases. 'Would you like a drink before you set off?'

'No thanks,' Ruth said. 'We've got a long journey and I'd like to get on the road.'

I nodded, and I looked at Dawn and Barbara as we stood awkwardly in the hall, not knowing what to say or do.

'I'll put Dawn's bags in the car,' Ruth said, 'while you two say goodbye.'

Dawn, Barbara and I moved down the hall a little, so that Ruth could get to Dawn's luggage. Adrian wrapped his arms tightly round Dawn's legs to stop her from going, and buried his face in them. She bent down to pick him up, but as she tried to lift him she grimaced and touched her wrists, as if the stitches had pulled. She knelt down to cuddle him instead.

'All the best,' I said to Barbara, as Dawn hugged Adrian. 'Take care and have a safe journey. You will let me know how Dawn is doing, and when we can visit?'

'Of course, Cathy. And thanks for everything. I know you will always hold a special place in Dawn's heart, and I can't thank you enough for what you've done.' She put her arms around me and we hugged, as Ruth returned to the hall for more of Dawn's bags.

'Goodbye, then, little man,' Dawn said, finally straightening. 'I'm going to miss you.' She turned to me. 'Goodbye, Cathy.'

We looked at each other for a moment and then she fell into my arms and, burying her head in my shoulder, sobbed. 'I'm going to miss you, Cathy, and Adrian, and John. You will forgive me, won't you? I didn't mean any of it.'

'There's nothing to forgive, love,' I said, holding her and stroking her hair. 'Please stop blaming yourself. You're a good girl, and I know everything will work out fine. John sends his love; he's sorry he can't be here to say goodbye.' I glanced over Dawn's shoulder to Barbara, who was fighting back tears.

'All done,' Ruth said, returning to the hall.

I gave Dawn another big hug, and then gently eased her away. I looked into her eyes, wet with tears. 'Dawn, love, I want you to remember that none of this is your fault. And in time you will come to see that. We're going to miss you and we'll be thinking of you.'

She nodded and I wiped her wet cheeks with my hand. 'Now come on, I want to see you smile before you go. I don't want to remember you in tears.'

She sniffed, and then managed to raise a smile.

'Bye, then, Cathy,' Ruth called.

'Goodbye, love,' I said to Dawn; then, picking up Adrian, I followed Barbara and Dawn to the door. 'Take care both of you,' I called.

'And you,' Barbara said.

I watched as they went down the path to Ruth's car. Barbara got in the passenger seat and, fastening her belt, gave a wave through the window. Dawn was in the back, behind her mother, and looked directly at me as Ruth started the engine. 'Love you,' she mouthed, wiping her cheek again.

'Love you too,' I mouthed back.

As the car pulled from the kerb, Dawn managed a little smile. I smiled back as Adrian waved.

And that was the last time I saw Dawn, her face framed in the window of the car, fighting back the tears and making a brave attempt to smile. Goodbye, Dawn, love. Take care, and God bless you. I returned inside and closed the door.

Chapter Twenty-Seven

Proved Right

Six weeks after Dawn had left Barbara phoned me and said that Dawn had settled into her new home. Barbara said she still wasn't allowed to visit Dawn, but they were speaking on the phone twice a week. Dawn had told her mother that she liked the staff and had made friends with some of the other residents, and that she had begun therapy – meeting a psychiatrist three times a week. Dawn also told her mother that when she had lived in Ireland with her mother's aunt and uncle she had been repeatedly raped by their two sons, then aged sixteen and fourteen. Barbara was in tears on the phone as she told me, blaming herself for sending Dawn to live with them and allowing her to stay. I was shocked, but not altogether surprised that something so dreadful had happened to Dawn during her time in Ireland, for clearly something had caused her to become so distressed and disturbed.

Barbara said Dawn was obviously struggling to come to terms with what had been locked away in her subconscious for so many years, and was now being released in therapy. The psychiatrist had told her it would be some time before he felt it advisable for Dawn to have visitors. As Barbara spoke, apart from her shock and self-blame for what had happened, I also detected a warmth for and understanding of Dawn that hadn't been there before – a wish to make amends and to do what was best for her daughter, which I knew would lead to them having a better relationship in the future. I asked Barbara to give Dawn my love, and to phone again and let me know when we could visit.

After Dawn had left us, John and I did some careful thinking about fostering, and whether we should continue. For while we had come to love Dawn, and we recognised she wasn't responsible for her behaviour, caring for her had caused us much worry and upset. This had been made worse by our not being given crucial background information, which had left us ill-equipped to understand and deal with Dawn's behaviour, as well as placing us all in danger. We needed to make sure the same thing didn't happen again. We wanted to continue fostering because we still felt we had much to offer, and could help a child towards a better future, but understandably were cautious. After much thought and discussion, we decided we would tell the social services that we would prefer to look after younger children, who hopefully wouldn't have the history and therefore the dreadful problems Dawn had had. Two months later a five-year-old boy came to stay with us, but that is another story.

I had expected Barbara to phone again after that first call, but the months passed and I didn't hear anything further. I tried phoning her, but she was never in. When the phone was eventually answered, ten months after Dawn had left us, it was by a man. He said Barbara had moved, and he didn't have a contact number. I never saw or heard again from Barbara, or Ruth, so I had no way of knowing how Dawn was progressing. And while John and

I were sad to lose contact with Dawn, we recognised that the part we had played in her life was probably over, and assumed Barbara was now taking responsibility for Dawn and trying to be a better mother. Ultimately it was up to Barbara and Dawn whether they kept in touch and included us in their lives.

Adrian grew into a healthy, loving and inquisitive child who was into everything. When he was four, to our delight I found I was pregnant again, and I had a baby girl, Paula. Our family was complete, and with the fostering I was always very busy – happily so. I thought about Dawn often, and tried to picture what she was doing and where she was living. I prayed she was happy, and that life was good for her, for no one deserved a fresh start more than Dawn. As each of her birthdays came around on 6 January and she was a year older I tried to imagine what she looked like – how tall she was, how she did her hair – and wondered if I would recognise her if I passed her in the street.

Then one dismal November morning, five years after Dawn had left, the phone rang and, when I answered it, my heart skipped a beat and the grey November skies lifted. I'll always remember that morning. Adrian was at school, and I was in the lounge playing with Paula, who was then two, and Mary-Jane, a little girl of three I was fostering while her mother was in hospital. I moved away from the girls, who were playing with building bricks, to answer the phone on the corner table. I gave our number and waited. No one spoke.

'Hello?' I said. 'Can I help you?'

There was another pause. Then a voice asked, 'Cathy? Is that you?' And while the voice was older and more mature, I recognised it immediately.

'Dawn?' I cried in disbelief. 'Is that you?'

'Yes. I wondered if you would remember me.'

'Of course! Oh my! I can't believe it. How are you, Dawn? What are you doing? You're nineteen now!'

'I am,' she said with a little laugh. 'And I'm fine. I'm sorry I haven't phoned before. I nearly did a few times. But when I thought back to all the trouble I caused you and John I wasn't sure I should.'

'Oh, Dawn, you didn't cause us trouble – well, actually you did,' I said, laughing. 'But we understood and forgave you everything. Oh, Dawn, I'm so pleased you've phoned.'

She laughed again, easily and lightly. 'How are John and Adrian?' she said. 'I've still got a photograph of you all. Adrian will be a lot bigger now.'

'He is, and he's at school. And John's fine – he's at work.' I paused. I had so many questions I wanted to ask her, but time had passed and I recognised that Dawn wasn't the disturbed teenager who had left me but a self-possessed young lady. 'So what are you up to?' I said. 'Are you working?'

'No, I'm in my first year at college. I'm studying to be a teacher. I want to teach primary school children.'

'How wonderful! You must have done very well at school.'

'My grades were good,' she said, quietly and unassumingly.

'Well done. I thought you could do well.' Again I hesitated, wanting to know more but not sure I should ask. 'And what about your mum? Is she all right?'

'Yes. She's remarried, but not to that dope Mike. He's called Andy, and I like him very much. He has two grown-up children, and his son, Robert, my step-brother, is married and has two kids. It's great at Christmas when we all get together. We're a big family. And I still see my own dad sometimes.'

'That's fantastic, Dawn. Send my love to your mother, won't you?'

'I will, and say hi to Adrian and John for me. I'm pleased you are all OK. I've been wondering how you've been.'

'We're all fine, Dawn,' I said, 'and I've had another child – Paula. She's two now.'

'That's lovely. You're a good mum.'

'Thanks, love. That's nice of you to say so.' I paused again. 'Did everything work out for you at that home you went to? I've often wondered. Your mum phoned me at the beginning and said you were settling in.'

'Yes. I was there for over two years. I made some good friends and I'm still in touch with one girl. I left when I was nearly seventeen.'

'And where do you live now?'

'With Mum and Andy,' she said, slightly surprised that I hadn't realised.

'That's terrific. You're doing so well, Dawn, but I knew you would.'

'Did you?' she asked, her voice suddenly serious.

'Yes. I knew you had a lot of problems, but I always thought that with the right help you would come to terms with everything and get your life back. There was some-thing about you, an inner strength. You just needed some-one who you could talk to, someone who could guide and help you.'

'You were right, Cathy. And I probably should have talked to you, but at that time I couldn't talk to anyone. I couldn't even remember. It was frightening not remembering most of my childhood.'

'And do you now?' I asked tentatively.

'Yes. And it wasn't a good childhood. I had to face a lot of stuff, and still have to now. The things that happened in Ireland were so painful to remember. But now I know how to deal with them. And I know it wasn't my fault. Which is what you told me when I left.'

'I did!' I said surprised. 'You remember that.'

'Cathy, I can remember nearly everything you said to me, and did for me. And I want you to know I'm truly grateful.'

My eyes immediately filled with tears. 'That's sweet of you, Dawn. Thank you so much. It means a lot to me. We had some good times, didn't we? Times I still remember and will treasure. I'm pleased you remember them too.'

'I do, Cathy, and I always will.' She paused. 'Well, I'd better be going now. I've got a lecture soon, on the developmental stages of cognitive learning. Whatever that is!' She gave another small laugh; Dawn laughed easily and often. 'I just wanted to say hi, and thank you. I will never forget you, Cathy.'

'Thank *you* for phoning, Dawn. I won't forget you either. And if you ever want to visit, we'd be very pleased to see you. It's the same address.'

'I'll remember that. Bye, Cathy.'

'Bye, Dawn. Thanks again, and take care.'

I sat for a moment on the sofa, overwhelmed by Dawn's call. How lovely that she should phone after all this time, and what a success story! Dawn had completely turned her life around and was now studying to be a teacher! I had to smile. Who would have thought it, given her previous attitude to school? It just goes to show, I mused, that given the right help, determination and courage, what could be achieved. And if, in some small way, I had helped Dawn, if only by being there for her, then my feeling of reward was immeasurable.

I couldn't wait until John came home from work to tell him of Dawn's call, so I phoned him at the office. He was as surprised and delighted as I was.

'Well, well,' he said, bemused. 'I have to admit I had my doubts about her achieving anything.'

'Did you?' I asked. 'I didn't.'

'No, but then you always think the best of people, and fortunately now you have been proved right.'

Epilogue

I had hoped that Dawn would phone again and possibly even visit, but she didn't. And I came to realise that she wouldn't necessarily want to be reminded of that time, which was so traumatic for her and from which she had moved on so successfully. I was pleased for her, but not hearing from her didn't stop me from thinking about her. As the years ticked by, I imagined Dawn finishing college and starting her first job. Where she was living I didn't know, for Dawn had been living with her and her stepfather when she had phoned and her mother had moved away. Possibly she was still living with them, out of the area, or maybe they had returned – I'd no idea.

Dawn is thirty-six now, and very likely married with a family of her own. And I'm certain that if she does have children she will be the best mother ever, giving her family all the love, warmth and stability she didn't have as a child, and which she so dearly missed and deserved. Yet while Dawn hasn't visited or phoned, I haven't ruled out the possibility that she might yet. That one day, maybe on an impulse or remembering something of her time with us, she might pick up the phone or just pop in. For as Dawn's memory has stayed alive with me for over twenty-two years, I think the same might be true for her. The bond that formed between us was a little bit special and will remain with me always. I'm proud of Dawn and what she achieved: she not only survived a dreadful childhood but successfully turned her life around.

Dawn, if you are reading this, take care, and God bless.